NetBeans Platform 6.9 Developer's Guide

Create professional desktop rich-client Swing applications using the world's only modular Swing application framework

Jürgen Petri

BIRMINGHAM - MUMBAI

NetBeans Platform 6.9 Developer's Guide

First published: August 2010

Production Reference: 1020810

Published by Packt Publishing Ltd.
32 Lincoln Road
Olton
Birmingham, B27 6PA, UK.

ISBN 978-1-849511-76-6

www.packtpub.com

Cover Image by Vinayak Chittar (vinayak.chittar@gmail.com)

Credits

Author
Jürgen Petri

Special Thanks
Geertjan Wielenga

Acquisition Editor
Douglas Paterson

Development Editor
Rakesh Shejwal

Technical Editor
Gauri Iyer

Indexer
Rekha Nair

Editorial Team Leader
Aanchal Kumar

Project Team Leader
Priya Mukherji

Project Coordinator
Prasad Rai

Proofreader
Lynda Sliwoski

Production Coordinator
Shantanu Zagade

Cover Work
Shantanu Zagade

Foreword

NetBeans RCP – Das Entwicklerheft, Jürgen's original German book about the NetBeans Platform, was published in August, 2008. What's happened with the NetBeans Platform since then? Well, quite a lot, actually! NetBeans Platform 6.9 has been released, sporting a large set of features which Jürgen might only have dreamed of while working on his book. Most significantly, the new NetBeans Platform support for integrating OSGi bundles needs mentioning in this regard. Apart from that, there are many other new features, including new and changed APIs, which to a greater or lesser extent have an impact on the text and the code that the original book provided. Wherever relevant, and always as seamlessly as possible, these new features have been introduced into this translated and updated version.

The spirit of Jürgen's original book remains intact: this is not a complete reference guide to each and every detail that the NetBeans Platform provides Java desktop developers. For those purposes, "The Definitive Guide to the NetBeans Platform" (Apress) and "Rich Client Programming: Plugging into the NetBeans Platform" (Prentice Hall) continue to be the best sources, together with the many NetBeans Platform tutorials (`http://platform.netbeans.org/tutorials`), of course. However, after reading those books and documents, many readers have asked themselves: "OK, that's all very interesting, but how do I get started?" That's what this book is all about, taking you by the hand and showing you many aspects of the NetBeans Platform in step-by-step instructions, within one coherent whole.

Because of this approach, some readers may feel somewhat disappointed. For example, Maven-based applications are not addressed at all in this book, simply because that was not relevant to the particular application that Jürgen set about to create. And, most topics in this book could deserve more pages, more explanation, and deeper analysis. However, a balance had to be made between providing a practical guide to the newbie, which this book tries to do, and providing a complete and thorough reference guide, various forms of which already exist. Hopefully the reader will forgive us for any errors made in this balancing act.

The NetBeans Platform community pitched in and translated this book together. The translation team was as follows: Jean-Marc Borer, Zane Cahill, Costantino Cerbo, Stefan Alexander Flemming, Michael Holste, Peti Horozoglu, Martin Klähn, Victor Ott, Christian Enrique Portilla Pauca, Christian Pervoelz, Sven Reimers, Peter Rogge, Johannes Strassmayr, Florian Vogler, and Fionn Ziegler. Many thanks for their enthusiasm and hard work! I recommend them all as translators.

Many thanks also to the many reviewers, in particular Jaroslav Tulach, Anton Epple, and Tom Wheeler. In fact, in the Pantheon of NetBeans, Tom Wheeler is at least a minor deity on the order of Eos.

From the team at Packt, many people deserve praise and thanks. In particular, Prasad Rai and Douglas Paterson, for making this book possible, as well as Rakesh Shejwal and Gauri Iyer, for their endless patience and support.

Happy reading and learning about the NetBeans Platform!

Geertjan Wielenga
Technical Trainer & Writer
NetBeans

About the Author

Jürgen Petri is a Sun Certified Enterprise Architect with more than 12 years experience in developing enterprise Java applications.

He provides consulting services on Java and Java EE technology, and he also trains architects and developers on software engineering, enterprise architectures, and Java-related technologies. Although he is interested in many areas of software development, Jürgen has a distinct focus on great UI technologies like the NetBeans Platform.

Currently, he puts his knowledge in migrating the UI of a core banking system with a broad spectrum of technical cross cutting aspects into a web application using GWT.

Additionally, Jürgen is the author of *NetBeans RCP - Das Entwicklerheft* published in 2008 by O'Reilly.

Acknowledgement

First, I want to thank Geertjan Wielenga for his relentless work to publish an updated English version of my previous book *NetBeans RCP - Das Entwicklerheft* published in 2008 by O'Reilly. Without him this book would not exist. Geertjan is the author of several NetBeans Platform publications and author of a great and well-known blog (`http://blogs.sun.com/geertjan`). If you are starting to develop an application on this great platform, you should make sure to visit his blog. For me it has been a continuous source of inspiration. Geertjan mobilized members of the NetBeans community in order to translate and update the book. He did an excellent job in managing the translation and update.

I especially want to thank Christian Enrique Portilla Pauca, Sven Reimers, Peter Rogge, Johannes Strassmayr, Florian Vogler, Zane Cahill, Martin Klähn, Jean-Marc Borer, Victor Ott, Fionn Ziegler, Constantino Cerbo, Peti Horozoglu, Christian Pervoelz, Martin Klähn, and Stefan Alexander Flemming for contributing to the translation.

I want to thank Packt for giving me the opportunity to write this book and for putting up with me even though I had continuously missed upon the agreed dates.

Most importantly, I want to thank my wife who supported me in writing the book in the first place and my son Leonard for all the joy he brings to us.

Table of Contents

Preface

The NetBeans Platform is the world's only modular Swing application framework. It aims to drastically simplify desktop application development by providing a number of techniques, patterns, and full-blown Swing components.

Most desktop applications have very similar technical requirements, such as the following:

- Consistent user interface
- Extensibility
- Data display
- Configuration settings
- Help system
- Distribution mechanisms
- Online update function
- Cross-operating system support

Fulfilling these technical requirements over and over again for each new application is expensive, superfluous, and boring. The NetBeans Platform gives the developer a transparent, open source, extensible, and free framework that addresses all of these technical requirements.

This book doesn't aim to explicate all that the NetBeans Platform offers or to explore each and every corner of its many features. Rather, this book guides you through the development of a specific Java desktop application, while showing you everything that is relevant in the context of the particular application itself. That process, in turn, will lead you through the main features relevant to the development of most general applications on the NetBeans Platform.

The central driver of the book is, therefore, the creation of a complete Java desktop application, chapter by chapter, step-by-step, sequentially through the progression of chapters in this book.

What this book covers

Chapter 1, Module: A module is the basic building block of a NetBeans Platform application. In the chapter dealing with this theme, you learn why it makes sense to develop modular applications, while examining the features of modules, as well as their interdependencies. Moreover, you examine module versioning and the lifecycle of modules, as well as the entry points into that lifecycle.

Chapter 2, Forms: Almost every large desktop application needs to provide a number of forms that accept data from the user. You learn how forms are created for usage on the NetBeans Platform, how their layout is set, and how to implement the related handling of events.

Chapter 3, Window System: The NetBeans Window System, together with the API that it exposes, lets you arrange forms on the screen within a docking framework. You learn how to create windows, what their lifecycle looks like, and how to influence that lifecycle. In addition, you examine how a window is positioned within the layout of the application, how to influence the window layout, and how to create groups of related windows.

Chapter 4, Lookup: The Lookup API provides a communication mechanism, comparable to an event bus, which is of central significance in the creation of NetBeans Platform applications. You learn how to use the Lookup to find services so that loosely-coupled communication between modules can be established. You also learn how to listen to the Lookup so that content can be added dynamically to a NetBeans Platform application. You examine how a Lookup can act as a proxy for another Lookup and how this functions as the basis of context sensitivity, also known as "selection management", in NetBeans Platform applications.

Chapter 5, Actions: You learn how to create global actions and how to invoke them from menus and toolbars. You also examine how to connect actions to shortcuts, allowing them to be invoked from a keyboard.

Chapter 6, Nodes and Explorer Views: A sophisticated MVC implementation for displaying business objects is made available via a set of extensible Swing components, which you can use without very much work at all. You explore how generic hierarchical models, known as "nodes", can represent and display business objects in advanced Swing components called "explorer views". You use flat as well as hierarchical structures and are shown how easily one view can be exchanged for another and how they can be synchronized with each other.

You also spend some time learning about the asynchronous creation of nodes and how context sensitive actions are attached to a node. Last but not least, you learn how the properties of a node can be displayed in property views and how to create the related property editors.

Chapter 7, File System: The File System API lets you access a NetBeans Platform's virtual filesystem, which serves as the application's central registry. You learn how to access the configuration system, as well as other systems that can be created on top of the same API. Finishing up, you create new folders, files, and attributes in the filesystem.

Chapter 8, Data System: The Datasystems API gives you access to the content of files. You learn how to extend a NetBeans Platform application to provide support for custom data types. You also discover how the features available to data content can change in relation to the current status of the underlying file.

Chapter 9, Dialogs: The responsibilities of dialogs in an application extend from the display of simple messages to the management of step-by-step procedural wizards. In that context, you learn how to display simple messages, standard dialogs, and sophisticated multi-step wizards to the user.

Chapter 10, Settings: Large applications, such as those based on the NetBeans Platform, typically have many different kinds of users. Not all of them need all the application's features and not all of them use those features in the same way. As the application becomes larger, a centralized approach is needed, so that each module added to the application can contribute to a centralized Options window. That is the theme of this chapter, which introduces you to the most important APIs and the entry points into the centralized Options window.

Chapter 11, Help: HTML files constituting your documentation can be integrated into the application. When the user clicks on the Help buttons in the application, or when they invoke an Action to display the entire help content, your HTML files can be displayed to them. This chapter shows you how to configure the help system and gets you started with a few help topics, a table of contents, and an indexing system.

Chapter 12, Branding: Branding enables the application's ancillary details, such as icons and splash screens, to be customized. For example, you learn how to exchange the custom splash screen with your own.

Chapter 13, Distribution and Updates: To let you distribute applications, you examine the various distribution mechanisms for NetBeans Platform applications. You generate a distribution and an installer, with a special focus on how to let an application be updated online.

The Appendices are available for free at `http://www.packtpub.com/sites/default/files/1766_Appendices.zip`.

What you need for this book

To use this book, you need the following software:

- The Java SE Development Kit (JDK) 6.0 Update 13 or later is required to install NetBeans IDE. The 6.9 version of the IDE cannot be installed using JDK 5.0.
- NetBeans IDE 6.9. The "Java SE" distribution, which is one of the smallest distributions (54 MB) of the IDE is all you need. This distribution supports all standard Java SE development features, including tools that help you create NetBeans Platform applications. Get it here: `http://netbeans.org/downloads/index.html`.

For details, visit the following URL, which provides the complete installation instructions for NetBeans IDE 6.9: `http://netbeans.org/community/releases/69/install.html`

Who this book is for

This book is written for developers who are comfortable with Java and Swing and who would like to use a framework as the basis of their Swing applications. Zero knowledge of the NetBeans Platform is assumed.

The reader is typically a developer (or a group of developers) wanting to create large, distributed, and flexible Swing applications. The development team is typically large and distributed and members need to work independently on distinct parts of the application. The end user of the application typically needs to have the ability to install additional features at runtime, after the application has already been installed, without reinstalling the application.

Conventions

In this book, you will find a number of styles of text that distinguish between different kinds of information. Here are some examples of these styles, and an explanation of their meaning.

Code words in text are shown as follows: "The `manifest.mf` is extended to declare the required dependency on the **JavaHelp Support** module."

A block of code is set as follows:

```
[public class TaskIdGeneratorImpl implements TaskIdGenerator {
   private Random random = new Random();
   public String generateID() {
       String id = "000000" + this.random.nextInt();
       id = id.substring(id.length()-6);
       return id;
   }
}
```

New terms and **important words** are shown in bold. Words that you see on the screen, in menus or dialog boxes for example, appear in the text like this: "Right-click the **Overview** module and choose **New | Other | Module Development | JavaHelp Help Set**. Click **Next**".

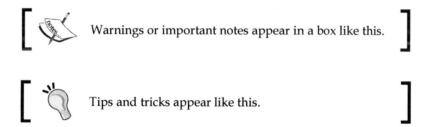

Warnings or important notes appear in a box like this.

Tips and tricks appear like this.

Reader feedback

Feedback from our readers is always welcome. Let us know what you think about this book—what you liked or may have disliked. Reader feedback is important for us to develop titles that you really get the most out of.

To send us general feedback, simply send an e-mail to feedback@packtpub.com, and mention the book title via the subject of your message.

If there is a book that you need and would like to see us publish, please send us a note in the **SUGGEST A TITLE** form on www.packtpub.com or e-mail suggest@packtpub.com.

If there is a topic that you have expertise in and you are interested in either writing or contributing to a book on, see our author guide on www.packtpub.com/authors.

Customer support

Now that you are the proud owner of a Packt book, we have a number of things to help you to get the most from your purchase.

Downloading the example code for this book

You can download the example code files for all Packt books you have purchased from your account at http://www.PacktPub.com. If you purchased this book elsewhere, you can visit http://www.PacktPub.com/support and register to have the files e-mailed directly to you.

Errata

Although we have taken every care to ensure the accuracy of our content, mistakes do happen. If you find a mistake in one of our books—maybe a mistake in the text or the code—we would be grateful if you would report this to us. By doing so, you can save other readers from frustration and help us improve subsequent versions of this book. If you find any errata, please report them by visiting http://www.packtpub.com/support, selecting your book, clicking on the **let us know** link, and entering the details of your errata. Once your errata are verified, your submission will be accepted and the errata will be uploaded on our website, or added to any list of existing errata, under the Errata section of that title. Any existing errata can be viewed by selecting your title from http://www.packtpub.com/support.

Piracy

Piracy of copyright material on the Internet is an ongoing problem across all media. At Packt, we take the protection of our copyright and licenses very seriously. If you come across any illegal copies of our works, in any form, on the Internet, please provide us with the location address or website name immediately so that we can pursue a remedy.

Please contact us at copyright@packtpub.com with a link to the suspected pirated material.

We appreciate your help in protecting our authors, and our ability to bring you valuable content.

Questions

You can contact us at questions@packtpub.com if you are having a problem with any aspect of the book, and we will do our best to address it.

1
Modules

In this chapter, you will cover the following topics:

- You learn about modules and modular application development
- You examine the role that modules play in NetBeans Platform applications while creating your first module
- You look at how to configure modules, especially at how to define module dependencies and versioning data
- You round this topic off by looking at the lifecycle of modules and how to programmatically access that lifecycle

Modular application development

Modularization becomes more important as an application's complexity increases. The old and trusted programming methodologies struggle to keep pace with continually shortened production cycles, gradually increasing feature sets, and the simultaneously rising importance of software quality. In particular, the pressure of time to market demands a solid application design, providing clear extension points, loosely-coupled components, and a reliable versioning mechanism. Without a strong foundation based on a sustainable architecture, each version increase and new feature introduces a new level of chaos, leading to a scenario where enhancements and bug fixes become impossible to implement, as each change causes increasingly detrimental side effects. An application of this kind can become so problematic that it needs to be rewritten from scratch but, because the underlying application architecture remains unchanged, a rewrite of this kind fails to solve the application's structural defects.

A solution to this problem entails the introduction of modules. A module is a self-contained software component with which other modules can communicate via well-defined interfaces, behind which their implementations are hidden. Each coarsely-grained feature of an application is created within a module, giving each module a clearly defined responsibility within the application. The chaos described above can, of course, continue to exist within a module, exactly as it had existed in the pre-modular application. However, as the classes within a module exist to provide a very specific feature, the module, as a whole, needs to function interdependently with the other modules in the application, meaning that the chances of complete chaos in your code are smaller than they were before. The limited responsibility of a module within the application enables it to be more focused and the application as a whole to be more cleanly designed.

Moreover, the worsening chaos described above is less likely to arise within a modular application, as the implementation of features can only take place via publicly exposed interfaces. The dependencies in the whole application are well-defined and never accidental. Breaking the contract with the interfaces, thereby introducing the chaos described above, can only be done intentionally.

Besides these advantages to the developer, a modular application also benefits the end user. As the NetBeans module system is dynamic, modules (that is, features) can be loaded and unloaded dynamically at runtime. The adaptability and flexibility of applications and the ease with which features can be added and removed by the user at runtime is of particular relevance to enterprise applications, which typically provide support for a variety of user profiles.

Let's now take a more concrete look at modules and their relationship to NetBeans Platform applications.

Characteristics of a module

Generically, a module needs to have certain characteristics to provide the desired advantages promised by modular application development.

Deployment format

It must be possible to make all resources required by a module available via a single deployment package. The closest concept in the Java world is the JAR archive. You can bundle an arbitrary number of resources into a JAR and provide metadata via the manifest file. NetBeans modules are packaged in a similar format, together with module-specific metadata in the related manifest file, into an NBM archive.

Uniqueness

Each module must have its own unique identity. The NetBeans module system provides an additional key in the manifest, **OpenIDE-Module**, which you use to define the application-wide unique name of a module.

Versioning

Each module must be able to specify its version. NetBeans modules differentiate between specification versions and implementation versions.

- The specification version indicates the version of the officially exposed interfaces. This version is defined via the OpenIDE-Module-Specification-Version key in the manifest file, using the Dewey format. Generally, the assumption is that new versions are backward-compatible.

- The implementation version indicates the implementation state of a module. This version is not assumed to be backward-compatible and can be used only within a specific version of the application. The OpenIDE-Module-Implementation-Version key in the manifest defines this version.

Exposed interfaces

Each module defines public interfaces, via which features can be accessed. Accepted methods of accessing dependencies in software rely strongly on conventions. One of these is that types in packages can only be accessed indirectly via facades. However, typically, these well-intended conventions are abandoned in the interests of time. On the other hand, component systems with their own lifecycle environment tend to demand that conventions of this kind are followed to the letter. Within a module, any class can be declared public, and thereby, be accessed by any other class within that module. However, other modules can only access a module's exposed classes, that is, classes that are found within explicitly exposed packages.

The NetBeans Platform is one of the systems that provide a mechanism of this kind. The packages that are to be exposed to other modules in the application are declared via the OpenIDE-Module-Public-Packages manifest key. The NetBeans Platform provides a system of ClassLoaders that provide access to those classes that are within the module, as well as those classes that are found within the publicly exposed packages of other modules upon which the module has declared a dependency.

Declarative dependencies

Each module must declare which, if any, of the other modules in the application are required for it to function. To this end, the NetBeans Platform provides the manifest key OpenIDE-Module-Dependencies. As mentioned previously, the NetBeans Platform module system lets other modules access only the explicitly exposed packages of modules within the application.

Lifecycle

Each module must have its own lifecycle, managed by the application's runtime. The NetBeans module system handles the loading and configuration of modules. It also handles the processing of installation code, if any, and the unloading of modules when the application shuts down.

Creating an application

Now that you've been exposed to a lot of theory, let's create a new application with two modules. You then configure them so that they can interact with each other via their publicly exposed interfaces.

You start by creating a new NetBeans Platform Application project. The application project serves as a container for modules and represents a single application, while providing a number of NetBeans Platform modules out of the box. You're also able to configure the NetBeans Platform and brand the application via this project type.

1. Choose **File | New Project**, which opens the **New Project** wizard. Then choose **NetBeans Modules | NetBeans Platform Application**, as shown in the following screenshot. Click **Next>**.

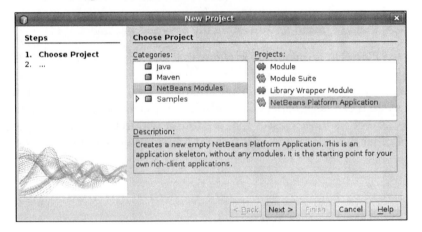

2. Type **TaskManager** as the application name, as shown in the following screenshot:

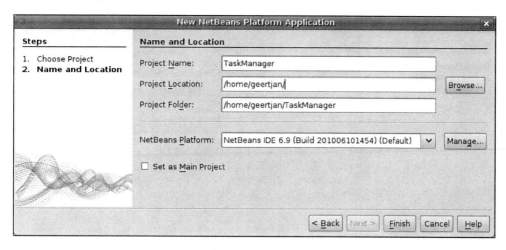

3. When you click **Finish**, you see that a new project structure is created for your application, which can be seen in the **Projects** window.

Now you add your first new module to the application.

1. In the **Projects** window, right-click the **Modules** node of the application and choose **Add New**. In the **New Module Project** wizard, enter **HelloService** as the name of the module, along with a location for storing it, as shown in the following screenshot:

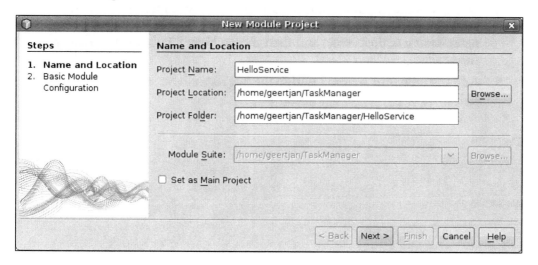

2. Click **Next>** and enter the **Code Name Base** of the module as **com. netbeansrcp.helloservice**, as shown in following screenshot:

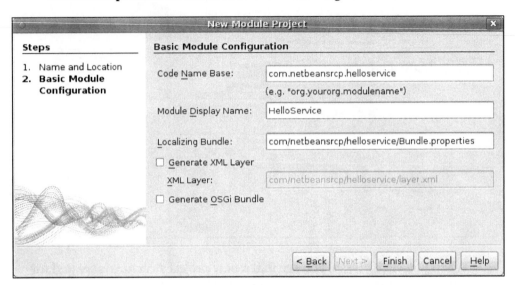

The **Code Name Base** is a string defining a unique ID by which the module is known to the rest of the application.

3. Click **Finish** and the module source structure will be shown in the **Projects** window.

4. Let us now add a public class `HelloService` to our module. Right-click the module's package node (under **HelloService | Source Packages | com. netbeansrcp.helloservice**) and then choose **New | Java Class**. Create a class called `HelloService`.

5. Add the following method within the `HelloService` class:

```
public void hello(String name) {
   System.out.println("Hello " + name + "!");
}
```

Let's take a look at what you've done so far. First, using a wizard in NetBeans IDE, you created a new module within a new NetBeans Platform application. The module contains various configuration files. You will later learn that the most important of these are the manifest.mf file and the layer.xml file. Both files are found within the **Important Files** node of the module. The layer.xml is discussed in detail in the later chapters. At the moment, the content of this file is not yet very interesting. The manifest file has been discussed already and, right now, has the following content:

```
Manifest-Version: 1.0
OpenIDE-Module: com.netbeansrcp.helloservice
OpenIDE-Module-Layer: com/netbeansrcp/helloservice/layer.xml
OpenIDE-Module-Localizing-Bundle: com/netbeansrcp/helloservice/Bundle.
properties
OpenIDE-Module-Specification-Version: 1.0
```

Setting dependencies

Now, of course, you'd like to be able to use the HelloService class from another module.

1. In the same way as explained previously, create the second module. Name it as **HelloClient** and add a class to it named **HelloClient**, containing the following method:

```
public static void main(String[] args) {
  new HelloService().hello("NetBeans");
}
```

The new class cannot be compiled yet, as the HelloService class cannot be found currently. It is not possible to add an import statement, as the module containing the required class is isolated from all the other modules via its module-specific classloader. Therefore, for a class in the **HelloClient** module to use a class in the **HelloService** module, two conditions must first be satisfied:

- The HelloService class must belong to the publicly exposed interfaces of the module in which it is defined

- The **HelloClient** module must declare its dependency on the **HelloService** module

2. First of all, you need to add the `HelloService` class to the module's publicly exposed interfaces. To that end, right-click the **HelloService** module in the **Projects** window and choose **Properties**. In the **API Versioning** tab, you see the list of packages in the module. Here, you can specify the packages containing the interfaces that you want to expose to the rest of the application, as shown in the following screenshot:

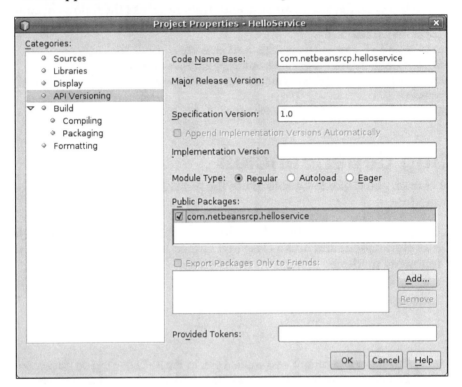

In this case, the package you want to expose is **com.netbeansrcp.helloservice**. Types in any other packages than those that have been exposed cannot be accessed by other modules.

1. Now you need to declare the dependency of **HelloClient** on **HelloService**. Right-click the **HelloClient** module and choose **Properties**. In the **Libraries** tab, set the dependencies between the current module and other modules in the application. Click **Add Dependency** and begin typing the name of the class that you would like to access. NetBeans IDE shows, while you are typing, the classes in the available modules that match the entered text, as shown in the following screenshot:

2. Choose the **HelloService** module and confirm your choice. Click **OK** to close the **Properties** dialog. If you have not created an import statement for the HelloService class in the HelloClient class yet, do so now. It should now be possible to compile the class.

At this point, you've used various tools in NetBeans IDE to define the public interface of the **HelloService** module. Next, in the **HelloClient** module, you set a dependency on the **HelloService** module. Now the classes in the **HelloClient** module can access the classes that are part of the public interface of the **HelloService** module.

Versioning

Along with the information defining the dependencies between modules, you need to specify exactly which version of the module you are depending on. The NetBeans Platform makes a distinction between the version of the specification and the version of the implementation of the module as follows:

- Specification versions are set using Dewey notation. In general, it consists of the main version number, that is, the version number that is incremented when new features are added, together with the minor version number, and the patch level. A version number of this kind is comparable to Mac OS X in the version 10.4.10.

- The implementation version indicates a concrete development state and should only be used after agreement with the module owner.

As an example, you set the **HelloService** module to version 2.1.5.

1. Next, let's configure **HelloClient** such that it requires **HelloService** to be set at version 2.1.5. Right-click the **HelloClient** module and click **Properties.** In the **Libraries** tab, select the **HelloService** dependency, and then click **Edit**. Enter the specification version as **2.1.5**, as shown in the following screenshot, and then close the dialog.

○ When you now attempt to build the project, you should see a message that the build is broken, because the **HelloService** module needs to be available in a version equal to or greater than 2.1.5, as follows:

```
Cannot compile against a module:

/home/geertjan/TaskManager/build/cluster/modules/com-
netbeansrcp-helloservice.jar

because of dependency: com.netbeansrcp.helloservice > 2.1.5

BUILD FAILED (total time: 2 seconds)
```

2. To let the build succeed, you need to declare that the specification version of the **HelloService** module is at least 2.1.5. Right-click the **HelloService** module, choose **Properties**, and use the **API Versioning** tab, as shown in following screenshot, to set the specification number:

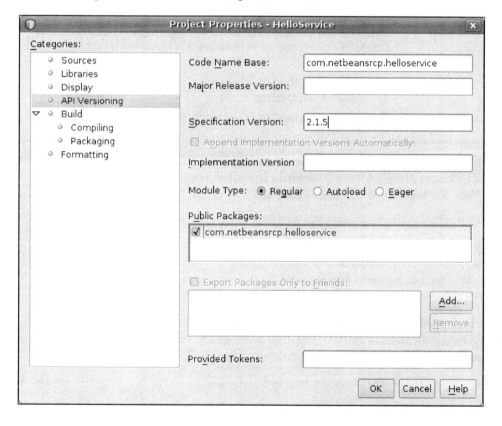

Try again to build the application. The build succeeds as the requested specification version now corresponds to the specification version of the **HelloService** module.

Installing modules

A module needs to be installed for the runtime container to manage its lifecycle. Installation takes place declaratively, with all the necessary files being generated by wizards in NetBeans IDE.

You might want to programmatically influence the lifecycle of a module. For that purpose, the ModuleInstall API class is provided by the NetBeans Platform. This class defines a module installer providing methods that interact with the runtime container at specific points in the lifecycle of a module. Generally, these methods are used to initialize settings in the application at the time when the module is installed or to uninitialize those settings when the application closes.

Method	Description
validate()	Override this method to prevent the module from being loaded. That might be something you want to do after failing to determine that certain preconditions, such as the presence of a license, have been met.
restored()	Override this method to initialize the module. Do this only when absolutely necessary, as performance is impacted by the initialization sequences.
closing()	Override this method to return false in order to prevent the application from closing.
close()	Override this method to provide information about the closed state of the application.

To create your own module installer, right-click the **Project** node of the **HelloService** project, choose **New | Other | Module Installer**, accept the default values, and complete the wizard (see figures 9 and 10).

Define the restored() method as follows:

```
@Override
public void restored() {
   System.out.println("HelloService() restored.");
}
```

Start the application by right-clicking the **Application Project** node and choosing **Run**. The application is started, together with all the modules that define it. In the **Output** window of the IDE, you should now see the following:

```
HelloService() restored
```

In other words, the module installer has been processed.

If you have changed a module, you do not need to restart the whole application. Instead, you can reload the changed module. Without stopping the application, change the definition of the `restored()` method, then right-click the **Module Project** node and choose **Reload in Target Platform**.

From the **Output** window, you can see that the **HelloService**, as well as the related **HelloClient** module, are shut down. Next, the **HelloService** is installed afresh and then both modules are enabled afresh. The **Output** window now shows the changed output of our module installer:

```
HelloService() restored - modified.
```

The NetBeans module system has dynamically reloaded the module. It has also managed the dependencies between the modules. You can now close the application.

In short, you have seen that you can programmatically influence the lifecycle of a module. You might want to do this to introduce an initialization sequence into the application, though doing so impacts the startup time of the application and should be done only after careful consideration of alternate approaches.

Integrating OSGi Bundles

A new feature in NetBeans Platform is its support for **OSGi**, the *de facto* standard module system that has seen wide adoption. In essence, OSGi attempts to provide the same features as the NetBeans module system and, as a result, the two are not very different from each other.

Two scenarios are envisioned when using OSGi in the context of the NetBeans Platform. Most typically, you have some OSGi bundles of your own that you would like to integrate into your NetBeans Platform application. For example, the domain model might have been designed in the **Eclipse Modeling Framework (EMF)**, meaning that you have OSGi bundles generated by EMF. Importing those bundles into your application is a seamless process, allowing you to immediately begin creating Swing components on top of your domain model, using the various Swing components described later in this book. A second approach is relevant when you want your entire application to be based on OSGi. Experimental support is available for generating OSGi bundles from all your NetBeans modules, including the modules that make up the NetBeans Platform.

To import OSGi bundles, go to the **Project Properties** dialog of your application, and browse to a folder containing your bundles, using the **Libraries** tab to do so. The IDE recognizes that the JARs in the folder are not NetBeans modules and requests to be permitted to add metadata to the folder containing the JARs. The metadata provides information such as when the bundle should be loaded, for example, lazily as needed or when the application starts up. The OSGi bundles now being part of your application, you can set dependencies on them and use the EMF-generated classes, just as you would use any other domain classes as the basis of your application.

The sample application

Over the coming chapters, you develop a complete application piece by piece.

The example application is a **TaskManager**, that is, a tool for managing various kinds of activities. For the purposes of this application, a **task** is an activity, and each task requires a short description and a long description to provide information about the activity to the user. Each task also has a priority, enabling users to sort the tasks in the categories "low", "medium", and "high". Each task has a due date and needs to be identifiable via a unique ID number.

As the tasks consist of subtasks, they are hierarchically structured, with parent tasks containing child subtasks. Each task therefore has a list for its subtasks and a reference to the parent task to which the child tasks belong. The parent task is the main model object, and, as you anticipate that many components within our application are interested in changes to the model, you add support for a PropertyChangeListener. These features are defined within an interface.

To that end, create a new NetBeans Platform application and name it **TaskManager**. Within the **TaskManager** application, create a module named **TaskModel**. Use **com. netbeansrcp.taskmodel** as the name of the main package.

Create a subpackage named **api** and define the **Task** interface as follows:

```
public interface Task extends Serializable {
  public java.lang.String getId();
  public java.lang.String getParentId();
  public java.lang.String getName();
  public void setName(java.lang.String name);
  public java.util.Date getDue();
  public void setDue(java.util.Date due);
  public enum Priority { LOW, MEDIUM, HIGH }
  public Priority getPrio();
  public void setPrio(Priority prio);
  public int getProgr();
```

```
  public void setProgr(int progr);
  public java.lang.String getDescr();
  public void setDescr(java.lang.String descr);
  public void addChild(Task subTask);
  public java.util.List<Task> getChildren();
  public boolean remove(Task subTask);
  public void addPropertyChangeListener(PropertyChangeListener listener);
  public void removePropertyChangeListener(
                                    PropertyChangeListener listener);
  public static final String PROP_NAME = "name";
  public static final String PROP_DUE = "due";
  public static final String PROP_PRIO = "prio";
  public static final String PROP_PROGR = "progr";
  public static final String PROP_DESCR = "descr";
  public static final String PROP_CHILDREN_ADD = "children_add";
  public static final String PROP_CHILDREN_REMOVE =
"children_remove";
}
```

Now that you have an interface, you need to implement it. In the implementation, you need to think about providing support for a `PropertyChangeListener` class. You delegate the management of the listener to a `PropertyChangeSupport` class, which handles the methods for adding and removing the listener. Then, for each relevant property change, you fire a `PropertyChangeEvent` via the `PropertyChangeSupport` class.

In this way, you end up with the following implementation, which you create in the **com.netbeansrcp.taskmodel** package:

```
public class TaskImpl implements Task {
  private String id = "";
  private String name = "";
  private String parentId = "";
  private Date due = new Date();
  private Priority prio = Priority.MEDIUM;
  private int progr = 0;
  private String descr = "";
  private List<Task> children = new ArrayList<Task>();
  private PropertyChangeSupport pss;
  public TaskImpl() {
    this("", "");
  }


  public TaskImpl(String name, String parentId) {

      this.id = "" + System.currentTimeMillis();
      this.name = name;
      this.parentId = parentId;
      this.due = new Date();
```

```
            this.prio = Priority.MEDIUM;
            this.progr = 0;
            this.descr = "";
            this.children = new ArrayList<Task>();
            this.pss = new PropertyChangeSupport(this);
        }
    public String getId() {
        return id;
    }
    public String getName() {
        return name;
    }
    public void setName(String name) {
        String old = this.name;
        this.name = name;
        this.pss.firePropertyChange(PROP_NAME, old, name);
    }
    public String getParentId() {
        return parentId;
    },
    public Date getDue() {
        return due;
    }
    public void setDue(Date due) {
        Date old = this.due;
        this.due = due;
        this.pss.firePropertyChange(PROP_DUE, old, due);
    }
    public Priority getPrio() {
        return prio;
    }
    public void setPrio(Priority prio) {
        Priority old = this.prio;
        this.prio = prio;
        this.pss.firePropertyChange(PROP_PRIO, old, prio);
    }
    public int getProgr() {
        return progr;
    }
    public void setProgr(int progr) {
        int old = this.progr;
        this.progr = progr;
        this.pss.firePropertyChange(PROP_PROGR, old, progr);
    }
    public String getDescr() {
        return descr;
    }
    public void setDescr(String descr) {
        String old = this.descr;
        this.descr = descr;
        this.pss.firePropertyChange(PROP_DESCR, old, descr);
    }
    public List<Task> getChildren() {
```

```
            return Collections.unmodifiableList(this.children);
        }
    public void addChild(Task subTask) {
        this.children.add(subTask);
        this.pss.firePropertyChange(PROP_CHILDREN_ADD, null, this.children);
        }
    public boolean remove(Task subTask) {
        boolean res = this.children.remove(subTask);
        this.pss.firePropertyChange(PROP_CHILDREN_REMOVE, null,
                                                    this.children);
        return res;
        }
    public synchronized void addPropertyChangeListener(
                            PropertyChangeListener listener) {
        this.pss.addPropertyChangeListener(listener);
        }
    public synchronized void removePropertyChangeListener(
                            PropertyChangeListener listener) {
        this.pss.removePropertyChangeListener(listener);
        }
    @Override
    public boolean equals(Object obj) {
        if (obj == null) {
            return false;
        }
        if (getClass() != obj.getClass()) {
            return false;
        }
        final TaskImpl other = (TaskImpl) obj;
        return this.id.equals(other.getId());
        }
    @Override
    public int hashCode() {
        int hash = 7;
        hash = 97 * hash + (this.id != null ? this.id.hashCode() : 0);
        return hash;
        }
    @Override
    public String toString() {
        return this.getId() + " - " + this.parentId + " - " +
                this.getName() +" - " + DateFormat.getInstance().
                format(this.due) + " - " + this.prio + " - " +
                this.progr + " - " + this.descr;
        }
}
```

Summary

Though you do not have code that can be run yet, you now have a Task interface, together with its implementation. You have completed the application's model.

Later, you need to make these classes available to the other modules in the application. You can prepare for this by exposing the API package to the rest of the application, as described earlier in this chapter, which adds the "Task" interface to the public interfaces of the module.

In the next chapter, you will continue learning about the NetBeans Platform and the development of the sample application.

2
Forms

In the following chapters, you will develop an example application for the management of tasks. As with every desktop application, the Task Manager needs a graphic surface with various views, which might also be referred to as "forms".

In this chapter, you examine the "Matisse" Form Builder in NetBeans IDE. You learn how to:

- Create your own forms
- Customize forms so that they exactly meet your needs
- Handle events
- Modify generated code
- Extend the palette

Form Builder

NetBeans IDE 5.0 revolutionized the design of graphical user interfaces for Java desktop applications. The "**Matisse**" **Form Builder**, in other words, the modules in NetBeans IDE for visual composition of forms, introduced the new "**GroupLayout**" layout manager, together with an optimized GUI builder to use it.

Unlike the previous layout managers, which were based on coordinates and the boxing of components, the GroupLayout introduced a new concept of distributing components according to their alignment to each other and according to the relative nearness to other components and the edges of the form. In short, this approach lets you design your forms far more intuitively than before, while providing a correspondence between design and deployment that had, until then, never been matched before.

The Form Builder consists of a number of views, which you look at in some detail during the remainder of this chapter. A global overview of all the views can be seen in the following screenshot, which shows the **TaskEditor** that you will create in this chapter.

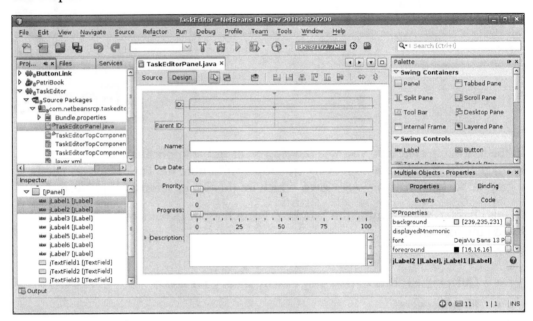

The Form Editor (as shown in the center of the screenshot above) has multiple views, derived from the NetBeans Core MultiView API. In other words, it provides different perspectives on the same component. You can switch between the views via the toggle buttons **Source** and **Design**. Unsurprisingly, the **Design** view shows the graphic view of the components, while the **Source** view shows the source code. In the **Design** view, you can arrange components onto a form via a standard drag-and-drop behavior. In the **Source** view, you can type the source code, with the parts that relate to the visual components being protected in blue blocks that cannot be directly edited in this view. The **Source** view provides access to all the code that is processed, once the application is up and running. NetBeans IDE creates supporting XML files for metadata relating to the visual composition of the form, but these files do not contain any of the code required for application processing.

The **Inspector** window (**Window | Navigating | Inspector**), as shown in the bottom-left of the screenshot above, gives you a hierarchical view of the component structure of the current form. By clicking on a component in the **Inspector** window, you can quickly gain access to it in the form.

The **Palette** (*Ctrl-Shift-8*), shown in the bottom-right of the screenshot on the previous page, shown in the top-right of the screenshot above, displays a list of components that you can drag-and-drop into the form. The standard palette includes all the Swing and AWT components, and you can extend it by adding your own components via the **Palette Manager**.

The **Properties** window (*Ctrl-Shift-7*) shows the properties of the current component. Wherever applicable, the **Properties** window also lets you modify the current component's properties. It's quite easy to modify properties, thanks to the special property editors provided for the most frequently used data types.

The **Connection** wizard simplifies the writing and registration of event listeners, though you do not use this wizard in the creation of the Task Manager.

The **Form Tester**, accessed via a button in the Form Editor's toolbar, gives you a quick preview of how your application appears when it is deployed. You can preview your form under different look-and-feels, while you can also register additional look-and-feels, if those provided prove insufficient.

Now that you have a general understanding of the "Matisse" Form Builder's main forms, let us take the next step in the creation of our Task Manager.

Creating a form

You now create a new form in the new module. In the same way as done in the previous chapter, create a new module. This time, name it **TaskEditor**. In the next section, you create a new form and add it to this newly created module. To create a new form, right-click the main package of the **TaskEditor** module and choose **New | Other**. In the category **Swing GUI Forms**, select **JPanel Form**, and then click **Next**.

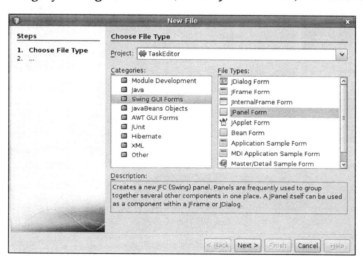

In the second wizard panel, type **TaskEditorPanel** as the name of the class and click **Finish**.

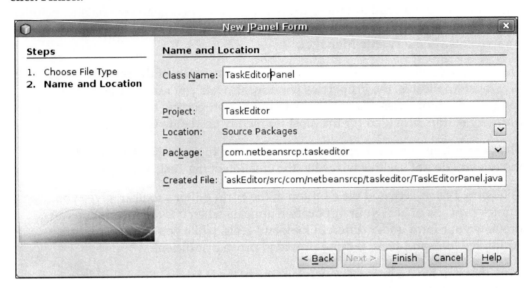

The Form Builder opens, and you can see the empty JPanel form, as shown in the following screenshot:

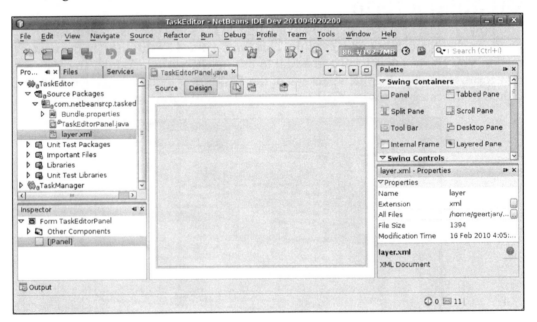

Laying out a form

The simplest way of laying out a form is by dragging components from the palette and dropping them onto the form. Alternatively, you can click on a component in the palette and then click the place on the form where you'd like the component to be created. In this case, when you hold down the *Shift* key, you can, very efficiently, create multiple components of the same type.

After returning to our **TaskEditorPanel** in the Form Builder, click the **Label** component in the palette, move the cursor over the form, and click your mouse again. A new label, with the name **JLabel1**, appears on the form, together with two anchors, showing the location of the label relative to the sides of the form.

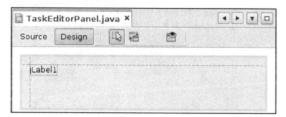

Aligning components on a form

The Form Builder uses GroupLayout as its default layout manager. As described earlier, GroupLayout relies heavily on the relationship of components with each other and with the edges of the form.

The Form Builder supports the design of components even before you add components to a form. As soon as you add a component near another component or near the edge of the form, the Form Builder attempts to determine the relative position of the component and how the component relates to the other components in the form.

While moving a component in the form, the currently chosen position of the component is shown in the Form Builder by means of dashed lines between the components and the edges, as well as a text display above the form, as shown in the following screenshot:

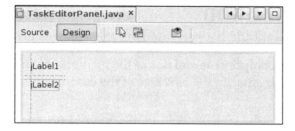

As soon as components are placed on the form, the display is updated. The dashed lines are replaced by full lines, showing the position of the sides of the component relative to the other components and the edges. In this way, the anchoring of the component relative to its surroundings is shown.

Now, add a second JLabel to the form. Use the Form Builder's guidance lines to suggest a desirable distance between the two components and position the new JLabel, so that it is right-aligned with the previously dropped JLabel.

Note that when you place the second JLabel on the form, the relative position to the first JLabel, as well as to the top and left edges of the form, can be seen, as shown in the following screenshot:

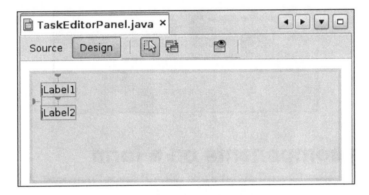

By double-clicking a JLabel, you can change its name.

Now add four JTextFields, two JSliders, a JTextArea, and seven JLabels to the form.

After double-clicking each of the JLabels, change their texts to **ID**, **Parent ID**, **Name**, **Due Date**, **Priority**, **Progress**, and **Description**.

Move the components around the form until they are placed as you would like them to be. Look at the screenshot on page 9 to see the design that is used throughout this book.

Space distribution

Now let's define what should happen when the user changes the size of the form.

Right-click one of the components and notice the menu item **Auto Resizing**. Using this menu item, you can specify the new size of the component after the form has been resized.

Select all the text fields as well as the text area. Then right-click and select **Auto-Resizing | Horizontal**. Next, select only the text area, right-click, and choose **Auto-Resizing | Vertical**.

Now click the **Preview Design** icon, which is in the toolbar to the right of the **Design/View** toggle buttons. The form appears in preview mode. Resize it and make sure that the components within the form are laid out as expected when the form resizes.

Properties window

When you select a component in the form, its properties are shown in the **Properties** window. You can modify the properties there, often via a property editor specifically created for the data type in question.

For our application, let's define some important properties for the components you created in the previous section.

The JTextFields for the ID and Parent ID serve no other purpose than to be displayed to the end user. Therefore, they should neither be editable nor active. Change the properties **editable** and **enabled** to **false**.

The JSlider showing the priority should start at **0**, have a maximum of **2**, and change in value in steps of 1. Change the **maximum property** to **2**, the **value** property to **0**, and the **majorTickspacing** property to **1**. Next, the ticks should be shown on the slider, while a snapping effect should occur as it is dragged left and right. Change the **paintTicks** and **snapToTicks** properties to **true**.

Next, let's look at the JSlider showing the progress of the tasks in the TaskManager. As done for the priority slider, make sure to let the user see the slider's ticks and let the slider snap from tick to tick as the user moves it left and right. In addition, let's show the numerical values to the end user in this case. Set the **paintLabels** property to **true**. The JSlider values should begin at **0** and end with a maximum of **100**. Therefore, set the **value** property to **0** and the **maximum** property to **100**. Movement of the slider should occur in steps of 5 percent and you mark each 25 percent setting so that the user can see the relative position of the current value. Therefore, set the **minorTickspacing** property to **5** and the **majorTickspacing** property to **25**.

Finally, empty the values of the texts in the text fields.

The form should now look as shown in the following screenshot:

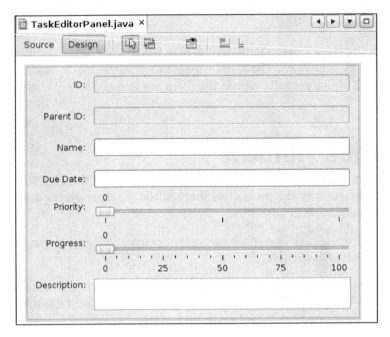

Event handling

Event handling is also supported by tools in the Form Builder. When you right-click a component in the Form Builder, the **Events** menu item contains all the events that are relevant to the current component. If you select an event in the list, a Listener is generated as an anonymous inner class, within the protected blue block in the **Source** view of the editor. In addition, the Listener is automatically registered to be used with the selected component.

In the code that follows, you provide the form with a task instance. Then you synchronize the properties of the task instance with the current values displayed in the form. To that end, you need to be able to access the **TaskModel** module. As shown in the previous chapter, set a dependency in the **TaskEditor** module on the **TaskModel** module. Make sure that the **TaskModel** module exposes its API package, which contains the Task interface.

Now that the API class is available, switch to the **Source** view of the panel and add an instance variable of the type Task:

```
private Task task = new TaskImpl();
```

Next, you need a method that writes the content of the form into the task:

```java
private void updateTask() {
  this.task.setName(this.jTextField3.getText());
  Date due = null;
  try {
      due =
DateFormat.getDateInstance().parse(this.jTextField4.getText());
    }
  catch (ParseException exception) {
      due = new Date();
    }
  this.task.setDue(due);
  if (!this.JSlider1.getValueIsAdjusting()) {
      switch (this.jSlider1.getValue()) {
          case 0:
              this.task.setPrio(Task.Priority.LOW);
              break;
          case 1:
              this.task.setPrio(Task.Priority.MEDIUM);
              break;
          case 2:
              this.task.setPrio(Task.Priority.HIGH);
        }
    }
    this.task.setProgr(this.jSlider2.getValue());
    this.task.setDescr(this.jTextArea1.getText());
}
```

You also need a method that updates the form with the values of the task:

```java
private void updateForm() {
  this.jTextField1.setText(this.task.getId());
  this.jTextField2.setText(this.task.getParentId());
  this.jTextField3.setText(this.task.getName());
  this.jTextField4.setText(DateFormat.getDateInstance()
                                    .format(this.task.getDue()));
  this.jTextArea1.setText(this.task.getDescr());
  if (Task.Priority.LOW.equals(this.task.getPrio())) {
      this.jSlider1.setValue(0);
    }
  else if (Task.Priority.MEDIUM.equals(this.task.getPrio())) {
      this.jSlider1.setValue(1);
    }
  else {
      this.jSlider1.setValue(2);
    }
  this.jSlider2.setValue(this.task.getProgr());
}
```

When you display the form, call the method for putting the values of the task into the form. Therefore, overwrite the constructor of the form as follows:

```
public TaskEditorPanel() {
  initComponents();
  this.updateForm();
}
```

Now let's register two ChangeListeners on the sliders. These call our update task method whenever the values of the sliders change. Right-click the first slider, select **Events**, and then **Change | stateChanged**. The Form Builder adds a new event in the **Source** view. Do the same for the second slider.

Implement the two events as follows:

```
private void jSlider1StateChanged(javax.swing.event.ChangeEventevt) {
  this.updateTask();
}
private void jSlider2StateChanged(javax.swing.event.ChangeEventevt) {
  this.updateTask();
}
```

You can treat changes in the text fields in the same way. In the next section, you look at a different way of doing this, so that you learn how to modify the generated code.

Modification of generated code

You've probably noticed that NetBeans IDE generates code in protected blue blocks that prevent you from making modifications directly in the **Source** view of the Form Builder. In this way, the Form Builder ensures that the metadata of the form description handled in the **Design** view remains synchronized with the source code in the **Source** view. If you want to change the code in the blue blocks, you need to use the **Code** tab of the **Properties** window, rather than the editor itself.

The properties in the **Properties** window correspond to specific places in the source code, parts of which can be edited in multiline editors in the **Properties** window. In this example, you use one of the multiline editors in the **Properties** window to register your own Listener on the text components in the panel.

Start by creating a `DocumentListener` and writing it to an instance variable:

```java
private DocumentListener docListener = new DocumentListener() {
    @Override
    public void insertUpdate(DocumentEvent evt) {
        TaskEditorPanel.this.updateTask();
      }
    @Override
    public void removeUpdate(DocumentEvent evt) {
        TaskEditorPanel.this.updateTask();
      }
    @Override
    public void changedUpdate(DocumentEvent evt) {
        TaskEditorPanel.this.updateTask();
      }
};
```

In the **Design** view, select the **Name** text field. Open the **Code** tab of the **Properties** window. Now click on the **...** button next to **Post-Listeners Code**. In the text area that appears on the screen, enter the following statement and click **OK**.

```java
this.jTextField3.getDocument().addDocumentListener(this.docListener);
```

Do the same for each of the other text fields.

Extending the palette

You've already used the palette to quickly and easily add components to your form. In this section, you'll add the panel as a new component to the palette that enables you to drag-and-drop the panel onto a window, in the next chapter, in the same way that you dragged and dropped `JLabels` and `JTextFields` earlier in this chapter.

Right-click in the palette, and choose the **Palette Manager** menu item to open the **Palette Manager**. In the **Palette Manager**, click **New Category** and type **My Category** in the **New Palette Category** dialog. Click **OK**. You should now see the **My Category** item at the top of the **Palette Manager**.

Again in the **Palette Manager**, click **Add from Project**. In the **Install Components to Palette** wizard, choose the **Task Manager** project and then select the **TaskEditor** module project. Click **Next**. From the JavaBeans available in the project, select our **TaskEditorPanel** and then select the new **My Category** category on the final page of the wizard. Click **Finish**.

Now the palette contains your own custom component, which contains the task editor panel that you will reuse in the next chapter.

Summary

In this chapter, you learned how to use the Matisse Form Builder and created a form required by the TaskManager. You familiarized yourself with the most important features of the Form Builder, so that you can use it comfortably and intuitively to create and lay out your forms.

In the next chapter, you will learn how to display forms in the windows of the **TaskManager**, after acquiring a general understanding of the NetBeans window system.

3
Window System

Large desktop applications need to provide many different views for visualizing data. These views have to be managed and shown and the NetBeans Platform handles these requirements for you out of the box via its docking framework.

While it once might have been sufficient for a docking framework to provide static fixed window layouts, today the user expects far more flexibility. Windows should be able to be opened, movable, and, generally, customizable at runtime. The user tends to assume that the positions of views are modifiable and that they persist across restarts of the application. Not only that, but applications are assumed to be so flexible that views should be detachable from the application's main window, enabling them to be displayed on multiple monitors at the same time. While once the simple fact of the availability of menus and toolbars was sufficient, today a far more dynamic handling is needed so that window content can be adapted dynamically. Connected to these expectations of flexibility, plugins are increasingly becoming a standard technology, with the user assuming their windows to be pluggable, too.

In short, the requirements for window management have become quite complex and can only be met by means of an external docking framework, otherwise all these various concerns would need to be coded (and debugged, tested, and maintained) by hand. The NetBeans Platform provides all of these features via its docking framework, known as the NetBeans Window System. It also provides an API to let you programmatically access the window system. Together, the window system and its API fulfill all the requirements described above, letting you concentrate on your domain knowledge and business logic rather than on the work of creating a custom window management facility for each of your applications.

This chapter teaches you the following:

- How to define views
- How to position views in the main window
- How to customize the default window layout
- How to group views so that they open and close as a unit
- How to change the persistence of views across restarts of the application

Creating a window

The NetBeans Window System simplifies window management by letting you use a default component for displaying windows. The default component, that is, the superclass of all windows, is the TopComponent class, which is derived from the standard JComponent class. It defines many methods for controlling a window and handles notification of main window system events.

The WindowManager is the central class controlling all the windows in the application. Though you can implement this class yourself, this is seldom done as normally the default WindowManager is sufficient. Similarly, you typically use the standard TopComponent class, rather than creating your own top-level Swing components. In contrast to the TopComponent class, the default WindowManager cannot manage your own top-level Swing components, so these cannot take advantage of the Window System API.

Now let's create a TopComponent and let it be an editor for working with tasks. This is done easily by using the **New Window** wizard.

1. In the **Projects** window, right-click the **TaskEditor** module project node and choose **New | Window**.

2. On the first page of the wizard select **Editor** for **Window Position** and **Open on Application Start**. Click **Next**.

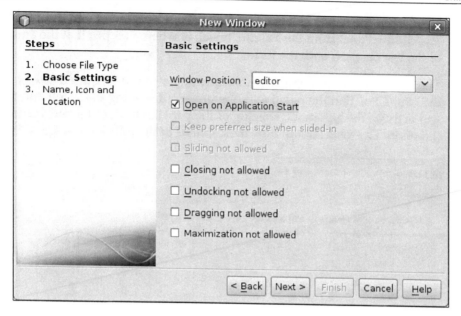

3. In the next page of the wizard, type **TaskEditor** in **Class Name Prefix**. This prefix is used for all the generated files. It is possible to specify an icon that will be displayed in the tab of the new window, but let's skip that for the moment. Click **Finish** and all the files are generated into your module source structure.

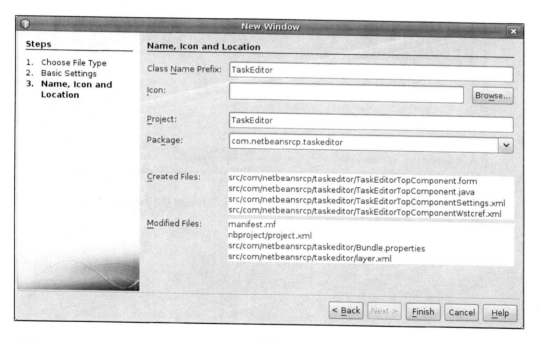

4. Next, open the newly created **TaskEditorTopComponent** and drag the **TaskEditorPanel** from the **Palette**, which is where you put it at the end of the last chapter, onto the form.

5. The size of the component automatically adjusts to the required size of the panel. Position the panel with the preferred spacing to the left and top and activate the automatic resizing of the panel in horizontal and vertical direction. The form should now look similar to the following screenshot:

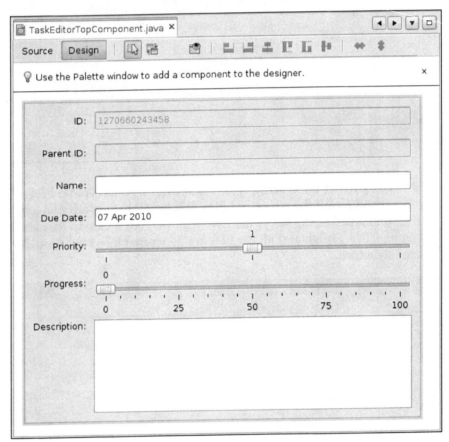

6. Start the application. You now see a tab containing the new **TaskEditor Window**, which holds your form.

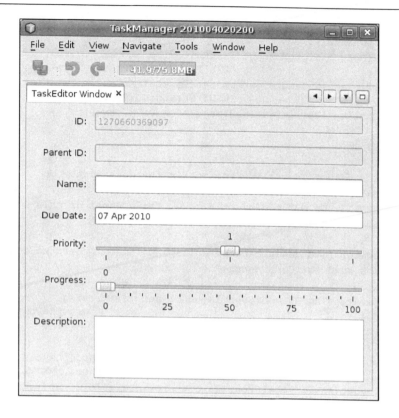

Examining the generated files

You have used a wizard to create a new TopComponent. However, the wizard did more than that. Let's take a look at all the files that have been created and at all the files that have been modified, as well as how these files work together.

The only Java class that was generated is the TopComponent that will contain the **TaskEditor**, shown as follows:

```
@ConvertAsProperties(dtd = "-//com.netbeansrcp.taskeditor//TaskEditor//
EN", autostore = false)
public final class TaskEditorTopComponent extends TopComponent {
  private static TaskEditorTopComponent instance;
  /** path to the icon used by the component and its open action */
//    static final String ICON_PATH = "SET/PATH/TO/ICON/HERE";
  private static final String PREFERRED_ID = "TaskEditorTopComponent";
```

```
    public TaskEditorTopComponent() {
    initComponents();
    setName(NbBundle.getMessage(TaskEditorTopComponent.class,
                            "CTL_TaskEditorTopComponent"));
    setToolTipText(NbBundle.getMessage(TaskEditorTopComponent.class,
                            "HINT_TaskEditorTopComponent"));
//    setIcon(ImageUtilities.loadImage(ICON_PATH, true));

    }


    /**This method is called from within the constructor to
     * initialize the form.
     * WARNING: Do NOT modify this code. The content of this method is
     * always regenerated by the Form Editor.
     */
    // <editor-fold defaultstate="collapsed" desc="Generated Code">
    private void initComponents() {

        javax.swing.GroupLayout layout = new javax.swing.
                                                GroupLayout(this);
        this.setLayout(layout);
        layout.setHorizontalGroup(
            layout.createParallelGroup(javax.swing.GroupLayout.
                Alignment.LEADING).addGap(0, 555, Short.MAX_VALUE));
        layout.setVerticalGroup(layout.createParallelGroup(
                javax.swing.GroupLayout.Alignment.LEADING)
            .addGap(0, 442, Short.MAX_VALUE)
        );
    }// </editor-fold>

    // Variables declaration - do not modify
    // End of variables declaration
    /**
     * Gets default instance. Do not use directly: reserved for
     *.settings files only,
     * i.e. deserialization routines; otherwise you could get a
       non-deserialized instance.
     * To obtain the singleton instance, use {@link #findInstance}.
     */
    public static synchronized TaskEditorTopComponent getDefault() {
        if (instance == null) {
            instance = new TaskEditorTopComponent();
        }
        return instance;
    }
```

```java
/**
 * Obtain the TaskEditorTopComponent instance. Never call {
 *                                 @link #getDefault} directly!
 */
public static synchronized TaskEditorTopComponent findInstance() {
    TopComponent win = WindowManager.getDefault().findTopComponent
                                               (PREFERRED_ID);
    if (win == null) {
        Logger.getLogger(TaskEditorTopComponent.class.getName()).
        warning("Cannot find " + PREFERRED_ID + " component.
        It will not be located properly in the window system.");
        return getDefault();
    }
    if (win instanceof TaskEditorTopComponent) {
        return (TaskEditorTopComponent) win;
    }
    Logger.getLogger(TaskEditorTopComponent.class.getName()).
    warning("There seem to be multiple components with the '" +
    PREFERRED_ID
            + "' ID. That is a potential source of errors and
              unexpected behavior.");
    return getDefault();
}


@Override
public int getPersistenceType() {
    return TopComponent.PERSISTENCE_ALWAYS;
}


@Override
public void componentOpened() {
    // TODO add custom code on component opening
}
@Override
public void componentClosed() {
    // TODO add custom code on component closing
}


void writeProperties(java.util.Properties p) {
    // better to version settings since initial version
        as advocated at
    // http://wiki.apidesign.org/wiki/PropertyFiles
    p.setProperty("version", "1.0");
    // TODO store your settings
}

Object readProperties(java.util.Properties p) {
    if (instance == null) {
        instance = this;
```

```
        }
        instance.readPropertiesImpl(p);
        return instance;
    }

    private void readPropertiesImpl(java.util.Properties p) {
        String version = p.getProperty("version");
        // TODO read your settings according to their version
    }

    @Override
    protected String preferredID() {
        return PREFERRED_ID;
    }

}
```

As expected, the class `TaskEditorTopComponent` extends the `TopComponent` class.

Let's look at it more closely:

- For efficient resource usage, the generated `TopComponent` is implemented as a singleton. A private constructor prohibits its incorrect usage from outside by disallowing direct instantiation of the class. The static attribute `instance` holds the only instance in existence. The static method `getDefault` creates and returns this instance if necessary on demand. Typically, `getDefault` should never be called directly. Instead of this, you should use `findInstance`, which delegates to `getDefault` if necessary. `findInstance` tries to retrieve the instance using the Window Manager and the ID of the `TopComponent` before falling back to the singleton instance. This ensures the correct usage of persistent information.

- The constructor creates the component tree for the `TaskEditorTopComponent` by calling the method `initComponents()`. This method contains only code generated via the NetBeans "Matisse" Form Builder and is read-only in the NetBeans Java editor. You can change the code in this method using the Form Builder's Property Sheet, as will be shown later.

- The static property `PreferredID` holds the `TopComponent` ID used for identification of the `TopComponent`. As indicated by its name, the ID can be changed by the Window System, if name clashes occur. The ID is used throughout all the configuration files.

- The methods `componentOpened()` and `componentClosed()` are part of the lifecycle of the `TopComponent`.

- You learn about the method `getPersistenceType()` later, in the section about the persistence of `TopComponents`.

What does the Java code do and not do?

The Java code only defines the visual aspects of the `TaskEditorTopComponent` and manages the singleton instance of this component. In no way does the code describe how and where the instance is shown. That's the task of the two XML files, described below.

Two small XML files are created by the wizard. The first is the `TopComponent`'s settings file:

```xml
<?xml version="1.0" encoding="UTF-8"?>
<!DOCTYPE settings PUBLIC "-//NetBeans//DTD Session settings 1.0//EN"
"http://www.netbeans.org/dtds/sessionsettings-1_0.dtd">
<settings version="1.0">
    <module name="com.netbeansrcp.taskeditor" spec="1.0"/>
    <instanceof class="org.openide.windows.TopComponent"/>
    <instanceof class="com.netbeansrcp.taskeditor.
        TaskEditorTopComponent"/>
    <instance class="com.netbeansrcp.taskeditor.TaskEditorTopComponent"
        method="getDefault"/>
</settings>
```

The settings file describes the persistent instance of the `TopComponent`. As you can see, the preceding configuration describes that the `TopComponent` belongs to the module **TaskEditor** in the specification version "1.0" and that it is an instance of the types `TopComponent` and `TaskEditorTopComponent`. Also described is that the instance that is created is done so using the method call `TaskEditorTopComponent.getDefault()`.

```xml
<?xml version="1.0" encoding="UTF-8"?>
<!DOCTYPE tc-ref PUBLIC "-//NetBeans//DTD Top Component in Mode Properties
2.0//EN" "http://www.netbeans.org/dtds/tc-ref2_0.dtd">
<tc-ref version="2.0" >
    <module name="com.netbeansrcp.taskeditor" spec="1.0"/>
    <tc-id id="TaskEditorTopComponent"/>
    <state opened="true"/>
</tc-ref>
```

The WSTCREF (window system creation file) describes the position of the `TopComponent` within the main window. This becomes clearer with the following file. The other important information in the WSTCREF file is the opened state at application start.

Typically, you do not have to change these two configuration files by hand. This is not true for the following file, the `layer.xml`, which you often need to change manually, to register new folders and files in the filesystem.

```xml
<?xml version="1.0" encoding="UTF-8"?>
<!DOCTYPE filesystem PUBLIC "-//NetBeans//DTD Filesystem 1.2//EN" "http://
www.netbeans.org/dtds/filesystem-1_2.dtd">
  <filesystem>
    <folder name="Actions">
    <folder name="Window">
    <file name="com-netbeansrcp-taskeditor.TaskEditorAction.instance">
     <attr name="component"
                methodvalue="com.netbeansrcp.taskeditor.
                TaskEditorTopComponent.findInstance"/>
     <attr name="displayName"
                bundlevalue="com.netbeansrcp.taskeditor.
                Bundle#CTL_TaskEditorAction"/>
    <attr name="instanceCreate" methodvalue="org.openide.windows.
                TopComponent.openAction"/>
    </file>
    </folder>
    </folder>
    <folder name="Menu">
    <folder name="Window">
      <file name="TaskEditorAction.shadow">
        <attr name="originalFile" stringvalue="Actions/Window/com
        netbeansrcp-taskeditor-TaskEditorAction.instance"/>
      </file>
    </folder>
    </folder>
    <folder name="Windows2">
    <folder name="Components">
      <file name="TaskEditorTopComponent.settings"
                url="TaskEditorTopComponentSettings.xml"/>
    </folder>
    <folder name="Modes">
    <folder name="editor">
      <file name="TaskEditorTopComponent.wstcref"
                url="TaskEditorTopComponentWstcref.xml"/>
    </folder>
    </folder>
    </folder>
  </filesystem>
```

The `layer.xml` is integrated into the central registry (also known as the `SystemFileSystem`) using the via a registration entry in the module's **manifest** file. The `SystemFileSystem` is a virtual filesystem for user settings. Each module can supply a layer file for merging configuration data from the module into the `SystemFileSystem`.

The Window System API and the Actions API reserve a number of folders in the central registry for holding its configuration data. These folders enable specific subfolders and files relating to window system registration to be added to the filesystem.

- Let's have a look at the folder `Windows2`. `Windows2` contains a folder named `Components`, which contains a virtual file with the name of the `TopComponent` and the extension `.settings`. This `.settings` file redirects to the real settings file. It is used to make the configuration known to the Window System.

- In addition, the `Windows2` folder contains a folder named `Modes`, which contains a folder named `editor`. Modes represent the possible positions at which `TopComponents` can be shown in the application. The `editor` folder contains a `.wstcref` file for our `TopComponent`, which refers to the real `WSTCREF` file. This registers the `TopComponent` in the mode `editor`, so it shows up where typically editor windows are opened, which is the central part of the main window.

- Next, take a look at the folder `Actions`. It contains a folder named `Window` which contains a file declaring the action opening the `TaskEditorTopComponent`. The name is typically following Java class naming conventions with dots replaced by dashes and ending in `.instance`. The declaration of the virtual file itself consists of three critical parts. The attribute `component` describes how to create the component (`methodvalue` declares which method to call). The attribute `displayName` describes the default action name as shown in the example, in menu items. A possible declaration is the `bundle value` which describes the bundle and key to use to retrieve the display name. The attribute `instanceCreate` uses a static method call to create a real action to use.

- The folder `Menu` describes the application main menu. The folder `Window` contains a `.shadow` file. The attribute `originalFile` uses the full path in the `SystemFileSytem` to delegate to the original action declaration. As described above, `.shadow` files are used as symbolic links to real-defined virtual files. This declaration adds the action to the real menu bar of the application.

As a result, important parts of the Window System API are not called programmatically, but are simply used declaratively. Declarative aspects include configuration and the positioning of windows, as well as the construction of the menu.

In addition, you discovered that the wizard for creating `TopComponents` always creates singleton views. If you would like to change that, you need to adapt the code created by the wizard. For the time being, it is sufficient to use the singleton approach, particularly as it is more resource-friendly.

Automatic window lifecycle management

A further major advantage of the NetBeans Window System is that it provides a WindowManager that controls the lifecycle of all the windows defined in the application. The WindowManager notifies all `TopComponents` about state changes using callback methods, listed as follows:

`componentOpened()`	It is called after the `TopComponent` has been opened. If multiple `TopComponents` are opened into the same position (called `mode`), the NetBeans Window System uses a tabbed container, with one `TopComponent` per tab. Of all available `TopComponents` found within a shared tabbed container, only the content of the selected `TopComponent` is visible.
`componentShowing()`	It notifies the component that its content is now visible. This `TopComponent` is now either selected or is the only component in a separate container.
`componentActivated()`	It is called after the `TopComponent` has gained the input focus or has become the selected component.
`componentDeactivated()`	It is called after the `TopComponent` has lost the input focus.
`componentHidden()`	It notifies the `TopComponent` that its content is no longer visible.
`componentClosed()`	It is called after the `TopComponent` has been closed.

Let's illustrate this lifecycle via an example that logs all the callback methods to the output window of NetBeans IDE, which is your development environment on top of the NetBeans Platform.

1. Create a new NetBeans Platform application and name it **WindowSystemExamples**.

2. Add a new module named **LifeCycle**, with **Code Name Base** `com.netbeansrcp.lifecycle`.

3. Add a `TopComponent`, with **Class Name Prefix** prefix `LifeCycleDemo`, making sure to indicate that it should be automatically opened in the editor area at application startup.

4. Override the lifecycle methods as follows:

```java
public void componentOpened() {
  super.componentOpened();
  System.out.println("componentOpened()");
}


protected void componentShowing() {
    super.componentShowing();
    System.out.println("componentShowing()");
}


protected void componentActivated() {
  super.componentActivated();
  System.out.println("componentActivated()");

}


@Override
protected void componentDeactivated() {
  super.componentDeactivated();
  System.out.println("componentDeactivated()");
}


@Override
    protected void componentHidden() {
  super.componentHidden();
  System.out.println("componentHidden()");
}


@Override
    public void componentClosed() {
  super.componentClosed();
  System.out.println("componentClosed()");
}
```

Start the new application. The `TopComponent` `LifeCyleDemoTopComponent` is automatically opened at startup. Select the `TopComponent` and inspect the output in the NetBeans IDE Output Window. You should see the following:

```
componentOpened()
componentShowing()
componentActivated()
```

The `TopComponent` has passed the first half of its lifecycle and is now activated.

Close the `LifeCyleDemoTopComponent` and inspect the output again, to understand the second half of the `TopComponent` lifecycle. You should see the following output:

```
componentHidden()
componentDeactivated()
componentClosed()
```

You have learned that the `TopComponent`'s lifecycle is automatically controlled by the NetBeans Platform. Between the start and the end of the `TopComponent`'s lifecycle are six different states, all managed by the NetBeans Platform, and with notifications sent via callbacks.

Programmatically managing the Window lifecycle

You can manage the lifecycle of a `TopComponent` programmatically. For this purpose, the `TopComponent` provides the following methods:

- `open()`: Opens the `TopComponent`
- `requestVisible()`: Requests to select to `TopComponent`
- `requestActive()`: Requests to transfer the input focus to the `TopComponent`

Let's now modify the `LifeCycleDemoTopComponent` for demonstration purposes.

1. Add a JButton to the `TopComponent`, as follows:

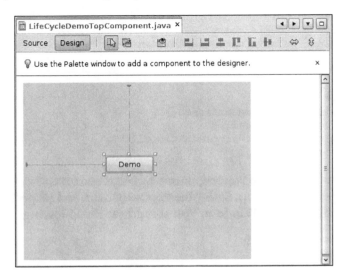

2. Implement an `ActionEventListener` as follows:

```java
private void jButton1ActionPerformed(java.awt.event.ActionEvent evt) {

    this.close();
    RequestProcessor.getDefault().post(new java.lang.Runnable() {
        public void run() {
            java.awt.EventQueue.invokeLater(new java.lang.Runnable() {
    public void run() {
    com.netbeansrcp.lifecycle.LifeCycleDemoTopComponent.this.open();
    }
                });
        }
    }, 3000);


        RequestProcessor.getDefault().post(new java.lang.Runnable() {

        public void run() {
            java.awt.EventQueue.invokeLater(new java.lang.Runnable() {

                public void run() {
                    com.netbeansrcp.lifecycle.
                    LifeCycleDemoTopComponent.this.requestActive();
                }
            });
        }
    }, 6000);
}
```

3. Restart the application. When you click the button, the `LifecycleDemoTopComponent` is closed via the `close()` method, called above in the first line of the code you entered.

The `RequestProcessor` provides a thread pool. The default instance of this pool lets you execute a `Runnable` after a short delay, thanks to the `post()` method. As the `TopComponent`'s lifecycle method should be called from the AWT event thread, you do not call them directly in the `run()` method, but by posting a new `Runnable` to the `EventQueue`, which in the end calls the Window System API methods.

The argument `3000` ensures that the execution of the `Runnable` is delayed for `3000` ms so that the `TopComponent` is opened again after 3 s.

After six seconds the second `Runnable` posted to the `EventQueue` is executed and `requestActive()` is called for your `LifecycleDemoTopComponent`. Your `TopComponent` is now shown in the foreground, if it had been behind other windows previously.

You have learned how to manage the lifecycle of a TopComponent. Via the example you have seen how to open a TopComponent and make it focusable.

Positioning of windows

The NetBeans Window System divides the available space in the main window into areas that are called "modes". Each mode represents a specific area of the main window, providing a container for windows in a predefined position in the frame. You can add windows, that is, TopComponents, to a mode, either declaratively or programmatically.

A standard layout is provided by the NetBeans Window System, corresponding to the layout of NetBeans IDE. For example, the predefined modes correspond to the names used in the corresponding positions in NetBeans IDE, such as "editor" and "explorer". If needed, you can define your own modes, too. No wizard is provided for this purpose in NetBeans IDE, so you need to create the mode definition files yourself manually.

In the previous section you learned about the layer.xml file. To create a default layout for an application, each TopComponent needs to be declaratively registered within the Windows2 | Modes folder, within a subfolder named after the mode in which the TopComponent should be docked.

To demonstrate declarative registration of TopComponents, edit the layer.xml in the **LifeCycle** module, changing the folder name Windows2 | Modes | editor to Windows | Modes | rightSlidingSide, as shown in the following code snippet:

layer.xml

```
//
  <folder name="Windows2">
    <folder name="Components">
      <file name="LifecycleDemoTopComponent.settings"
        url="LifecycleDemoTopComponentSettings.xml"/>
    </folder>
    <folder name="Modes">
      <folder name="rightSlidingSide">
        <file name="LifecycleDemoTopComponent.wstcref"
          url="LifecycleDemoTopComponentWstcref.xml"/>
      </folder>
    </folder>
  </folder>
//
```

Select **Clean and Build** on the application node in the **Projects** window, to remove the build folder containing the last used window layout, and start the application again. When the application starts up, notice that the LifecycleDemoTopComponent is not opened in the editor mode. Instead, it is represented by a button on the right sidebar of the application (as shown in the screenshot below). That is the rightSlidingSide mode, providing a container for minimized windows.

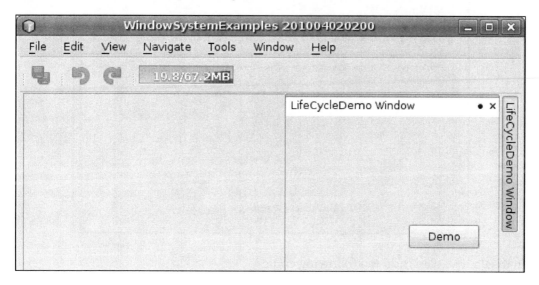

As you have seen, providing a default layout via declarative registrations of TopComponents is rather easy. You only need to create an entry in the layer.xml for the TopComponent, in a folder with the name of the desired mode, within the **Windows2 | Modes** folder.

Sometimes declarative registration alone is too static for your business needs. Fortunately, positioning of TopComponents can also be done programmatically. In the next example, you create a TopComponent that moves to new modes via a click of a button.

1. Add to the **WindowSystemExamples** application a new module named **Modes**, with the **Code Name Base** com.netbeansrcp.modes.

2. Within the module, create a TopComponent called **ModesDemo**, which is opened when the application starts into the "editor" mode.

Add two JButtons to the TopComponent with the texts **Back** and **Forward**, as well as a JLabel with an empty initial text. The TopComponent should look as shown in the following screenshot:

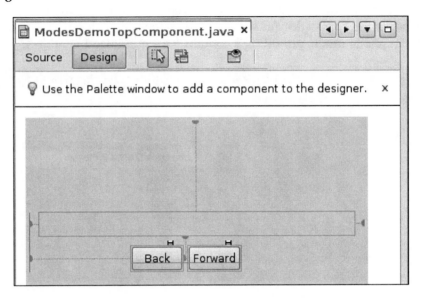

In the Source view, add the following code:

```
private static final String[] MODES = new String[] {
    "properties", "commonpalette", "rightSlidingSide",
    "bottomSlidingSide", "output", "debugger", "navigator",
    "explorer", "leftSlidingSide", "editor"
};
private void changeMode(boolean next) {
    Mode currentMode = WindowManager.getDefault().findMode(this);
    String currentModeName = currentMode.getName();

    String nextModeName = "editor";
    for (int i = 0; i < MODES.length; i++) {
        String modeName = MODES[i];
        if (modeName.equals(currentModeName)) {
            if (next) {
                nextModeName = (i + 1 < MODES.length) ? MODES[i + 1]
                               : MODES[0];
            }
            else {
                nextModeName = (i - 1 >= 0) ? MODES[i - 1] :
                    MODES[MODES.length - 1];
            }
```

```
                break;
              }
            }
          }

      Mode nextMode = WindowManager.getDefault().findMode(nextModeName);
          if (nextMode != null) {
              this.jLabel1.setText(nextModeName);
              nextMode.dockInto(this);
              this.open();
              this.requestActive();
          }
    }
    private void jButton2ActionPerformed(java.awt.event.ActionEvent evt) {
        this.changeMode(true);
    }
    private void jButton1ActionPerformed(java.awt.event.ActionEvent evt) {
        this.changeMode(false);
    }
```

The static string array contains the names of the most important modes. These modes can also be identified dynamically, by calling `WindowManager.getDefault().getModes()`.

The `ActionListener` delegates the call to the method `changeMode()` and gives the desired back/forward direction. This method determines via `WindowManager.getDefault().findMode(this)` the mode in which the `TopComponent` is displayed, as well as the name of the current mode.

The string array is then searched and `dockInto(this)` is called to dock the `TopComponent` into a different mode.

How to revert to the default layout?

As the layout of the NetBeans Platform is persisted when the application shuts down, first perform a **Clean and Build** on the application project. With the removal of the `build` folder, the layout settings are also deleted, so that the default layout is used when the application starts again.

Using the two buttons, you can let the `TopComponent` be docked in some of the most commonly used modes (as shown in the screenshot below).

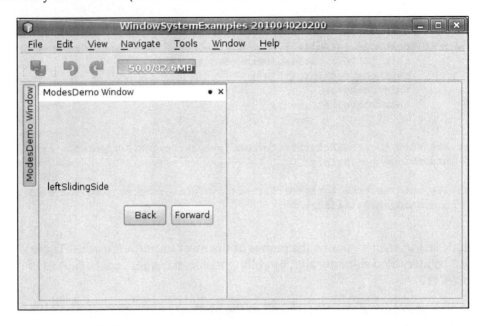

You have programmatically docked a `TopComponent` into various places within the available modes in the application. In the process, you have learned how `TopComponent`s can be docked dynamically, that is, at runtime, into desired positions. Both the declarative and the programmatic approaches to docking should now be familiar to you.

Creating custom modes

You can get quite far with the standard modes provided by the NetBeans Platform. Still, sometimes you may need to provide a custom mode, to provide a new position for the `TopComponent`s within the application. A custom mode is created declaratively in XML files, rather than programmatically in Java code.

In the following example, you create two new modes that are positioned side by side in the lower part of the application using a specific location relative to each other.

1. Create a new module named **CustomModes**, with **Code Name Base** `com.netbeansrcp.custommodes`, within the existing **WindowSystemExamples** application.

2. Right-click the module project and choose **New | Other** to open the **New File** dialog. Then choose **Other | Empty File**, as shown in the following screenshot:

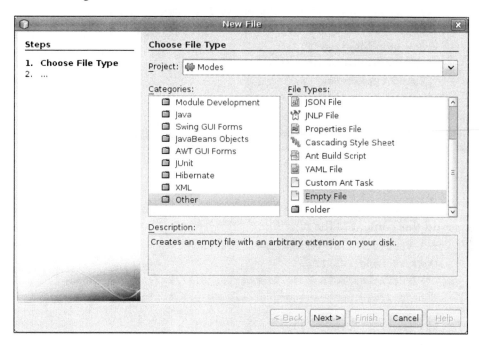

3. Type **model.wsmode** as the new filename and file extension, as shown in the following screenshot. Click **Finish**.

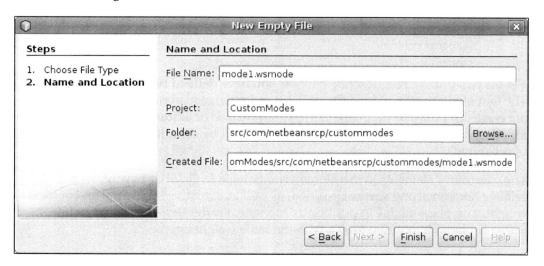

4. Define the content of the new **model.wsmode** as follows:

```xml
<?xml version="1.0" encoding="UTF-8"?>
<!DOCTYPE mode PUBLIC
  "-//NetBeans//DTD Mode Properties 2.3//EN"
  "http://www.netbeans.org/dtds/mode-properties2_3.dtd">
<mode version="2.3">
  <name unique="model" />
  <kind type="view" />
  <state type="joined" />
    <constraints>
      <path orientation="vertical" number="20" weight="0.2"/>
      <path orientation="horizontal" number="20" weight="0.5"/>
    </constraints>
  </mode>
```

5. Create another file to define the second mode and name it `mode2.wsmode`.
   Add this content to the new file:

```xml
<?xml version="1.0" encoding="UTF-8"?>
<!DOCTYPE mode PUBLIC
  "-//NetBeans//DTD Mode Properties 2.3//EN"
  "http://www.netbeans.org/dtds/mode-properties2_3.dtd">
<mode version="2.3">
  <name unique="mode2" />
  <kind type="view" />
  <state type="joined" />
  <constraints>
    <path orientation="vertical" number="20" weight="0.2"/>
    <path orientation="horizontal" number="40" weight="0.5"/>
  </constraints>
</mode>
```

Via the two `wsmode` files described above, you have defined two custom modes. The first mode has the unique name `model`, with the second named `mode2`. Both are created for normal `TopComponents` (**view** instead of **editor**) that are integrated into the main window, rather than being undocked by default (**joined** instead of **separated**).

The constraints elements in the files are comparable to **GridBagLayout**, with a relative horizontal and vertical position, as well as a relative horizontal and vertical weight. You place model in position `20/20` with a weighting of `0,5/0,2`, while `mode2` is placed in position `20/40` with the same weighting.

If all the other defined modes have TopComponents opened within them, the TopComponents in the two new modes should lie side by side, right above the status bar, taking up 20% of the available vertical space, with the horizontal space shared between them.

1. Let us now create two new TopComponents and register them in the layer.xml file so that they will be displayed in your new modes. Do this by using the **New Window** wizard twice in the **CustomModes** module, first creating a window called **Class Name Prefix Red** and then a window with **Class Name Prefix Blue**.

What should I set the window position to?

In the wizard, in both cases, it does not matter what you set to be the window position, as you are going to change that setting manually afterwards. Let both of them open automatically when the application starts.

2. In the **Design** mode of both **TopComponents**, add a JPanel to each of the **TopComponents**. Change the **background** property of the panel in the **RedTopComponent** to red and in the **BlueTopComponent** to blue.

3. Edit the layer.xml of **CustomModes** module, registering the two **.wsmode** files and ensuring that the two new **TopComponents** open in the new modes:

```xml
<folder name="Windows2">
  <folder name="Components">
    <file name="BlueTopComponent.settings"
      url="BlueTopComponentSettings.xml"/>
    <file name="RedTopComponent.settings"
      url="RedTopComponentSettings.xml"/>
  </folder>
  <folder name="Modes">
    <file name="mode1.wsmode" url="mode1.wsmode"/>
    <file name="mode2.wsmode" url="mode2.wsmode"/>
      <folder name="mode1">
        <file name="RedTopComponent.wstcref"
          url="RedTopComponentWstcref.xml"/>
      </folder>
      <folder name="mode2">
        <file name="BlueTopComponent.wstcref"
          url="BlueTopComponentWstcref.xml"/>
      </folder>
  </folder>
</folder>
```

4. As before, perform a **Clean and Build** on the application project node and then start the application again. It should look as shown in the following screenshot:

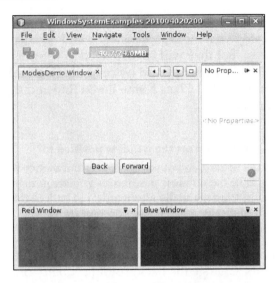

In the summary, you defined two new modes in XML files and registered them in the module's `layer.xml` file. To confirm that the modes work correctly, you use the `layer.xml` file to register two new `TopComponents` so that they open by default into the new modes. As a result, you now know how to extend the default layout of a NetBeans Platform application with new modes.

Creating window groups

Some windows should always open and close together with other windows. For example, in NetBeans IDE, the Matisse GUI Builder's Design mode always opens together with the **Inspector**, the **Palette**, and the **Properties** window. That combination of windows constitutes a workspace to use when laying out an application's user interface. To achieve this yourself in your own application, you need to define a `TopComponentGroup`.

In the following example, you group the two `TopComponents` you have created in the previous sections and open and close them together as a single unit.

1. To get started, within the **CustomModes** module, create a new empty file named `colorgroup.wsgrp`, with the following content:

```xml
<?xml version="1.0" encoding="UTF-8"?>

<!DOCTYPE group PUBLIC
   "-//NetBeans//DTD Group Properties 2.0//EN"
   "http://www.netbeans.org/dtds/group-properties2_0.dtd">
   <group version="2.0">
   <name unique="colorgroup" />
   <state opened="false" />
</group>
```

   You have now defined a group named **colorgoup** and you have specified that initially the `TopComponents` within the group are closed.

2. Let us now specify which `TopComponents` belong to the group. Create two new files called `RedTopComponentWstcgrp.xml` and `BlueTopComponentWstcgrp.xml`, with the content shown in the following code snippets:

```xml
<?xml version="1.0" encoding="UTF-8" ?>
<!DOCTYPE tc-group PUBLIC "-//NetBeans//DTD Top Component in Group
Properties 2.0//EN" "http://www.netbeans.org/dtds/tc-group2_0.dtd">
<tc-group version="2.0">
    <module name="com.netbeansrcp.custommodes" spec="1.0"/>
    <tc-id id="RedTopComponent" />
    <open-close-behavior open="true" close="true" />
</tc-group>
<?xml version="1.0" encoding="UTF-8"?>
<!DOCTYPE tc-ref PUBLIC "-//NetBeans//DTD Top Component in Mode
Properties 2.0//EN" "http://www.netbeans.org/dtds/tc-ref2_0.dtd">
<tc-ref version="2.0" >
    <module name="com.netbeansrcp.custommodes" spec="1.0"/>
    <tc-id id="BlueTopComponent"/>
    <open-close-behavior open="true" close="true" />
</tc-ref>
```

   You now have a file per `TopComponent`, providing the `TopComponent`'s unique ID, while declaring the state of the `TopComponent` when the group to which it belongs is opened or closed.

3. Now modify the `layer.xml` to register the two files created in the previous step, within the **Windows2 | Groups** folder:

```
<folder name="Groups">
  <file name="colorgroup.wsgrp" url="colorgroup.wsgrp"/>
    <folder name="colorgroup">
      <file name="RedTopComponent.wstcgrp"
        url="RedTopComponentWstcgrp.xml"/>
      <file name="BlueTopComponent.wstcgrp"
        url="BlueTopComponentWstcgrp.xml"/>
    </folder>
</folder>
```

The file `colorgroup.wsgrp` declares the group to the Window System and refers to the group definition file of the same name. The subfolder `color-group` describes the contents of the group and adds references to the file for each `TopComponent`, so that they now belong to the group.

4. Use the **New Action** wizard to create two new **Always Enabled** actions, **OpenRedBlueAction** and **CloseRedBlueAction**, with display names **OpenRedBlue** and **CloseRedBlue**, for opening/closing the group. Within the **ActionListener** classes generated by the **New Action** wizard, define the code to be invoked as follows:

```
public void actionPerformed(ActionEvent evt) {
    TopComponentGroup myGroup
        WindowManager.getDefault().findTopComponentGroup("colorgroup");
        if (myGroup != null) {
           myGroup.open();
        }
}


public void actionPerformed(ActionEvent evt) {
    TopComponentGroup myGroup = WindowManager.getDefault()
      .findTopComponentGroup("colorgroup");
    if (myGroup != null) {
       myGroup.close();
    }
}
```

5. Modify the files `BlueTopComponentWstcref.xml` and `RedTopComponentWstcref.xml`, to ensure that their individual default states are set to closed:

```
<state opened="false"/>
```

6. Choose **Clean and Build** on the application to remove the `build` folder that contains the user settings persisted from the last deployment of the application. Start the application again. Select **Window | OpenRedBlue** and notice that both `TopComponents` open. Then select **Window | CloseRedBlue** and notice that both `TopComponents` close.

In the summary, you have learned how to define a group of `TopComponents` that open and close together as a unit.

Extending the default TopComponent persistence

You've probably noticed that when you restart the application, its layout is not reset to its default state. Instead, the layout settings from the last deployment are reused whenever you restart the application. That is what the user typically expects, though this may be inconvenient during development. During development, if you'd like the default layout to be used when you run the application, you need to select **Clean and Build** on the application node. This menu item deletes the application's `build` folder, which contains the `testuserdir` folder, where the settings from the previous deployment are stored.

It is this feature, that of automatic persistence, that we now look at more closely. In this section, we extend the persistence of our application, as the NetBeans Platform allows us to access the persistence feature and to save additional data when the application is closed.

In the next example, we create a simple form with content that is restored when the application restarts.

1. Create a new NetBeans Platform application, containing a new module, with a `TopComponent` created via the **New Window** wizard. The `TopComponent` should have `PersistenceDemo` as its **Class Name Prefix**, it should be positioned within the editor mode, and it should open when the application starts. Design the content of the new `TopComponent` as shown the following screenshot:

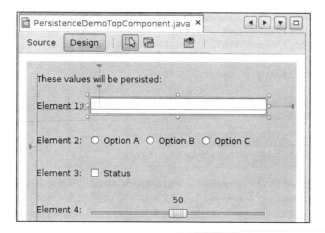

The Window System API provides special support for serialization of configuration data. To store configuration data, and to reload them at restart, we need to override the methods `writeProperties` and `readProperties`, which are generated by the **New Window** wizard when you created the `TopComponent`. These methods are required so that the `@ConvertAsProperties` annotation, declared at the top of the `TopComponent` class, is able to generate the code at compile time, persisting the specified settings.

To fine-tune the `TopComponent` persistence outlined above, you have two additional values that need to be set, but which are set by default when you use the **New Window** wizard to create your `TopComponent`:

- The value returned by the `preferredID()` method. The returned value uniquely identifies the `TopComponent` to the window system.

- The value returned by the `getPersistenceType` method. This value determines the conditions under which the `TopComponent` is persisted. The value `TopComponent.PERSISTENCE_ALWAYS` specifies that the content of the `TopComponent` will be persisted, in so far as you have specified settings for persistence. `PERSISTENCE_NEVER` specifies that when the application closes, nothing set in the `TopComponent` will be persisted. Finally, `PERSISTENCE_ONLY_OPENED` specifies that a `TopComponent` is only persisted if it is open when the application shuts down. The latter is useful if the `TopComponent` is some kind of editor, for example, as in the cases of the editor windows in NetBeans IDE, which reopen on startup if they had been closed when the application shut down.

2. Specify that the `PersistenceDemoTopComponent` should persist if it was open when the application shut down. Next, define the `writeProperties` and `readProperties` methods as follows:

```
void writeProperties(java.util.Properties p) {
    // better to version settings since initial version as advocated
    // at http://wiki.apidesign.org/wiki/PropertyFiles
    p.setProperty("version", "1.0");
    p.setProperty("element1", jTextField1.getText());
    if (jRadioButton1.isSelected()) {
        p.setProperty("element2", "1");
    }
    if (jRadioButton2.isSelected()) {
        p.setProperty("element2", "2");
    }
    if (jRadioButton3.isSelected()) {
        p.setProperty("element2", "3");
    }
    p.setProperty("element3", String.valueOf(jCheckBox1.isSelected()));
    p.setProperty("element4", String.valueOf(jSlider1.getValue()));
}
```

```
Object readProperties(java.util.Properties p) {
    if (instance == null) {
        instance = this;
    }
    instance.readPropertiesImpl(p);
    return instance;
}

private void readPropertiesImpl(java.util.Properties p) {
    String version = p.getProperty("version");
    jTextField1.setText(p.getProperty("element1","empty"));
    if (p.getProperty("element2").equals("1")) {
        jRadioButton1.setSelected(true);
    }
    if (p.getProperty("element2").equals("2")) {
        jRadioButton2.setSelected(true);
    }
    if (p.getProperty("element2").equals("3")) {
        jRadioButton3.setSelected(true);
    }
    if (p.getProperty("element3").equals("true")) {
        jCheckBox1.setSelected(true);
    } else {
        jCheckBox1.setSelected(false);
    }
    jSlider1.setValue(Integer.parseInt(p.getProperty("element4")));
}
```

3. Restart the application. Enter some values into the TopComponent and then close the application. When you restart the application, notice that the values you specified are restored as shown in the following screenshot:

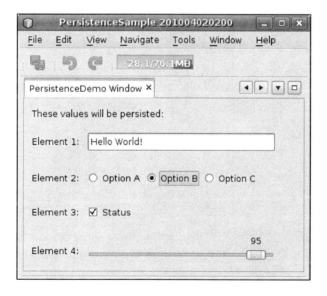

When you close the application, do a **Clean and Build** on the **TaskManager** project node. Then, now that the application user directory is removed, restart the application and notice that all the values are set back to their defaults.

In summary, you have extended the persistence of the TopComponent, so that the values specified in the TopComponent at the time the application shuts down are restored when the application is restarted.

Summary

You have been introduced to all of the most important topics relating to working with the NetBeans Window System. Not only did you learn how to create new windows, that is, TopComponents, but you also learned how to position them, group them, and extend their persistence.

In the next chapter, you focus on one of the key topics of modular architectures, that is, how a module can communicate with another module, without even the need to know that it exists! This is a key requirement for modular architectures ensuring that modules are loosely coupled from each other.

4
Lookup

"Lookup" is the NetBeans Platform's response to the need for loose coupling at all levels of software architecture. On the level of modules, lookups enable service providers to centrally register their services and consumers to find them. On the level of individual components, lookups enable the exchange of information between a provider and any number of consumers. The information can either be messages, data, or information about component state and capabilities.

The topics covered in this chapter will teach you the following:

- How to register and find services
- How to create extension points
- How to enable loosely-coupled communication
- How to handle dynamic changes and notifications
- How to handle selection management

Registering and finding services

In a modular system, the implementation of a service should be interchangeable. Simultaneously, it should also be possible for there to be several implementations of a single service. Users of those services need a central mechanism to find service providers. As a result, you need to be able to register an implementation of a service and also the possibility of finding registered services.

NetBeans provides a so-called "default `Lookup`" to find registered services. The API of a `Lookup` is similar to `Map<Class, Collection<Object>>`, where the key is a type and the values are instances of the type.

The result of a `Lookup` might not only be one or more objects but also an observable `Lookup.Result`, which provides access to several other stored objects. The default `Lookup` is a `Lookup` that evaluates the service declarations in the `META-INF/services` folder. It is callable through the `Lookup.getDefault()` method. By asking for a service interface in this way, you receive instances of implementing classes registered in the `META-INF/services` folder.

To demonstrate this approach, you continue to develop the **TaskModel** module in the next sections, as the **TaskModel** module should not only provide a new Task but also add a unique ID to it. This can be done in several ways, which is the reason why you do not work with a direct implementation, but with a service around which you provide replaceable implementations. In this simple scenario, the standard implementation is defined in the same module as the service definition.

1. In the **TaskManager**, create a new module named **TaskIDGenerator**, with **com.netbeansrcp.taskidgenerator** as the **Code Name Base**.

2. In the new module, create an interface named **TaskIdGenerator**, within a package named **com.netbeansrcp.taskidgenerator.api**, using the following code snippet:

```
public interface TaskIdGenerator {
    public String generateID();
}
```

3. Create an implementation, named **TaskIdGeneratorImpl**, in the package **com.netbeansrcp.taskidgenerator**, with this code:

```
public class TaskIdGeneratorImpl implements TaskIdGenerator {
  private Random random = new Random();
  public String generateID() {
      String id = "000000" + this.random.nextInt();
      id = id.substring(id.length()-6);
      return id;
    }
}
```

Now the service is to be registered, using the standard JDK 6 Java extension mechanism. That mechanism entails the creation of a folder named `META-INF/services`, containing a file named after the interface, containing a list of names of implementing classes.

1. Instead of creating that file manually, add a dependency on the NetBeans Lookup API, and then annotate the `TaskIdGeneratorImpl` class as follows:

```
@ServiceProvider(service=TaskIdGenerator.class)
public class TaskIdGeneratorImpl implements TaskIdGenerator {
```

2. Declare the package `com.netbeansrcp.taskidgenerator.api` as part of the public interface of the module.

This is all you need to do to register the new service. Next, you need to be able to find the service, from the **TaskModel** module.

1. The implementation of the Task should use the `TaskIdGenerator` to generate an ID and assign it to the id attribute. Therefore the **TaskModel** module needs to declare a dependency to the **TaskIdGenerator** module.

2. As already mentioned, it's very easy to find a service. The only thing you need to do is to ask for the interface of the service using the default `Lookup`:

```
public TaskImpl(String name, String parentId) {
    TaskIdGenerator idGen = Lookup.getDefault().lookup
        (com.netbeansrcp.taskidgenerator
        .api.TaskIdGenerator.class);
    this.id = idGen.generateID();
    this.name = name;
    // ...
```

Manage your dependencies!

To use the `Lookup` class above, you need to declare a dependency in the **TaskModel** module on the Lookup API module.

3. Now start the application. The **TaskEditor** should show a generated six-digit ID, as you can see in the screenshot below:

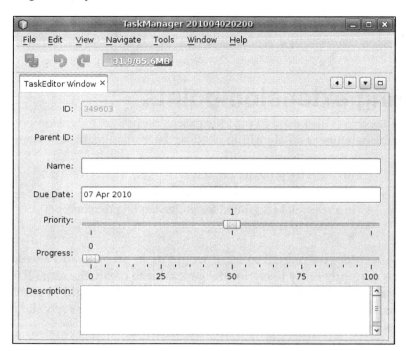

To summarize, you have been introduced to the default Lookup mechanism for finding services. In order to register a service, you only need to annotate a class with the @ServiceProvider annotation to fulfill the Java extension mechanism requirement, as this annotation causes the META-INF/services folder to be created at compile time, together with the required service provider registration. The default Lookup finds the files created at compile time in the META-INF/services folder, evaluates them, and gives back instances of registered implementing classes.

When you look in the **Files** window *Ctrl-2*, the build folder shows the META-INF/services folder with its content that has correctly been created at compile time thanks to the @ServiceProvider annotation:

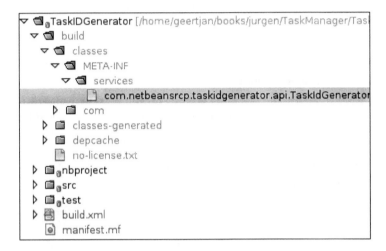

Creating extension points

The default Lookup is also used to provide extension points. Extension points are made available whenever an algorithm needs to be exchangeable or extensible.

> **Think "service provider interface"**
>
> Readers familiar with the term "Service Provider Interface" have a relevant background for understanding the concepts addressed in this section.

For the ID generator you've built so far, it would make sense to add a validator. After all, it is currently fairly likely for the generator to create the same ID twice or to return a negative ID. The number of types of validators that could be relevant for the ID is endless, hence you need to make it possible for any number of validators to be made available dynamically.

1. Start by creating a validation service. Do this by defining an interface named `IdValidator` in the package **com.netbeansrcp.taskidgenerator.api**.

2. As an implementation of the interface, create a class named `UniqueIdValidator` in the package **com.netbeansrcp.taskidgenerator**. The implementation pseudo-checks the uniqueness of IDs.

3. The code for the interface and its implementation is shown as follows:

```
public interface IdValidator {
  boolean validate(String id);
}
@ServiceProvider(service=IdValidator.class)
public class UniqueIdValidator implements IdValidator {
  public boolean validate(String id) {
  System.out.println("UniqueIdValidator.validate(" + id + ")");
  return true;
  }
}
```

4. Now you need to define an extension point. This extension point consists of logic in `TaskIdGeneratorImpl` that searches for all `IdValidators` and calls their `validate(String)` method.

   ○ In addition, the extension point consists of documentation stating that all `TaskIdGenerators` embed services made available by `IdValidators`. To this end, you need to rewrite `TaskIdGeneratorImpl`. Again you use the default `Lookup`. This time, though, you won't only search for one instance but for all instances of a type. This means you receive all registered implementations of the service.

   ○ In addition, you work with a `Lookup.Result` object, which encapsulates the search result and is able to dynamically notify listeners when the lookup content changes. You read about this feature later in the chapter. The `Lookup.Result` either holds a collection of found instances or a collection of `Lookup.Items`. `Lookup.Items` does not only allow access to found instances but also to metadata such as types, IDs, and display names.

   ○ After requesting the found instances, you are able to call them at well-defined and documented parts of the software. This way, you create software that is extensible by yourself or third-party vendors.

```
@ServiceProvider(service=TaskIdGenerator.class)
public class TaskIdGeneratorImpl implements TaskIdGenerator {

    private Random random = new Random();
```

```
                    public String generateID() {
                        Lookup.Result<IdValidator> rslt =
                            Lookup.getDefault().lookupResult(IdValidator.class);
                        String id = null;
                        boolean valid = false;
                        while (!valid){

                            id = this.getId();

                            valid = true;
                            for (IdValidator validator : rslt.allInstances()) {

                                valid = valid & validator.validate(id);
                            }
                        }
                        return id;
                    }

                private String getId() {
                    String id = "000000" + this.random.nextInt();
                    return id.substring(id.length() - 6);
                }
            }
```

- ○ The `generateID()` method uses `Lookup.getDefault().` `lookup(...)` to receive a `Lookup.Result<IdValidator>` from the default `Lookup` that holds all registered implementations of the `IdValidator` interface.

- ○ The found instances are used to validate the generated IDs. Therefore, the `valid` flag is set to `true` and all found `IdValidator` instances are asked if they accept the ID. If a validator does not accept the ID, the flag is set to `false`, a new ID is generated, and validated again. This step is repeated until all the validators accept the ID.

5. Start your application and look at the output. You should find the output includes the following line:

```
UniqueIdValidator.validate(954566)
```

The message above proves that the `IdValidator` is found and called.

In summary, you have created an extension point and used it in the **TaskManager**. As an exercise, you can create another service provider to make available another implementation of the service and reuse the extension point.

Using extension points externally

In the previous section, the extension point is defined in the same module as where it is used. In order to connect to the extension point from an external module, you need to do the same as before. You need to read the documentation, find out about the extension points of the application, and implement the relevant service interfaces. As before, once you have implemented a service interface, use the `@ServiceProvider` annotation to register the implementation.

Let's look at this process using the **TaskManager** application.

1. In the **TaskManager**, create a new module named **NotNegativeIdValidator**, with **com.netbeansrcp.notnegativeidvalidator** as the code name base.

2. In the new module, declare a dependency on the modules **TaskIDGenerator** and **Lookup**.

3. Create a new class as the service provider, named `NotNegativeIdValidator`, defined as follows:

    ```
    @ServiceProvider(service=IdValidator.class)
    public class NotNegativeIdValidator implements IdValidator {
      public boolean validate(String id) {
          System.out.println("NotNegativeIdValidator.validate(" + id +
            ")");
          return !id.startsWith("-");
      }
    }
    ```

4. Start the application and look at the output. It should include lines as follows:

    ```
    UniqueIdValidator.validate(357769)
    NotNegativeIdValidator.validate(357769)
    ```

As you can see, the module **NotNegativeIdValidator** extended another module.

In summary, for a moment you switched to the role of an external programmer. The external programmer extended your own `IdValidator`. From the documentation of the **TaskManager**, the external programmer found the name of the `IdValidator` interface. As a result, the external programmer created a new module and then implemented the interface. After using the `@ServiceProvider` annotation to register the interface, the service was found and used automatically when the application started.

Enabling loosely-coupled communication

Apart from its involvement in the registration and finding of services, the Lookup has another important purpose. The Lookup is the primary mechanism enabling objects to exchange information without being dependent on each other.

To make loose coupling possible, an information provider is able to administer its own Lookup, providing it to anyone interested in its information. Into its Lookup, the provider can put objects that the consumer might find useful. The consumer only needs to find the Lookup and get the objects, based on their type.

The ability to administer and provide a Lookup is defined via the Lookup.Provider interface:

```
Lookup getLookup()
```

In this section, you create a new window in a new module. The new window shows a log of previously created Tasks, without the module that contains the window having a dependency on the **TaskEditorTopComponent** window. This scenario reflects a typical Master/Detail relationship implemented on the NetBeans Platform. A different approach is described in the chapter on Nodes and Explorer views.

1. The main source for new Tasks in the example is the TaskEditorTopComponent. It does not hold a reference to the Task being edited. Instead, the Task is handled by the TaskEditorPanel only. To make the Task publicly available, change its modified from private to public in the TaskEditorPanel, shown as follows:

```
public Task task = new TaskImpl();
```

2. The TaskEditor should handle a Lookup and provide it using the Lookup.Provider interface. The TopComponent class already implements Lookup.Provider and therefore your TaskEditorTopComponent doesn't need to do so explicitly. In addition to implementing Lookup.Provider, TopComponents provide a method for resetting the Lookup. Therefore, you need to extend the constructor of TaskEditorTopComponent to create a new Lookup and set it for the TopComponent. Instead of implementing your own Lookup, you use the Lookup class, which creates a Lookup with one single object:

```
private TaskEditorTopComponent() {
        initComponents();
// ...
        this.associateLookup
        (Lookups.singleton(((TaskEditorPanel)
        this.taskEditorPanel1).task)
);
}
```

That's all that needs to be done on the side providing the information, which is, in this case, the Task.

Loosely-coupled consumption

You have now exposed data that any other part of your application can consume. To that end, you create a new module containing a new TopComponent, where the Task is consumed.

1. Create a new module named **TaskLog**, with **org.netbeansrcp.tasklog** as the **Code Name Base**.

2. Set a dependency on the **TaskModel** module.

3. Use the **New Window Component** wizard to create a new TopComponent. The window should appear in the **properties** mode and the class name prefix is **TaskLog**.

4. The Tasks consumed by the TopComponent are displayed in a JList. In the IDE, drag a JList and drop it on the TopComponent. Let it take up the TopComponent's complete vertical and horizontal space and remove the default content so that it is empty as shown in the following screenshot:

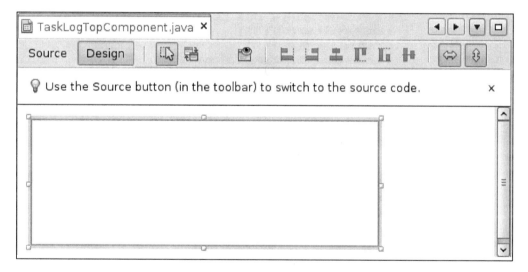

5. Switch to the **Source** view of the `TopComponent` and add an instance variable for a `DefaultListModel`, which you will use to store Tasks. After the `TopComponent` is opened, the currently edited Task is shown in the `JList`.

6. To synchronize the data in the view with the editor, implement a `PropertyChangeListener` for the `TaskLogTopComponent`. When the `TopComponent` opens, add the `PropertyChangeListener` and remove it when the `TopComponent` closes.

   The preceding code is listed as follows:

```
final class TaskLogTopComponent extends TopComponent implements
   PropertyChangeListener {
       private DefaultListModel listModel = new DefaultListModel();
// ...

       public void componentOpened() {
           Task task = WindowManager.getDefault().
             findTopComponent("TaskEditorTopComponent").
             getLookup().lookup(Task.class);
           this.listModel.addElement(task);
           task.addPropertyChangeListener(this);
         }
       public void componentClosed() {
           for ( Enumeration e = this.listModel.elements();
             e.hasMoreElements(); ) {
             ((Task)e.nextElement())
                .removePropertyChangeListener(this);
           }
         }
       }
// ...
     public void propertyChange(PropertyChangeEvent arg0) {
         this.jList1.repaint();
       }
```

7. To link the `DefaultListModel` to the `JList`, select the `JList` open the **Code** section of the **Properties** window, and add the following line to the **Custom Creation Code** property:

```
new JList(this.listModel);
```

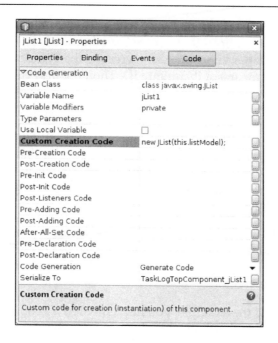

8. Run the application. On the right side of the application, that is, in the **Properties** mode, you see the **TaskLog**. The only item in the list is the item for the currently edited Task. As you edit the Task, the **TaskLog** in the JList is updated.

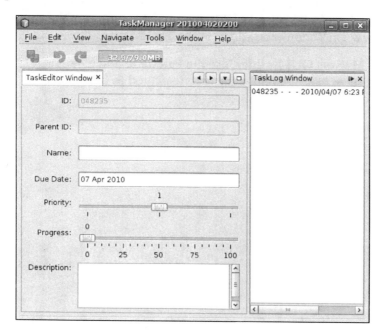

In summary, you added the current Task to the `Lookup` of the `TaskEditorTopComponent`. You then created another module, containing another `TopComponent`. In the latter `TopComponent`, you use the **WindowManager** to find the first `TopComponent` by means of its unique ID. Then the first `TopComponent`'s `Lookup` is queried for its `Task` object.

The second `TopComponent` acquired data from the first `TopComponent` without there being a dependency between the two. Of course, you do still have a different kind of dependency between the two `TopComponents` as you hardcoded the name of the first `TopComponent` in order to enable the **WindowManager** to find it. That part of the example changes later in this chapter, to remove even that semi-dependency between the two modules.

You have now seen how two loosely-coupled objects can exchange data with each other. The potential number of consumers of the data is unlimited. It is also irrelevant whether the consumer is part of the original application or contributed by an external third-party vendor.

For current purposes of the example, you implemented a `PropertyChangeListener`, to keep the two `TopComponents` synchronized. A later chapter shows a better way of doing this, in the context of working with Nodes and Explorer views.

Creating new tasks

Let us now prevent Tasks from being created automatically whenever the `TopComponent` opens. Instead, let's let the user click a button in the `TopComponent` whenever a new Task should be added to the **TaskManager**.

1. In the **Matisse GUI Builder**, use the **Palette** to add a `JButton` to the `TaskEditorPanel`. Change the text displayed in the `JButton` to **Create New Task**.

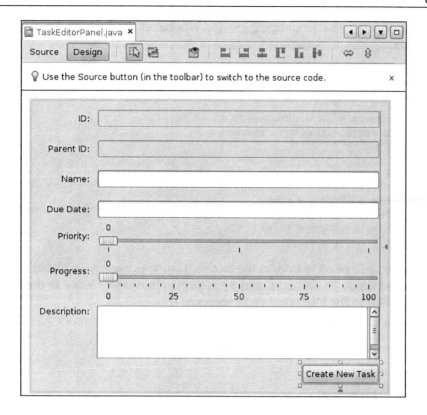

2. Double-click the `JButton` so the **Source** view opens, with the cursor in the definition of a new `actionPerformed` event. Use the event to create a new Task and update the form, as shown in the following code snippet:

```
private void jButton1ActionPerformed(java.awt.event.ActionEvent
evt) {
    this.task = new TaskImpl();
    this.updateForm();
}
```

3. To prevent a task from being created whenever the form opens, which is currently the case, change the code in the panel as follows:

```java
public class TaskEditorPanel extends javax.swing.JPanel {
    // ...
    private boolean noUpdate = false;
    // ...
    private void updateTask() {
    if (this.noUpdate)  return;
    // ...

    // ...
    private void updateForm() {
    this.noUpdate = true;
    // ...
    this.noUpdate = false;
}
```

4. Finally, you need to inform the `TaskEditorTopComponent` about newly created tasks. To that end, add a `PropertyChangeListener` to the JPanel, as shown in the following code snippet:

```java
public class TaskEditorPanel extends javax.swing.JPanel {
    public static final String PROP_TASK = "TASK";
    private PropertyChangeSupport pcs;
    // ...

    @Override
    public synchronized void
        addPropertyChangeListener(PropertyChangeListener listener) {
      if (pcs == null) {
         pcs = new PropertyChangeSupport(this);
         }
      this.pcs.addPropertyChangeListener(listener);
    }

    @Override
    public synchronized void
      removePropertyChangeListener(PropertyChangeListener listener) {
      if (pcs != null) {
          this.pcs.removePropertyChangeListener(listener);
         }
    }

    private void
            jButton1ActionPerformed(java.awt.event.ActionEvent evt) {
        Task oldTask = this.task;
        this.task = new TaskImpl();
        this.pcs.firePropertyChange(PROP_TASK, oldTask,this.task);
        this.updateForm();
      }
    // ...
```

Run the application again. Edit some of the values in the form and notice that the form is cleared and a new Task ID is assigned whenever you click the JButton.

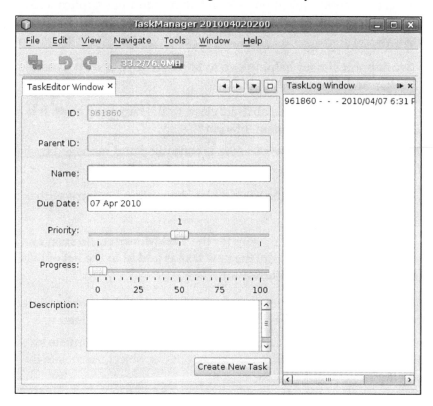

However, the list in the **TaskLog** remains unchanged. It only shows the initial task. Neither the TaskEditorTopComponent nor the TaskLogTopComponent currently support the ability to be dynamically updated. Part of the reason for this is that the **TaskLog** only looks into the Lookup once for a task, that is, when the **TaskLog** opens. Another part of the reason for the lacking dynamic update support is that the Lookup you are using is itself not observable. A Lookup created via Lookups.singleton() can only contain a fixed object, which is certainly insufficient for applications requiring dynamic handling of custom objects, such as, in this case, Tasks.

In the next section, you learn how to dynamically update the content of a Lookup and how consumers can be dynamically notified about changes to the Lookup.

Dynamic changes and notifications

As a vital aspect of a communication mechanism for modular applications, Lookup supports dynamic content, as well as consumer notifications when the dynamic content changes.

There are two support classes helping you to implement your own dynamic Lookup: AbstractLookup and InstanceContent.

- AbstractLookup is not an abstract class, as the name suggests. It is a full-featured Lookup implementation
- The content of an AbstractLookup is controlled and managed by the class InstanceContent

Together, these classes provide the basis for implementing Lookups with dynamic content.

Let's now implement a dynamic Lookup for the **TaskManager**. As soon as a new task has been created in the TaskEditor, the new task is added to the list of logs in the **Task Logs** window, shown as follows:

1. Modify the TaskEditorTopComponent. To control the Lookup content, create an InstanceContent object and store it as a member for later use.

2. In the constructor of the TaskEditorTopComponent, instantiate an AbstractLookup using that InstanceContent object. Associate the Lookup with the TaskEditorTopComponent.

3. Now the Lookup content needs to be updated, if a new task is created. To achieve this, register a PropertyChangeListener on the **TaskEditorPanel** and add new tasks to the InstanceContent.

The following code is the result of the above steps:

```
final class TaskEditorTopComponent extends TopComponent {
    // ...
    private InstanceContent ic = new InstanceContent();
    private PropertyChangeListener taskChangeListener =
      new ListenForTaskChanges();
    // ...

    private TaskEditorTopComponent() {
        initComponents();
        this.taskEditorPanel1.addPropertyChangeListener
            (taskChangeListener);
        this.ic.add(((TaskEditorPanel)
          this.taskEditorPanel1).task);
```

```
        this.associateLookup(new AbstractLookup(this.ic));
    }

    private class ListenForTaskChanges implements
      PropertyChangeListener {

        public void propertyChange(PropertyChangeEvent arg0) {

            If(TaskEditorPanel.PROP_TASK.equals
            (arg0.getPropertyName())) {

                List newContent = new ArrayList();
                    newContent.add(((TaskEditorPanel)
                       TaskEditorTopComponent.this.taskEditorPanel1).
                          task);

                TaskEditorTopComponent.this.ic.set(
                                        newContent, null);

            }
        }
    }

}
```

That's all that is needed to make the current task available in the `Lookup` of the `TaskEditorTopComponent`.

Next, `TaskLogTopComponent` needs to be notified about changed tasks in the `Lookup` of `TaskEditTopComponent`. In the previous example, you already used `Lookup.Result` to search for objects. However, there is one essential feature of `Lookup.Result` that you have not yet used. That is the ability of `Lookup.Result` to notify `LookupListeners` about changes in the requested result.

To use the `LookupListener` and receive notifications, change `TaskLogTopComponent` to implement the `LookupListener` interface. Register the `LookupListener` on the `Lookup.Result` that is created while the component is opening:

```
final class TaskLogTopComponent extends TopComponent
        implements PropertyChangeListener, LookupListener {

    // ...
    private Lookup.Result<Task> result;

    // ...
    public void componentOpened() {
        this.result =
          WindowManager.getDefault().
            findTopComponent("TaskEditorTopComponent").
              getLookup().lookupResult(Task.class);
        this.result.addLookupListener(this);
        for (Task task : this.result.allInstances()) {
            this.listModel.addElement(task);
            task.addPropertyChangeListener(this);
        }
```

```
        }

    public void componentClosed() {
        for (Enumeration e = this.listModel.elements();
                         e.hasMoreElements();) {
        ((Task)e.nextElement()).removePropertyChangeListener(this);
        }
        this.result = null;
    }
    public void resultChanged(LookupEvent evt) {
        Lookup.Result<Task> rslt = (Result<Task>) evt.getSource();
        for (Task task : rslt.allInstances()) {
            this.listModel.addElement(task);
            task.addPropertyChangeListener(this);
        }
    }
}
// ...
}
```

Run the application again.

When you click the JButton to create a task, the new task is added to the list of already defined tasks in the `TaskLogTopComponent`. Now, although `TaskEditorTopComponent` and `TaskLogTopComponent` are not dependent on each other, they exchange information dynamically.

In summary, you learned how to create and manage Lookups with dynamic content. For these purposes, the classes AbstractLookup and InstanceContent provide everything you need. Furthermore, you have explored the usage of LookupListeners as monitors for Lookups and you have used them to receive notifications about changes in the Lookup. All in all, in just a few lines of code, you saw how two objects can exchange information without being directly dependent on each other.

Creating an additional TaskProvider

At this stage, there are still a few imperfections to clean up. Firstly, a hardcoded ID is used to find the TaskEditorTopComponent via the **WindowManager**. The section after this one presents a solution to that problem. Secondly, and that is the focus of the current section, the architecture you currently have could be more flexible. If there were to be a second source of tasks, you want to be able to show those tasks in the TaskLogTopComponent.

Currently, only tasks provided by the TaskEditorTopComponent can be displayed in the TaskLogTopComponent. To demonstrate the problem, you create yet another module. The module provides a new window, where Tasks can be created. As in the case of the TaskEditorTopComponent, the created tasks will be made accessible via the TopComponent's Lookup.

1. In the **TaskManager**, create a new module named **TaskDuplicator**, with org.netbeansrcp.taskduplicator as the **Code Name Base**.

2. In the new module, add a dependency on the **TaskModel** module.

3. In the new module, use the **New Window Component** wizard to create a new TopComponent with **TaskDuplicator** as the **Class Name Prefix**. Choose **explorer** as the window position and also select **Open on Application Start**.

4. Add two JLabels to the TopComponent for each of the following properties: **Name, Due Date, Priority, Progress**, and **Description**. The first of each pair of JLabels shows the name, while the second shows the value.

5. Add a `JButton` for creating new tasks. The `TopComponent` should now look as shown in the following screenshot:

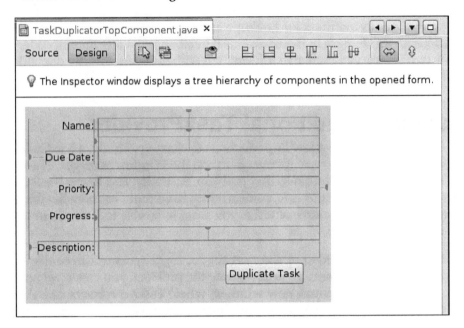

6. Switch to the **Source** view of the `TaskDuplicatorTopComponent`. You want the `TaskDuplicatorTopComponent` to behave similarly to the `TaskLogTopComponent`. That means that the `TopComponent` should monitor the `Lookup` of the `TaskEditorTopComponent` and show the values of the current task. In addition, the `TaskDuplicatorTopComponent` provides a `Lookup` containing the created tasks. Therefore, the following code needs to be added to the `TaskDuplicatorTopComponent`:

```
final class TaskDuplicatorTopComponent extends TopComponent
    implements PropertyChangeListener, LookupListener {

    private Lookup.Result<Task> result;
    private Task task;
    private InstanceContent ic = new InstanceContent();

    // ...
    private TaskDuplicatorTopComponent() {

        // ...
        this.associateLookup(new AbstractLookup(this.ic));
```

```
    }

    public void componentOpened() {
        this.result = WindowManager.getDefault().
          findTopComponent("TaskEditorTopComponent").
            getLookup().lookupResult(Task.class);
        this.result.addLookupListener(this);
        this.task = (Task) (this.result.allInstances().toArray())[0];
        this.task.addPropertyChangeListener(this);
    }

    public void componentClosed() {
        this.task.removePropertyChangeListener(this);
        this.result = null;
    }

    public void propertyChange(PropertyChangeEvent arg0) {
        this.updateTaskInfo();
    }
    public void resultChanged(LookupEvent arg0) {
        Task[] tasks = this.result.allInstances().
          toArray(new com.netbeansrcp.taskmodel.TaskImpl[]{});
          Task newTask = tasks[tasks.length - 1];

        this.task.removePropertyChangeListener(this);
        this.task = newTask;
        this.task.addPropertyChangeListener(this);

        this.updateTaskInfo();
    }

    private void updateTaskInfo() {
        this.jLabel6.setText(this.task.getName());
          this.jLabel7.setText(DateFormat.getInstance()
            .format(this.task.getDue()));
          this.jLabel8.setText("" + this.task.getPrio());
          this.jLabel9.setText("" + this.task.getProgr());
          this.jLabel10.setText(this.task.getDescr());
    }
    private void jButton1ActionPerformed(java.awt.event.ActionEvent
        evt) {
        Task t = new TaskImpl();
        t.setName(this.task.getName());
        t.setDue(this.task.getDue());
        t.setPrio(this.task.getPrio());
        t.setProgr(this.task.getProgr());
        t.setDescr(this.task.getDescr());
```

```
        List<Task> tasks = new ArrayList<Task>();
        tasks.add(t);
        this.ic.set(tasks, null);
    }
// ...
```

Let's look carefully at the preceding code. In the constructor of the `TopComponent`, you created a dynamic `Lookup` using `AbstractLookup` and `InstanceContent`, and you associated the dynamic `Lookup` with the `TopComponent`.

When the `TopComponent` opens, the `TaskEditorTopComponent` is found via its ID. The `Lookup` of the `TaskEditorTopComponent` is requested and a `LookupListener` is registered on it. The `LookupListener` is triggered when changes to a Task are made available to the `Lookup` of the `TaskEditorTopComponent`.

You register a `PropertyChangeListener` on the currently available task, so that you can be notified of changes to the task. In the related `propertyChange` method, you update the values of the labels in the form, so that the data is always current. When the `TopComponent` is closed, you detach the listener.

When the `Lookup` of the `TaskEditorTopComponent` changes, you use the `resultChanged` method to retrieve all the Tasks from the `Lookup`. You detach the `PropertyChangeListener` from the old task, as you are only interested in changes to the new task, so that you then attach the `PropertyChangeListener` to the new task.

You also need to react to clicks in the `TaskDuplicatorTopComponent`. Whenever the button in the `TaskDuplicatorTopComponent` is clicked, you create a new task, set its values to those of the currently edited task, and add the new task to the `InstanceContent` of the `TaskDuplicatorTopComponent`. That makes the new task available via the `Lookup` of the `TaskDuplicatorTopComponent`.

You now have two sources of new tasks, the `TaskEditorTopComponent` and the `TaskDuplicatorTopComponent`. The next challenge is to change the `TaskLogTopComponent` in such a way that both sources of tasks are consumed, with the tasks created by both `TopComponent`s being made available in the JList in the `TaskLogTopComponent`.

Proxy Lookups

As the name suggests, there is a way to hide several Lookups behind a single `Lookup` instance. The Lookup API provides a class called `ProxyLookup` to support this. The class can take an array of Lookups in its constructor and delegate to them. Importantly, the order of objects in the array is taken into account. For a normal `Lookup.lookup(<class>)` call, the first result found in the `Lookup` is returned. In that case, one `Lookup` can hide the content of another `Lookup`.

Let's make use of `ProxyLookup` in the **TaskManager**. With the help of a `ProxyLookup`, you can easily hide the fact that there are now two sources of tasks, `TaskEditorTopComponent` and `TaskDuplicatorTopComponent`.

Introducing the `ProxyLookup` means making a very small change to `TaskLogTopComponent`. You need to query both Lookups and create a `ProxyLookup` for them, though for right now you continue to use hardcoded IDs to find the `TopComponents`.

The Module shall provide a service, which allows a unified access to sources of tasks. The service implementation shall create the `ProxyLookup` aggregating the Lookups of `TaskEditorTopComponent` and `TaskdDuplicatorTopComponent`.

1. In the **TaskManager**, create a new module called **TaskSource**, with **org. netbeansrcp.tasksource** as the **Code Name Base**.

2. Declare dependencies on the Lookup API and the Windows System API.

3. Define the service interface `com.netbeansrcp.tasksource.api. TaskSource`. The only object you want to export is a `Lookup` providing access to created tasks in the system, so it is enough to extend the interface `Lookup.Provider`.

    ```
    public interface TaskSource extends Lookup.Provider {
    }
    ```

4. Expose the package containing the interface defined above to the other modules in the application. Right-click the module project, choose **Properties**, and use the **API Versioning** tab to make the package containing the service public.

    ○   Define the implementation of the service. Define the `getLookup()` method as discussed above, searching the `TopComponents`, creating the `ProxyLookup` for the returned `TopComponents`, and returning a `ProxyLookup`:

    ```
    @ServiceProvider(service=TaskSource.class)
    public class TaskSourceImpl implements TaskSource {
        public Lookup getLookup() {
            Lookup l1 = WindowManager.getDefault().
                findTopComponent("TaskEditorTopComponent").
                                                        getLookup();
            Lookup l2 = WindowManager.getDefault().
                    findTopComponent("TaskDuplicatorTopComponent")
                    .getLookup();
            return new ProxyLookup(new Lookup[]{l1, l2});
        }
    }
    ```

5. Now everything is ready. You can clean up the code in the `TaskLogTopComponent`. In the **TaskLog** module, start by adding a dependency on the new **TaskSource** module. Then remove the code causing the unwanted dependencies on a specific `TopComponents` and, instead, use the **TaskSource** service implemented previously:

```
public void componentOpened() {

    this.result =
      Lookup.getDefault().lookup(TaskSource.class).
      getLookup().lookupResult(Task.class);

    this.result.addLookupListener(this);

    // ...
}
```

6. Run the application again. As expected, all tasks are shown in the **TaskLog** as before, no matter if they are created by the **TaskEditor** or the **TaskDuplicator**. The `ProxyLookup` is doing its job, that is, it merges the two Lookups correctly.

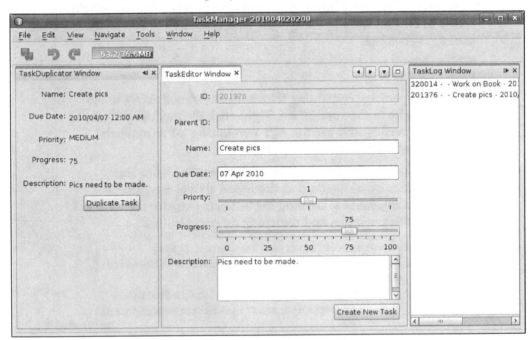

In summary, you have now been introduced to `ProxyLookups`. You used this new concept to combine two Lookups behind a single `Lookup`. This gives you the possibility to reduce dependencies on a lot of `Lookup.Providers` to just a single dependency on one `ProxyLookup`. Overall, `ProxyLookups` are a further way to reduce dependencies and increase the flexibility of your architecture.

At this point, the example looks a lot better than it did at the beginning of this chapter. You have minimized dependencies as far as possible, though there is still one further step to take in that direction as you are using a string to identify the name of the `TaskEditorTopComponent`. If the ID of the `TaskEditorTopComponent` changes, the `TaskLogTopComponent` will not be able to find it anymore. The next section shows how this problem can be solved.

Listening to the selection

You created the **TaskSource** module to decouple the `TaskLogTopComponent` from the Lookups of the `TaskEditorTopComponent` and `TaskDuplicatorTopComponent`. The latter two `TopComponent`s can both provide new data, in this case tasks, based on user interaction. As `TopComponent`s are the primary user interface of a NetBeans Platform application, their Lookups play an important role in communicating information resulting from user interactions. For user interfaces, this kind of communication is a very typical use case and whenever there are any such typical patterns, the NetBeans Platform tends to provide some kind of special support. One support method that you can now begin making sense of is `org.openide.util.Utilities.actionsGlobalContext`.

The static method `Utilities.actionsGlobalContext()` gives you access to the `Lookup` of whichever `TopComponent` currently is the activated `TopComponent`.

As the user can only work on one `TopComponent` at a time, there is always at most one active `TopComponent`. With that in mind, you never needed to merge the Lookups of the two `TopComponent`s at all. You can simply remove the **TaskSource** module without any loss of functionality, if you change the `TaskLogTopComponent` in the following way:

Old:

```
public void componentOpened() {
    //...
    this.result = Lookup.getDefault().lookup(TaskSource.class)
      .getLookup().lookupResult(Task.class);
    //...
    }
```

New:

```
public void componentOpened() {
    this.result =
      Utilities.actionsGlobalContext().lookupResult(Task.class);
  }
```

Such a small change! But now the **TaskLog** has no dependencies on the IDs of the two TopComponents anymore.

You now have three modules exchanging information without knowing about each other. That means that there are no methods in one of these modules making use of methods in one of the other modules. As a result, you can focus on the business logic of each module, without needing to worry about integration problems caused by changes in one of the other modules.

> **The Power of Flexibility**
>
> Note the flexibility of the communication mechanism based on Lookup. At any time, you can add either new sources of tasks or new consumers of tasks. When you do so, none of the other modules are affected in any way. In particular, when you are dealing with Master-Detail views, this flexibility is very powerful.

Creating a service facade

Lookups are one of the fundamental patterns of the NetBeans Platform. Most of the chapters that follow make use of it. However, before you turn to another chapter, let's refactor the **TaskModel** a bit. As you have learned how services can be defined and how you can access them using the default Lookup, let's provide a service for creating and managing tasks.

The problem is that you currently have many classes accessing the **TaskModel** directly. Hence, the creation and management of tasks is dispersed all over the code. To clean this up, you introduce the class **TaskManager**, which is a service facade. The **TaskManager** is responsible for the creation and removal of tasks, as well as for providing access to existing tasks.

1. In the **TaskModel** module, define an interface named TaskManager in the **com.netbeansrcp.taskmodel.api** package.

2. Move the Task class to the **com.netbeansrcp.taskmodel.api** too. Make this package publicly available to all the modules in the application, by right-clicking the module, choosing **Properties**, and then using the **API Versioning** tab to specify that this package is public. The other package, that is, the main package, should contain the TaskImpl class and, later, the TaskManagerImpl class too. In this way, you hide the implementing classes from other modules, so that they cannot accidentally be used by someone else.

3. Define the `TaskManager` interface as follows:

```
public interface TaskManager {

    Task createTask();

    Task createTask(String name, String parentId);

    void removeTask(String id);

    List<Task> getTopLevelTasks();

    Task getTask(String id);
    static final String PROP_TASKLIST_ADD = "TASK_LIST_ADD";
    static final String PROP_TASKLIST_REMOVE = "TASK_LIST_REMOVE";

    public void addPropertyChangeListener(java.beans.
                                PropertyChangeListener listener);

    public void removePropertyChangeListener(java.beans.
                                PropertyChangeListener listener);
}
```

The **TaskManager** interface suits your purposes, as it provides the following:

- A method to create parents tasks and a second method to create tasks using a parent ID.
- For deleting tasks, just one method is necessary, taking a Task ID as argument.
- Two query methods are also available. One returns all available parent tasks, the other allows direct access to a task using its ID.
- The last part of the code defines methods for adding and removing `PropertyChangeListeners` and two constants used as property names via the `PropertyChangeEvents` for added and removed tasks.

  Create the class `TaskManagerImpl` in the main package, that is, **com.netbean-srcp.taskmodel**, which means that it cannot be used by other modules, and implement the **TaskManager** interface as follows:

```
@ServiceProvider(service=TaskManager.class)
public class TaskManagerImpl implements TaskManager {

    private List<Task> topLevelTasks;
    private PropertyChangeSupport pss;
    public TaskManagerImpl() {
        this.topLevelTasks = new ArrayList<Task>();
        this.pss = new PropertyChangeSupport(this);
```

```
        }

    public synchronized Task createTask() {
        Task task = new TaskImpl();
        this.topLevelTasks.add(task);
        this.pss.firePropertyChange(PROP_TASKLIST_ADD, null, task);
        return task;

    }


    public synchronized Task createTask(String name, String parentId) {
        Task task = new TaskImpl(name, parentId);
        Task parent = this.getTask(parentId);
        if (null != parent)
         parent.addChild(task);
         this.pss.firePropertyChange(PROP_TASKLIST_ADD, parent, task);
         return task;

    }
    public synchronized void removeTask(String id) {
        Task task = this.getTask(id);
        if (null != task) {
            Task parent = this.getTask(task.getParentId());
            if (null != parent) {
                parent.remove(task);
              }
             this.topLevelTasks.remove(task);
             this.pss.firePropertyChange(PROP_TASKLIST_REMOVE,
                                        parent, task);

           }
         }


    public List<Task> getTopLevelTasks() {
        return Collections.unmodifiableList(this.topLevelTasks);
      }

    public Task getTask(String id) {

        for (Task task : this.topLevelTasks) {

            Task found = this.findTask(task, id);
            if (null != found)
              return found;
          }

        return null;
        }
```

```
    private Task findTask(Task task, String id) {
        if (id.equals(task.getId()))     return task;
        for ( Task child : task.getChildren() ) {
          Task found = this.findTask(child, id);
          if (null != found)
            return found;
        }
        return null;
    }

    public synchronized void
      addPropertyChangeListener(PropertyChangeListener listener) {
        this.pss.addPropertyChangeListener(listener);
      }

    public synchronized void
      removePropertyChangeListener(PropertyChangeListener listener) {
        this.pss.removePropertyChangeListener(listener);
      }
}
```

This is how the preceding code works:

- The constructor is simple. You create a list as storage for `TopLevelTasks` and a `PropertyChangeSupport` to manage and notify the Listeners.

- The `createTask()` method instantiates new tasks, adds them to the list, and fires a creation event.

- The `create` method instantiates a task, adds it to the list of `TopLevelTasks`, and fires an event that notifies all registered listeners about the change.

- The second create method needs to do a bit more. It creates a task for a given parent, so that you can create child elements in a hierarchy. To find the related task, you use `getTask`, which you use immediately, adding a new child task. You synchronize these methods as multiple threads can make use of these methods.

- Removal of tasks is made possible via the `removeTask` method, which uses the `getTask` method to find the task it needs to delete. If there are subtasks, these need to be deleted too. Finally you fire a `PropertyChangeEvent` to send a notification of the deletion.

- To return existing tasks, you have the methods `getTopLevelTasks`, which returns an unmodifiable list of `TopLevelTasks`, and `getTask`, which lets you return a single task. The latter method searches through `TopLevelTasks` and lets `findTask` determine whether the task is available in the hierarchy. If the task is found, it is returned. Next, the code determines whether the Task found is the root element or not. If it is not the root element, the subtasks are searched recursively until the ID is found.

When you now try to build your application, you will encounter a problem! After all, until now you have been directly accessing `TaskImpl`, which now no longer belongs to the publicly accessible interfaces of your application. The NetBeans Platform prevents the build from succeeding in this scenario, which is one of the advantages of using the NetBeans runtime container, as it prevents you from using types that are not part of the publicly declared packages.

As a result, you need to slightly rewrite parts of your code, to make use of **TaskManager** instead of `TaskImpl`. For example, you can see the rewritten parts of the classes `TaskEditorPanel` and `TaskDuplicatorTopComponent` as follows:

```
public class TaskEditorPanel extends javax.swing.JPanel {

    // ...
    private TaskManager taskMgr;
    // ...
    public TaskEditorPanel() {

        if (null == this.taskMgr) {
            this.taskMgr =
                Lookup.getDefault().lookup(TaskManager.class);
        }

        if (null != this.taskMgr) {
            this.task = this.taskMgr.createTask();
        }

        initComponents();
        this.updateForm();
        this.pss = new PropertyChangeSupport(this);
    }
    // ...
}



final class TaskDuplicatorTopComponent extends TopComponent
    implements PropertyChangeListener, LookupListener {
    // ...
    private void jButton1ActionPerformed(java.awt.event.ActionEvent
        evt) {

        TaskManager taskMgr =
            Lookup.getDefault().lookup(TaskManager.class);
        if (null != taskMgr) {

            Task t = taskMgr.createTask();
```

```
        t.setName(this.task.getName());
        t.setDue(this.task.getDue());

    // ...
        }

    // ...
        }
    // ...
    }
```

Summary

In this chapter, you learned how to use the Lookup classes, that is, the classes that enable modules and components to communicate in a loosely-coupled manner. On the level of modules, Lookups enable service providers to centrally register their services and consumers to find them. On the level of individual components, Lookups enable the exchange of information between a provider and any number of consumers. All the central concerns of Lookups have been addressed, together with relevant code samples.

5
Actions

In Swing, an `Action` object provides an `ActionListener` for Action event handling, together with additional features, such as tool tips, icons, and the Action's activated state. One aim of Swing Actions is that they should be reusable, that is, can be invoked from a menu item as well as a related toolbar button and keyboard shortcut.

The NetBeans Platform provides an Action framework enabling you to organize Actions declaratively. In many cases, you can simply reuse your existing Actions exactly as they were before you used the NetBeans Platform, once you have declared them. For more complex scenarios, you can make use of specific NetBeans Platform Action classes that offer the advantages of additional features, such as more complex displays in toolbars and support for context-sensitive help.

In this chapter, you focus on "Global" Actions, that is, those that should always be enabled. These types of Actions are not very different from standard Swing Actions. For example, you might want to create "New Task" and "Edit Task" Actions that can be invoked from the menubar and toolbar of the **TaskManager**.

The topics covered in this chapter will teach you the following:

- How to create global `Actions`
- How to add menu items
- How to add toolbar buttons
- How to add keyboard shortcuts

Preparing to work with global actions

Before you begin working with global `Actions`, let's make some changes to our application. It should be possible for the `TaskEditorTopComponent` to open for a specific task. You should therefore be able to pass a task into the `TaskEditorTopComponent`. Rather than the `TaskEditorPanel` creating a new task in its constructor, the task needs to be passed into it and made available to the `TaskEditorTopComponent`.

On the other hand, it may make sense for a `TaskEditorTopComponent` to create a new task, rather than providing an existing task, which can then be made available for editing. Therefore, the `TaskEditorTopComponent` should provide two constructors. If a task is passed into the `TaskEditorTopComponent`, the `TaskEditorTopComponent` and the `TaskEditorPanel` are initialized. If no task is passed in, a new task is created and is made available for editing.

Furthermore, it is currently only possible to edit a single task at a time. It would make sense to be able to work on several tasks at the same time in different editors. At the same time, you should make sure that the task is only opened once by the same editor. The `TaskEditorTopComponent` should therefore provide a method for creating new or finding existing editors. In addition, it would be useful if `TaskEditorPanels` were automatically closed for deleted tasks.

1. Remove the logic for creating new tasks from the constructor of the `TaskEditorPanel`, along with the instance variable for storing the **TaskManager**, which is now redundant:

```
public TaskEditorPanel() {
    initComponents();
    this.pcs = new PropertyChangeSupport(this);
}
```

2. Introduce a new method to update a task:

```
public void updateTask(Task task) {
    Task oldTask = this.task;
    this.task = task;
    this.pcs.firePropertyChange(PROP_TASK, oldTask, this.task);
    this.updateForm();
}
```

3. Let us now turn to the `TaskEditorTopComponent`, which currently cannot be instantiated either with or without a task being provided. You now need to be able to pass a task for initializing the `TaskEditorPanel`. The new default constructor creates a new task with the support of a chained constructor, and passes this to the former constructor for the remaining initialization of the editor.

4. In addition, it should now be able to return several instances of the `TaskEditorTopComponent` that are each responsible for a specific task. Hence, the class should be extended by a static method for creating new or finding existing instances. These instances are stored in a `Map<Task, TaskEditorTopComponent>` which is populated by the former constructor with newly created instances. The method checks whether the map for the given task already stores a responsible instance, and creates a new one if necessary. Additionally, this method registers a `Listener` on the **TaskManager** to close the relevant editor for deleting a task. As an instance is now responsible for a particular task this should be able to be queried, so we introduce another appropriate method. Consequently, the changes to the `TaskEditorTopComponent` looks as follows:

```
private static Map<Task, TaskEditorTopComponent> tcByTask =
    new HashMap<Task, TaskEditorTopComponent>();

public static TaskEditorTopComponent findInstance(Task task) {
    TaskEditorTopComponent tc = tcByTask.get(task);
    if (null == tc) {
       tc = new TaskEditorTopComponent(task);
     }
    if (null == taskMgr) {
       taskMgr = Lookup.getDefault().lookup(TaskManager.class);
       taskMgr.addPropertyChangeListener(newListenForRemovedNodes());
     }
    return tc;
  }


private class ListenForRemovedNodes implements PropertyChangeListener {
```

```
    public void propertyChange(PropertyChangeEvent arg0) {
        if
          (TaskManager.PROP_TASKLIST_REMOVE.equals
            (arg0.getPropertyName())) {
              Task task = (Task) arg0.getNewValue();
              TaskEditorTopComponent tc = tcByTask.get(task);
              if (null != tc) {
                  tc.close();
                  tcByTask.remove(task);
              }
          }
        }
    }

private TaskEditorTopComponent() {
    this(Lookup.getDefault().lookup(TaskManager.class));
}

private TaskEditorTopComponent(TaskManager taskMgr) {
    this((taskMgr != null) ? taskMgr.createTask() : null);
}

private TaskEditorTopComponent(Task task) {
    initComponents();

// ...

    ((TaskEditorPanel) this.jPanel1).updateTask(task);
    this.ic.add(((TaskEditorPanel) this.jPanel1).task);

    this.associateLookup(new AbstractLookup(this.ic));
    tcByTask.put(task, this);
}

public String getTaskId() {
    Task task = ((TaskEditorPanel) this.jPanel1).task;
    return (null != task) ? task.getId() : "";
}
```

With that our preparations are complete and you can turn to the following discussion on Actions.

Creating global actions

Let's start by creating an `Action` to add new `TopLevelTasks`. It will create a new Task and display it in the **TaskEditorPanel**. The wizard that you will use in this section will simply create a new **ActionListener** and register it in the `layer.xml` file.

1. Right-click the **TaskEditor** module project node and choose **New | Action**. Choose **Always Enabled** as the **Action type** as shown in the following screenshot. Click **Next>**.

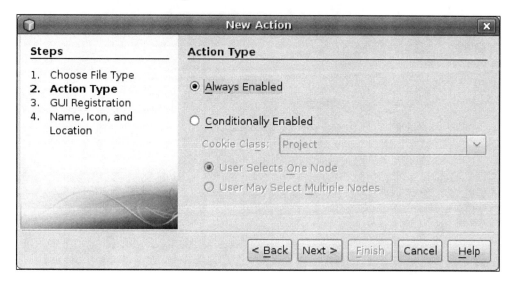

2. Choose **Edit** as the category of the Action, which determines where in the **Options** window's Keymap section it will be displayed.

3. Check the **Global Menu Item** checkbox. Now you can specify where the Action should appear in the menu bar. Choose **Edit** and then choose any position you want within the **Edit** menu. Click **Next>**.

 You do not need to insert the Action in the toolbar at this time, nor assign a keyboard shortcut.

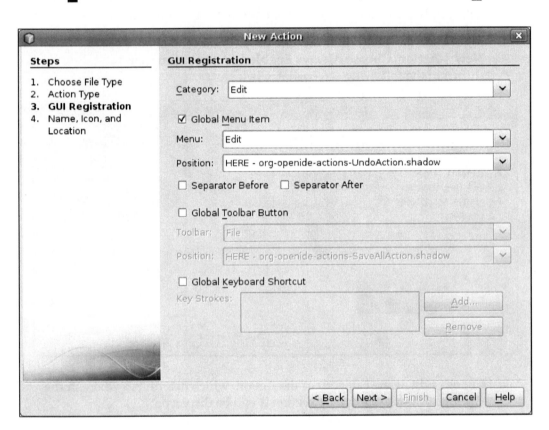

4. Name the `Action` **NewTaskAction**, with **New** as the **Display Name**. Optionally, specify an icon.

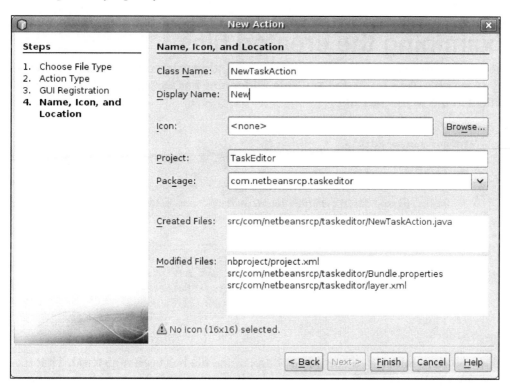

5. The `actionPerformed` method of the generated class `NewTaskAction` should create a new task and display it in a **TaskEditor**. Therefore, implement the method as follows:

```java
public void actionPerformed(ActionEvent e) {
    TaskManager taskMgr =
      Lookup.getDefault().lookup(TaskManager.class);
    if (null != taskMgr) {
        Task task = taskMgr.createTask();
        TaskEditorTopComponent win =
          TaskEditorTopComponent.findInstance(task);
        win.open();
        win.requestActive();
    }
}
```

6. Run the application again. In the **Edit** menu there is now a **New** menu item. When you select the menu item, a new task is created in the **TaskEditor**.

To summarize, you have used the **New Action** wizard to create and register a new global action.

Examining the created files

The wizard created a simple `ActionListener` and registered it declaratively in the `layer.xml` file. As a result, the `Actions` folder now has an `Edit` subfolder, with this content in the `layer.xml` file:

```
<folder name="Actions">
  <folder name="Edit">
    <file name="com-netbeansrcp-taskeditor-NewTaskAction.instance">
      <attr name="delegate"
              newvalue="com.netbeansrcp.taskeditor.NewTaskAction"/>
      <attr name="displayName" bundlevalue="com.netbeansrcp.
              taskeditor.Bundle#CTL_NewTaskAction"/>
      <attr name="iconBase"
              stringvalue="com/netbeansrcp/taskeditor/icon.png"/>
      <attr name="instanceCreate"
              methodvalue="org.openide.awt.Actions.alwaysEnabled"/>
      <attr name="noIconInMenu" boolvalue="false"/>
    </file>
  </folder>
</folder>
```

Below the `Edit` folder, you see that an `.instance` file has been registered. That file represents an instance of the class for which it is registered. A set of attributes have been defined for the file:

Attributes	Description
delegate	The task to be performed when the `Action` is invoked.
displayName	The name of the `Action`, optionally pointing to a key in a bundle file.
iconBase	The location of the icon displayed for the `Action`.
instanceCreate	The instance created by the `Action` registration.
noIconInMenu	True if the `Action` does not display an icon.

In addition to the `Action` registration, the wizard has also created a Menu registration in the `layer.xml` file:

```
<folder name="Menu">
    <folder name="Edit">
        <file name="com-netbeansrcp-taskeditor-NewTaskAction.shadow">
            <attr name="originalFile" stringvalue="Actions/Edit/
                                        com-netbeansrcp-taskeditor-
                                        NewTaskAction.instance"/>
```

```
                        <attr name="position" intvalue="100"/>
                    </file>
                </folder>
            </folder>
```

Within the **Edit** menu, a shadow file has been registered. Shadow files do not represent an instance, but serve as a symbolic reference, which is a familiar concept from the Unix world. If the `Action` instance had been directly attached to the menu, deleting the menu registration would cause the removal of the `Action` also. Thanks to the shadow files, removing the menu registration does not mean that the `Action` registration itself is removed, as the `Action` is registered separately. Also, when you decide to let the user invoke the `Action` from a toolbar or keyboard shortcut, you will again use shadow files. The `Action` will then be instantiated once, not each time it is invoked from the various places where the user invokes it from.

Enabling Users to Invoke actions

Let us now allow the user to invoke the action from both a toolbar button and a keyboard shortcut. After all, you can connect Actions to a variety of places. Actions are often attached, for example, to context menus within **Explorer** views, files of certain MIME types, or the editor. Often these Actions only make sense if they react in a context-sensitive way to the element from whose context menu they are called. This too is supported by the NetBeans Platform.

In this case, though, you simply want to have the `Action` always enabled and present in the toolbar, as well as from the menu bar where it is already found.

Toolbar

You have already seen how Actions are attached to menus. All that is involved is registering the corresponding `Action` class in the appropriate position in the `layer.xml` file. The same approach applies to toolbar buttons, where a new toolbar button is registered within a subfolder of the `Toolbars` folder, as follows in the `layer.xml` file:

```
<folder name="Toolbars">
  <folder name="Edit">
    <file name="com-netbeansrcp-taskeditor-NewTaskAction.shadow">
      <attr name="originalFile" stringvalue="Actions/Edit/com
        netbeansrcp-taskeditor-NewTaskAction.instance"/>
    </file>
  </folder>
</folder>
```

Toolbar buttons must have an icon

For toolbar buttons, it is important that you register an `Action` for which an icon has been registered in the `layer.xml` file. Otherwise no icon will be shown for the `Action` in the toolbar.

Run the application. The `Action` is now visible in the **Edit** toolbar.

In summary, you have attached an `Action` declaratively to a toolbar. You simply had to add a shadow file entry to the relevant location in the `layer.xml` file.

Keyboard

Actions can be triggered by pressing key combinations on a keyboard. As with menus and toolbars, a keybinding is implemented within the NetBeans Platform declaratively. The relevant folder in this case is `Shortcuts`, while the file that you need to register there is again a shadow file.

Consequently, the name of the shadow file does not relate to the name of the Action that is to be triggered, but instead indicates the key combination in an Emacs-like notation, consisting of a modifier followed by a key designator. A hyphen is required between the modifier and designator.

The valid modifiers are listed as follows:

C   *Ctrl* key

A   *Alt* key

S   *Shift* key

M   *Meta* key, for example, **Command** button

As the *Ctrl* key on the Mac is different to what it is on a conventional PC, the NetBeans Platform further provides us a wildcard, with a corresponding key that varies depending on the operating system:

D   Standard Acceleration Key

      (for example, PC: *Ctrl* Key, Mac: *Command* Key)

O   Alternative Acceleration Key

      (for example, PC: *Alt* Key, Mac: *Ctrl* Key)

As a key designator, the name of each key constant is derived from `java.awt.event.KeyEvent`, with the leading `VK_` of the constant name removed.

You now want to bind your action to the key combination *standard accelerator key-A*, which on the Mac is *Command-A*, while on the PC it is *Ctrl-A*.

Following the preceding description, register the `Action` to be invoked from a shortcut as follows in the `layer.xml` file:

```
<folder name="Shortcuts">
  <file name="D-A.shadow">
    <attr name="originalFile" stringvalue="Actions/Edit/
             comnetbeansrcp-taskeditor-NewTaskAction.instance" />
  </file>
</folder>
```

Run the application again. Press *Ctrl-A* on a PC or *Command-A* on a Mac. When you do so, you should see that the **TaskLog** registers the creation of a new task.

In summary, you have now declaratively bound an `Action` to a keyboard shortcut.

Summary

In this chapter, you continued working on the **TaskManager**, while learning about global `Actions`. First you created the Actions, and then you hooked them up to menu items, toolbar buttons, and keyboard shortcuts.

Next, you will learn about nodes and explorer views, which help you to create loosely-coupled views. While working through that chapter, you will also create Actions that are sensitive to their context, as not all Actions should be globally enabled, unlike the Actions discussed in the current chapter.

6

Nodes and Explorer Views

The Nodes API and the Explorer & Property Sheet API, in combination with the previously discussed Lookup API, help to implement one of the most powerful features of the NetBeans Platform: its loosely-coupled views.

The topics covered in this chapter will teach you the following:

- How and why to use nodes
- How to display nodes in explorer views
- How to create context-sensitive actions for nodes
- How to decorate nodes
- How to create property sheets for nodes

Multiple models in pure Swing

Suppose you want to represent a list of TopLevelTasks in a standard Swing application; you would probably use a JList. If you want to display additional attributes for the Tasks, such as the due dates, you would use a JTable. Finally, if you want to represent the whole hierarchy of TopLevelTasks and subtasks, you would logically use a JTree or a JXTreeTable from the SwingLabs project, if additional properties should be displayed.

Problems arise when you want to change the UI representation after having chosen one of the approaches described above, as each of these Swing components has its own data model. And, unfortunately, each of these data models is incompatible with each of the others. As a result, switching from one visual representation of data to another is difficult and time-consuming because it involves rewriting a lot of plumbing code. In particular, of course, newbies to Swing suffer from this problem, as they need to learn multiple data models at the same time, which shouldn't be necessary, as these models represent the same data. The Nodes API and the Explorer & Property Sheet API were created to solve exactly these issues in Swing.

The Explorer & Property Sheet API, which is a single API, provides a variety of ready-made UI view components, such as a list, a tree, and a tree table, similar to those outlined above. Each of these views shares the same data model, which is a hierarchy of nodes. Nodes are lightweight objects very similar to JavaBeans, wrapping actual domain data. They expose presentation information, such as a display name, icon, properties, and actions. Importantly, nodes can expose other nodes as their children. As all views use the same model and the same controller, so switching from one visual representation to another takes little time and effort. It is usually only a matter of changing one or two lines of code.

As nodes are abstractions of the domain model, you typically create a new node class for each class of the domain model. On the face of it, that might sound like a lot of work, though that is mitigated by the fact that only a few lines of code need to be written when actually defining a node.

Nodes and the global Lookup

You already know that each `TopComponent` and, therefore, each independent view within a NetBeans Platform application, has its own `Lookup`. It is very important to understand that as soon as a view receives input focus (that is, it becomes "the activated `TopComponent`"), its `Lookup` is proxied, that is, exposed to the global `Lookup` of the application, which is the ActionsGlobalContext Lookup. Therefore, any component that is interested in information provided by the activated `TopComponent` needs to register a `LookupListener` on the ActionsGlobalContext `Lookup`. An object that does this is notified whenever the `Lookup` content changes, which is typically after the user does something in the application.

Nodes and explorer views are ideal partners within this mechanism. Each node has its own `Lookup`, in which it stores its domain model object. Meanwhile, each explorer view also has a `Lookup`, which automatically contains all the `Lookup` data of the node it contains. The domain model objects are thus automatically made available to the `Lookup` of the explorer view. The latter has a helper method that exposes the content of the selected node's `Lookup` to the `TopComponent`'s `Lookup`. As a result, an object interested in the current data only needs to observe the ActionsGlobalContext `Lookup` via its registered `LookupListeners`.

Before diving deeper into all the related details, remember these three key points:

1. A `Node` is a lightweight object that wraps the model object, which may also be known as a "domain object". A `Node` is itself not a model object, that is, it does not itself represent data, but it wraps the model object that represents the data, so that an explorer view can display it.

2. An explorer view is a Swing component that can display nodes in different ways and can be easily interchanged.

3. An `ExplorerManager` is a universal controller, mediating between a `Node` and an explorer view, while making possible the interchangeability of the explorer views.

Multiple node implementations

A node is purely a container object, without any extensive logic. It wraps a model object and exposes it to interested objects through its `Lookup`. It also provides presentation-specific information, such as a localized display name, together with an optional state-dependent icon, properties, and actions.

Nodes are organized hierarchically, that is, you can ask each node for its children, each of which can again have their own children. Alternatively, you can create a flat list of nodes. A flat list of nodes is a root node that provides leaf nodes only, that is, one-level deep children only. As a result, both a hierarchical and a flat organization of data can be handled within the same structure.

The Nodes API provides several classes, depending on whether you want to manage the children as a list, a map, or as a set of keys, either sorted or unsorted. However, in most cases, you will want to work with the lighter, key-based variant. Many details on the recommended key-based approach follow later in this chapter.

The Nodes API provides several node implementations. Normally, you use one or more of the following node classes, depending on your current business requirements:

Class	Description
AbstractNode	An AbstractNode is, typically, the class you extend in production code when you need to create your own node. Despite its name, the class is not abstract. You should see it as the convenience node class, ideal for subclassing, instead of the base Node class itself.
BeanNode	A BeanNode is a very handy class for prototyping purposes and for situations where the underlying model object corresponds to the JavaBean specification. In that case, a BeanNode exposes the properties of the model object automatically, as Property objects, simplifying integration with the **Properties** window. For production code, however, you are more likely to need a more finely-tuned and performant node than that provided by the BeanNode, though even in production code a BeanNode could be sufficient, if you assess the pros and cons adequately.
DataNode	A DataNode represents data from files. Refer to the chapter on the DataSystems API for more information on this node implementation.
FilterNode	A FilterNode lets you decorate a node, whether the node is provided by your own module or a module over which you have no control. When using this node implementation, you replace the original node with a FilterNode, which enables you to modify the original node and even extend it with your own functionality.

In the discussions that follow, you learn how to choose which node implementation to use, as well as how to actually implement nodes in real business scenarios.

Creating a node

In this, the first example, you want to create a new view listing all the tasks that are due in a given calendar week.

1. Create a new module named **DueList**, with **Code Name Base com.netbeansrcp.duelist**.

2. As dependencies, select the Lookup API for the Lookup class, the **TaskModel** module, so that you have access to the domain model, as well as the Nodes API and the Explorer & Property Sheet API.

The following steps describe the code snippet that follows!

1. The first step is to wrap the Tasks in `TaskNodes`. Start by deciding which base class, in other words, which node implementation, to use for the node. As you do not have special requirements of any kind, you should take the standard node base class, which is `AbstractNode`.

2. Therefore, create a new class named `TaskNode`, within the main package of the module **DueList**. Let your new class extend `AbstractNode`. There is no node-specific wizard for creating Nodes, because there is nothing particularly complex or extensive to do here. As shown below, you need to do no more than ensure that the wrapped model object can be handed over to the constructor, where it will be stored in the Node `Lookup`. Usually you will also set a name, as well as a display name.

3. You must create a constructor that takes a Task as argument, storing it in its `Lookup`. This is done by creating a new `Lookup` with the help of the previously used `Lookups.singleton()`, putting the Task into it and passing it to the constructor of the `AbstractNode` superclass.

4. The super constructor needs a `Children` factory object too, which will be responsible for creating child elements of the `TaskNodes`. As you want to display a flat list of due tasks, no child elements appear below the `TaskNodes`. In a tree, nodes without children are called `leaves`. The Nodes API provides the `Children.LEAF` constant to indicate that a node is a leaf node.

5. Set the name of the node, as its identifier, which should not change during the lifecycle of the node. Also set the display name, which can change at any time, and probably will.

6. Actually, you want the display name to be able to change. A Task can be displayed in the list while it is being modified in a **TaskEditor**, where it gets its new name. Therefore, register a `PropertyChangeListener` that listens to changes of the task name property. When this occurs, the display name is updated accordingly.

That's a lot of words for a few lines of code! Here they are:

```
public class TaskNode extends AbstractNode {

    public TaskNode(Task task) {

        super(Children.LEAF, Lookups.singleton(task));

        this.setName(task.getId());
        this.setDisplayName(task.getName());
        task.addPropertyChangeListener(new PropertyChangeListener() {

            public void propertyChange(PropertyChangeEvent arg0) {
```

```
                    if (Task.PROP_NAME.equals(arg0.getPropertyName())) {
                        setDisplayName(arg0.getNewValue() + "");
                    }
                }
            });
        }
    }
```

With these statements, the `TaskNode` is completely implemented. You can see that a node-specific wizard in the IDE is not really necessary.

Usually, as in the case above, most of the code does not go into the implementation of the node, but into the creation of child elements. As you'll see you'll be creating a `ListView`, you might wonder why you need to create child elements for display in a list. However, don't forget that nodes are hierarchically organized. The `ExplorerManager`, which is the controller of the explorer views, will need a root node element. The `ListView` will not use the root node but, instead, its children. Later, you will therefore create, in the `DueListTopComponent`, an `AbstractNode` that will be the root node. You will then add the Task as `TaskNodes` to this root node.

Each node has its own `Children` object. `Children` is a container for child nodes, which are the node's subnodes. The `Children` class is responsible for the creation, addition, and structure of the child nodes. `Children` is itself a concrete class, though the actual implementation of the different strategies for the management of child elements is provided by the classes `ChildFactory`, `Children.Array`, `Children.SortedArray`, `Children.Map`, `Children.SortedMap`, `Children.Keys` or, if there are no subnodes, `Children.LEAF`.

The steps below explain the code that follows.

Create a new class named `TaskChildren`, extending `Children.Array`.

1. Override the method `initCollection()`, where you add the due tasks in the form of `TaskNodes`, so that they can be displayed in the explorer view.

2. Next, you need to create some UI where the user can select the calendar week for which the due tasks should be shown. In the view, use a `JSpinner` to let the user select a calendar week. The `TaskChildren` object must react whenever a change occurs in the calendar week, dynamically changing its child elements, which are then displayed. You need to, therefore, register a `ChangeListener` on the `JSpinner` responsible for updating the children to display.

3. The displayed child elements list should also change if new tasks are created or deleted in another place within the application. This can easily be done by registering a `PropertyChangeListener` on the **TaskManager**, informing its listeners about additions or deletions of tasks.

4. The display names of the nodes should also change dynamically when tasks are modified. Again you use a `PropertyChangeListener`, but this time you need to register a listener for each Task.

The above steps bring you to the following implementation:

```
public class TaskChildren extends Children.Array
   implements PropertyChangeListener, ChangeListener {

    private long startTime;
    private long endTime;
    private JSpinner spinner;
    private TaskManager taskMgr;


    public TaskChildren(JSpinner spinner) {

        this.spinner = spinner;
        this.spinner.addChangeListener(this);


        this.taskMgr = Lookup.getDefault().lookup(TaskManager.class);
        if (null != this.taskMgr) {
           this.taskMgr.addPropertyChangeListener(this);
           }

      }



    @Override
    protected Collection<Node> initCollection() {

        Calendar cal = Calendar.getInstance();
        System.out.println((Integer) this.spinner.getValue());
        cal.set(Calendar.WEEK_OF_YEAR, (Integer)
        this.spinner.getValue());
        cal.set(Calendar.DAY_OF_WEEK, cal.getFirstDayOfWeek());
        this.startTime = cal.getTimeInMillis();

        cal.add(Calendar.WEEK_OF_YEAR, 1);
        this.endTime = cal.getTimeInMillis();


        List<Task> dueTasks = new ArrayList<Task>();

        if (null != this.taskMgr) {

            List<Task> topLevelTasks = this.taskMgr.getTopLevelTasks();
```

```
                for (Task topLevelTask : topLevelTasks) {
                    this.findDueTasks(topLevelTask, dueTasks);
                }
            }

        Collection<Node> dueNodes = new
                                ArrayList<Node>(dueTasks.size());
        for (Task task : dueTasks) {
            dueNodes.add(new TaskNode(task));
            task.addPropertyChangeListener(this);
        }

        return dueNodes;
    }


    private void findDueTasks(Task task, List<Task> dueTasks) {

        long dueTime = task.getDue().getTime();

        if (dueTime >= this.startTime && dueTime <= this.endTime) {
            dueTasks.add(task);
        }

        for (Task subTask : task.getChildren()) {
            this.findDueTasks(subTask, dueTasks);
        }
    }


    private void updateNodes() {
        remove(getNodes());
        add(initCollection().toArray(new Node[]{}));
    }

public void propertyChange(PropertyChangeEvent arg0) {
    if ( (arg0.getSource() instanceof Task) &&
      TaskManager.PROP_TASKLIST_ADD.equals(arg0.getPropertyName()) ||
      TaskManager.PROP_TASKLIST_REMOVE.equals
      (arg0.getPropertyName())) {
        this.updateNodes();
    }
    if ( (arg0.getSource() instanceof TaskManager) &&
        TaskManager.PROP_TASKLIST_ADD.equals(arg0.getPropertyName()) ||
        TaskManager.PROP_TASKLIST_REMOVE.equals(arg0.getPropertyName())) {
            this.updateNodes();
    }
```

```
    public void stateChanged(ChangeEvent arg0) {
        this.updateNodes();
    }
}
```

In the preceding code, take note of the following, in particular:

- You pass a JSpinner to the constructor, store it, and register the TaskChildren object as its ChangeListener, with a stateChange() method that calls updateNodes().

- You get the **TaskManager** and register the TaskChildren, again as a PropertyChangeListener. The appropriate propertyChange() method checks whether the **TaskManager** is the source of the event and whether the property for the list of the managed tasks is triggered. If that is the case, updateNodes() is called again.

- initCollection() is responsible for creating child elements. It first determines the beginning and the end of the calendar week selected in the JSpinner. Then findDueTasks() finds all TopLevelTasks and their direct and indirect subtasks fall within the desired period. This list contains tasks that must be displayed.

- However, the result of initCollection() must not be a list of tasks, but of Nodes. The tasks are therefore wrapped in **TaskNodes**, which are added to the collection to be returned. To be notified about changes in the task, the TaskChildren object needs to register itself as a PropertyChangeListener of its tasks. The propertyChange() method checks whether the source of the event is a task and whether it concerns the name of the property. In this case, updateNodes() is called again.

- updateNodes() is responsible for recalculating the list of the child elements. First, the list of nodes is cleared by getting all current Nodes with getNodes() and remove()-ing them. Then you reinvoke the initCollection() method to generate a list of the child elements again. This list of Nodes is now transformed into a node array, where the child elements are added to the collection with add(). That is how the child elements are updated dynamically.

Your model is now ready to be used by one or more explorer views!

Multiple explorer view implementations

Explorer views are JComponents that can display nodes in several ways. As you already know at this point, nodes are always hierarchical, though they need not necessarily be displayed exactly as shown in the current example.

All explorer views extend JScrollPane from where they obtain their scroll bars. This is particularly interesting in the context of the Matisse GUI Builder, because by default Matisse doesn't know about explorer views, if you look in the IDE's Component Palette. However, as explorer views are JScrollPanes, that is, Swing components following the JavaBeans specification, it is possible to extend the Component Palette to include the explorer views, so that you can drag-and-drop them on the Matisse GUI Builder's Design view when you design your TopComponents.

The Explorer & Property Sheet API offers the following explorer views:

Class	Description
BeanTreeView	The **BeanTreeView** represents the nodes as tree. It is actually a JTree.
OutlineView	The **OutlineView** is a table view with a tree. The tree is in the leftmost column and makes the rows expandable and collapsible. The remaining columns contain additional data (properties of the node) about the node, shown in the tree column.
ListView	The **ListView** represents the children of root nodes in a flat list similar to a JList.
IconView	The **IconView** represents the Nodes as a list of large icons with a name label. It looks somewhat like the Windows Explorer.
ChoiceView	The **ChoiceView** displays all the children of a root Node in the JComboBox.
MenuView	The **MenuView** shows the children of the root node as a menu and the children of the children as submenus and so on.
ContextTreeView	The **ContextTreeView** is similar to the **BeanTreeView** except that it controls the ExploredContext of the **ExplorerManager**. The view acts as the master view where the detail view is the selected node.
PropertySheetView	The **PropertySheetView** doesn't display nodes, but shows the **PropertySheet** editor for a given node.

Explorer views are controlled by an ExplorerManager. This is the class responsible for managing the node selection and updating the nodes that belong to the given root node.

Components that provide an `ExplorerManager` must implement the interface `ExplorerManager.Provider`, which defines the single method `getExplorerManager()`. This defines a standard way for finding the `ExplorerManager`.

Explorer views are not explicitly linked to an `ExplorerManager`. They discover it at runtime by walking up their component hierarchy until they find a component, which implements `ExplorerManager.Provider`. As soon as this is found, the explorer view gets its `ExplorerManager`.

Creating an explorer view

For the example application you're building, you now need to create a `TopComponent` that will contain a `ListView`, where due tasks are displayed for a selected calendar week.

1. Use the **New Window** wizard to create a `TopComponent` in the **properties** mode. Specify that the new `TopComponent` should open when the application starts. Set "DueList" as the class name prefix, so that the new class ends up being named `DueListTopComponent`.

2. Use the Matisse GUI Builder to add a `JScrollPane` to the `TopComponent`, together with a `JSpinner`, together with the `JLabel` **Week**, as shown in the following screenshot:

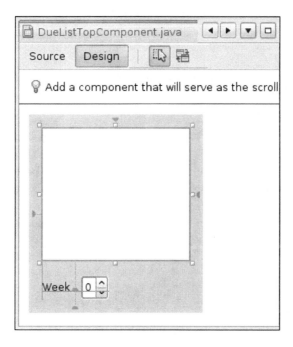

> You use a JScrollpane because you cannot create a **ListView** graphically, unless you add a ListView to the Component Palette yourself. So the trick here is to use a JScrollpane that acts as placeholder for the actual view. This is absolutely valid as ListView is a JScrollpane through inheritance.

3. Now you need to modify the creation code for the JScrollpane, letting it instantiate the ListView, instead of the JScrollPane. Select the JScrollpane and, in the **Properties** window's **Code** tab, set the **Custom Creation Code** property to the following:

    ```
    new ListView();
    ```

4. To the top of the class, add the import statement for the org.openide. explorer.view.ListView class.

5. You need to provide the JSpinner with a correct model, displaying numbers from 1 to 52 only, with increments of 1. The JSpinner must be initialized with the current calendar week. The constructor of the DueListTopComponent is therefore modified in the following way:

    ```
    private DueListTopComponent() {
        initComponents();
        int kw = Calendar.getInstance().get(Calendar.WEEK_OF_YEAR);
        SpinnerModel spinnerModel = new SpinnerNumberModel(kw, 1, 52, 1);
        this.jSpinner1.setModel(spinnerModel);
        // ...
    ```

Controlling views with the ExplorerManager

In the previous section, the ListView was added to the TopComponent to display the tasks. You now need to link the ListView to the task model. This is done through the use of an ExplorerManager, which acts as the controller between the view and the model. On the model side, the ExplorerManager maintains the model as a node hierarchy. On the view side, the ExplorerManager supplies the view with the data that can be displayed. The ExplorerManager also controls the nodes that should be displayed, while also managing the selection of nodes.

The selection is interesting for other components. With master-detail views, the first view shows node objects, while the second shows detailed information about the selected node. This mechanism can only work if the first view somehow communicates which nodes are currently selected. You have already seen an excellent mechanism that implements such functionality, that is, the Lookup and, in particular, the ActionGlobalContext. Explorer views and nodes insert themselves within this mechanism seamlessly.

Each node wraps an object model, which is stored in the node's Lookup. The nodes are shown in an explorer view, which in turn is contained within a TopComponent. To make the selection available to interested components, you need to first expose the Lookups of these nodes in the Lookup of the TopComponent. An interested component should then only need to listen to changes in the ActionsGlobalContext, grabbing the current domain model object as it appears there.

The class ExplorerUtils gives you a method for creating a Lookup, createLookup (...), which will be linked to an ExplorerManager. The ExplorerManager is responsible for the management of the selection, so that both the selected nodes and the content of their Lookups can be made available. The Lookup created in this way contains the selected nodes, as well as the domain model objects. If you specify this Lookup as the Lookup of the TopComponent, the ActionGlobalContext will always contain the selected nodes and domain model objects.

 In addition to the handling of the selection, the ExplorerManager also manages the actions of a view. It ensures that the correct context menu actions for an explorer view are enabled.

Creating an ExplorerManager

You now create an ExplorerManager and link it with the node model. The following steps describe the code that follows:

1. Instantiate an ExplorerManager and configure the ActionMap, as well as the input map of the TopComponent. Thanks to the LookupUtils.createLookup (ExplorerManager, ActionMap) method, you can create a Lookup that is linked to the ExplorerManager and the ActionMap of the TopComponent. Add it to the TopComponent's Lookup, enabling the Lookup to be accessed from other components.

2. Provide the data to be managed by the ExplorerManager. The ExplorerManager expects this data to be in the form of a node hierarchy, even though the view represents a flat list. A ListView does not show the root node, so that you can take a simple AbstractNode as the root and add the TaskNodes as children. You don't do this directly, but with the help of the TaskChildren instance that handles the task children.

3. Set a name for the root node. This name is used in the title of the ListView.

The complete constructor looks like this:

```
final class DueListTopComponent extends TopComponent implements
ExplorerManager.Provider {

    // ...
    private ExplorerManager em;
    private Lookup lookup;
    // ...

    private DueListTopComponent() {
        initComponents();
        int kw = Calendar.getInstance().get(Calendar.WEEK_OF_YEAR);
        SpinnerModel spinnerModel = new SpinnerNumberModel(
                                            kw, 1, 52, 1);
        this.jSpinner1.setModel(spinnerModel);
        this.em = new ExplorerManager();
        ActionMap map = this.getActionMap();
        InputMap keys = this.getInputMap(JComponent.WHEN_
                            ANCESTOR_OF_FOCUSED_COMPONENT);
        this.lookup = ExplorerUtils.createLookup(this.em, map);
        this.associateLookup(this.lookup);

        Children children = new TaskChildren(this.jSpinner1);

        Node root = new AbstractNode(children);
        this.em.setRootContext(root);
        this.em.getRootContext().setDisplayName("DueTasks");

        // ...
    }

    public ExplorerManager getExplorerManager() {
        return this.em;
    }

    // ...
```

Restart the application, which should look as shown in the illustration below. Edit the task opened in the task editor. Notice that the DueList and the data in the editor are synchronized. Continue to create some further tasks and assign the due dates from different calendar weeks. If a task gets a due date that does not fall within the current calendar week, it will not appear in DueList. Change the indicated calendar week afterwards with the help of the JSpinner. You will see that the displayed tasks change and that, hence, the explorer view works as expected.

To summarize, you have built the **TaskModel** with nodes and displayed these nodes with the help of an explorer view. To create this view, you had to implement very few things yourself. Compare again how much you coded for the view versus the business logic, which was in this case, the filtering of the tasks. Most of the coding went into the implementation of the business logic. The view was created in very few lines indeed.

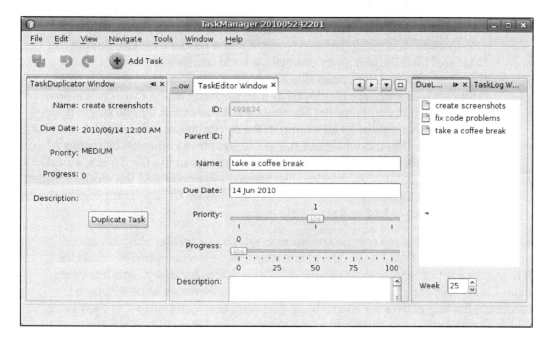

Key-based node hierarchies

In the previous section, you used a `Children` object and, upon instantiation, exactly one node was created for each model element. For most use cases, this is a sub-optimal pattern in which nodes are either created too early and possibly for no reason, because of the following reasons:

- Firstly, often the node doesn't need to be created and saved in its entirety. Instead, it is normally sufficient to determine the set of the model elements that need to be managed. Simply knowing that child elements exist is enough to provide for the node to be expandable or not. Then, and only when the user expands the node, is it necessary to actually create the child nodes. This concept is also known as "lazy initialization", helping to reduce the time required to create the view, while reducing the impact on the system resources and thereby improving performance.

- Secondly, unlike what we've assumed so far, there isn't necessarily a one-to-one relationship between a node and a model element. Taking the "Matisse" GUI Builder as an example, a form consists of two files, that is, the `.java` file and the `.form` file. Together, these files represent a logical entity and, as such, are displayed as a single node in the **Projects** window. In other words, multiple model elements are represented by one single node. Taking the **Navigator** as an example, the opposite can be seen to be true: for one Java file (the model element), the file structure is shown, by means of a large number of nodes, for each of the elements in the file. Hence, simply assuming a one-to-one relationship between the node and the model element is not correct, requiring us to be able to work with flexible mappings between model elements and nodes.

The class `Children.Keys` (or `ChildFactory`, which is a further simplification and enhancement of `Children.Keys`) is a response to the complexities described. It manages a set of keys and, as required, creates nodes for a key. This lets you delay creation of the node to the time the node actually needs to be displayed. Additionally, this allows for an arbitrary mapping between nodes and their keys, which decreases the resulting impact on resources and, hence, performance.

In addition to handling the more complex requirements outlined above, the `Children.Keys` (or `ChildFactory`) class lets you add, remove, and sort `Children` without losing selection. Combined, these features make `Children.Keys` (or `ChildFactory`) the most commonly used `Children` implementation.

Creating a key-based node hierarchy

In the next example, you create a view that lets the user browse the task hierarchy. To do so, you need to present tasks as nodes in an explorer view.

Creating subtasks is done via the subclass `Children.Keys` (which could also be the subclass `ChildFactory`).

1. Create a new module named **Overview**, with code name base **com.netbeansrcp.overview**.

2. As dependencies, select the **TaskModel** module, so that you have access to the domain model, as well as the Lookup API, Utilities API, the Nodes API, and the Explorer & Propery Sheet API.

3. You need a subclass of a `Node` implementation, for displaying tasks.

4. You want the `Node` to be able to display tasks as well as subtasks.

5. You want to modify the way the `Node` is displayed. The display name of a `Node` can contain a small set of HTML tags that are rendered accordingly. You want to use these HTML tags to display the priority of the task.

6. You also want to change the default icon to a Task-specific icon. You can do this by setting the `iconBase`. It specifies the base resource that is used to show an expanded and non-expanded node as well as different icon sizes.

7. Because of these changes, it is easier to create a new `TaskNode` than to reuse the `TaskNode` from the **DueList** module. You want to pass a Task to the new `TaskNode`, which the `TaskNode` uses to create an instance of `TaskChildren`. The `TaskChildren` in turn create `TaskNodes` for subtasks. Additionally, the `TaskNode` monitors its Task via the `PropertyChange` mechanism, modifying its display name accordingly.

After following the steps above, the `TaskNode` implementation looks as follows:

```
public class TaskNode extends AbstractNode implements
PropertyChangeListener {

    public TaskNode(Task task) {
        super(new TaskChildren(task), Lookups.singleton(task));

        this.setName(task.getId());
        this.setDisplayName(task.getName());
        this.setIconBaseWithExtension
          ("com/netbeansrcp/overview/Task.png");
        task.addPropertyChangeListener(this);
    }
```

```java
@Override
public String getHtmlDisplayName() {
    String html = "<font color='";
    Task task = this.getLookup().lookup(Task.class);
    switch (task.getPrio()) {
        case LOW:
            html += "0000FF";//blue
            break;
        case MEDIUM:
            html += "000000";//black
            break;
        case HIGH:
            html += "FF0000";//red
            break;
    }
    html += "'>" + task.getName() + "</font>";
    return html;
}

public void propertyChange(PropertyChangeEvent arg0) {
    if (Task.PROP_NAME.equals(arg0.getPropertyName())

    || Task.PROP_PRIO.equals(arg0.getPropertyName())) {
        setDisplayName(arg0.getNewValue() + "");
    }
}
}
```

Above, a Task is passed to the constructor of the TaskNode. A TaskChildren object, which you have not defined yet, and the Task in a singleton Lookup are passed to the super constructor. Additionally, the TaskNode is registered as a PropertyChangeListener with the Task, so that it can react to changes to the display name and priority.

The method getHtmlDisplayName() returns the display name wrapped in a font tag that colors the display name according to the priority. The method propertyChange() is used to modify the display name when changes to either the display name or the priority are made.

Next, you need a subclass of Children for creating the children of the TaskNode. The text that follows explains the code that comes after it:

1. Use Children.Keys, or ChildFactory, to make use of its built-in lazy initialization. Therefore, extend the class TaskChildren from Children. Keys and implement the method createNodes() and override the method addNotify().

2. The method `addNotify()` is called immediately before the `Children` object is first asked for its Nodes. Therefore it is the ideal place to determine the subtasks and to set them as the child elements keys.

3. The method `createNodes()` is called once for each key to return an array of nodes for that key. This method is the place where the mapping between keys and their nodes is done. A `TaskNode` is created for each subtask.

4. Furthermore, the `Children` object must react to changes to the list of subtasks of the Task and modify the set of keys of the `Children` instance. Therefore, the `TaskChildren` implements the interface `PropertyChangeListener` and is registered as a listener to the Task.

Taking the steps above results in the code that follows:

```
class TaskChildren extends Children.Keys<Task> implements
  PropertyChangeListener {

    private Task task;

    public TaskChildren(Task task) {
        this.task = task;
        task.addPropertyChangeListener(this);
    }

    @Override
    protected void addNotify() {
        super.addNotify();
        this.setKeys(task.getChildren());
    }

    protected Node[] createNodes(Task arg0) {
        return new TaskNode[]{new TaskNode(arg0)};
    }
    public void propertyChange(PropertyChangeEvent arg0) {
        if
          (TaskManager.PROP_TASKLIST_ADD.equals
          (arg0.getPropertyName())
        || TaskManager.PROP_TASKLIST_REMOVE.equals
          (arg0.getPropertyName())) {
            this.setKeys(this.task.getChildren());
        }
    }
}
```

Above, the constructor of the `TaskChildren` stores the Task that is passed and adds itself as a `PropertyChangeListener` to that Task. The method `addNotify()` determines the subtasks and registers them as the administered keys using the method `setKeys()`. Every key that was set is passed separately to the method `createNodes()`, which in this case returns a `TaskNode` for every subtask. In the method `propertyChange()`, changes to the list of subtasks are integrated in the `Children`'s keys. As `Children.Keys` automatically determines which keys were added or removed, you do not need to think about that.

With that, most of the Tasks are displayed. However, the `TopLevelTasks` still need to be displayed. You will use an `AbstractNode` as the root node, which is what you did before, too. Its child nodes are the `TopLevelTasks`. Therefore, create a new implementation of `Children` to display the `TaskNodes` of the `TopLevelTasks` and update it when necessary:

```java
public class TopLevelTaskChildren extends Children.Keys<Task>
    implements PropertyChangeListener {
      private TaskManager taskMgr;

      public TopLevelTaskChildren() {
         this.taskMgr = Lookup.getDefault().lookup(TaskManager.class);

            if (null != this.taskMgr) {
               this.taskMgr.addPropertyChangeListener(this);
            }
         }
      @Override
      protected void addNotify() {
         super.addNotify();
         if (null != this.taskMgr) {
            this.setKeys(this.taskMgr.getTopLevelTasks());
         }
      }

      protected Node[] createNodes(Task arg0) {
         return new Node[]{new TaskNode(arg0)};
      }

      public void propertyChange(PropertyChangeEvent arg0) {
         if (null != this.taskMgr) {
            If
(TaskManager.PROP_TASKLIST_ADD.equals(arg0.getPropertyName())
            || TaskManager.PROP_TASKLIST_REMOVE.equals(arg0.
getPropertyName())) {
               this.setKeys(this.taskMgr.getTopLevelTasks());
            }
         }
      }
   }
```

Above, the constructor attempts to find an instance of a **TaskManager** in the global `Lookup` and, if successful, registers itself as a `PropertyChangeListener` on it. Prior to first displaying the `TopLevelTasks` for the first time, the method `addNotify()` is called. There the **TaskManager** instance is queried for `TopLevelTasks` and the result is set as the keys of this `Children` instance. Those `TopLevelTasks` are passed to `createNodes()` separately, where a `TaskNode` is created and returned. The **TaskManager** notifies its `PropertyChangeListeners` of any change to its list of `TopLevelTasks`. In that case, the keys are updated automatically with the new list of `TopLevelTasks` in `propertyChange()`.

With that, everything is done for the presentation of the model. Now you can deal with displaying it.

Displaying nodes in an explorer view

Although, typically, the first choice for displaying hierarchies is a tree, with **BeanTreeView** providing the standard explorer view, let's use a simple list, for the time being. Especially for very large hierarchies, a list is easy to oversee, while it displays only a single branch offering navigation through the branches of the tree. For example, think of all those Norton Commander clones for file management. They are used in various operating systems and are able to handle very large file hierarchies easily.

1. In the **Overview** module, use the **New Window** wizard to create a new `TopComponent` in the explorer mode, which should open by default, and which should have `Overview` as the class name prefix.

2. Doing the same as in the `DueListTopComponent`, add a `JScrollPane` that is initialized by means of a `ListView`. Then add the code, as you did in the `DueListTopComponent`, and you end up with the following implementation:

```
final class OverviewTopComponent extends TopComponent implements
   ExplorerManager.Provider {

    private ExplorerManager em;
    private Lookup lookup;
// ...

    private OverviewTopComponent() {
        initComponents();
        this.em = new ExplorerManager();
        ActionMap map = this.getActionMap();
        InputMap keys = this.getInputMap(
          JComponent.WHEN_ANCESTOR_OF_FOCUSED_COMPONENT);
        this.lookup = ExplorerUtils.createLookup(this.em, map);
        this.associateLookup(this.lookup);
```

```
        Node root = new AbstractNode(new
          TopLevelTaskChildren());
        this.em.setRootContext(root);
        this.em.getRootContext().setDisplayName("Overview");
    // ...


    public ExplorerManager getExplorerManager() {
        return this.em;
    }
    // ...
```

To browse through the hierarchy, initialize the **TaskModel** with dummy values. To do this, modify the constructor of the TaskManagerImpl, which is in the **TaskModel** module, by creating a few Tasks, as shown in the following code snippet:

```
public TaskManagerImpl() {
    this.topLevelTasks = new ArrayList<Task>();
    this.pss = new PropertyChangeSupport(this);

    Task t1 = this.createTask();
    t1.setName("Todo 1");

    Task t2 = this.createTask("Todo 1.1", t1.getId());
    t2 = this.createTask("Todo 1.2", t1.getId());
    t2 = this.createTask("Todo 1.3", t1.getId());
    this.createTask("Todo 1.3.1", t2.getId());

    t1 = this.createTask();
    t1.setName("Todo 2");

    t2 = this.createTask("Todo 2.1", t1.getId());
    t2 = this.createTask("Todo 2.2", t1.getId());
    t2 = this.createTask("Todo 2.3", t1.getId());
    t1 = this.createTask("Todo 2.3.1", t2.getId());

    t2 = this.createTask("Todo 2.3.1.1", t1.getId());
    t2 = this.createTask("Todo 2.3.1.2", t1.getId());
}
```

When you restart the application, it should look as shown in the following screenshot. As soon as you modify the values of the currently displayed task in the editor, the changes are shown in the **Overview**. Double-clicking a node or pressing the *Enter* key lets you display the children of the selected node and jump one level deeper into the hierarchy. By pressing the *Backspace* key, you ascend one level. You can browse the task hierarchy, while large hierarchies are displayed effectively, with a minimum of required space.

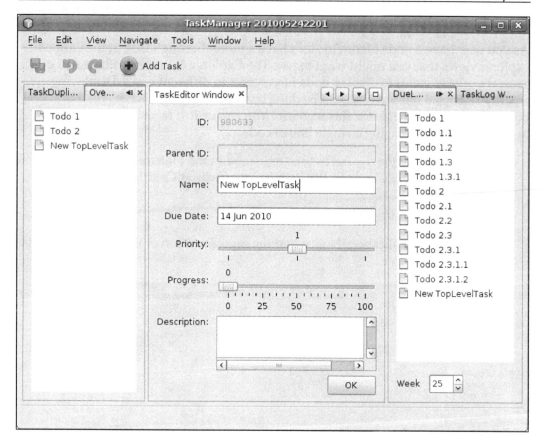

To summarize, in the previous example you have learned that tree structures can be displayed easily and efficiently using nodes and Children.Keys. Using Children.Keys, you can delay the creation of a Node's children, optimizing performance while still showing the user interface quickly. Additionally, you discovered how to map a model element to multiple nodes. To display the Node, you used a ListView, though a BeanTreeView would have been a more intuitive choice, as you would then also be able to see the children as subnodes beneath the main nodes. In the next example, you look at various other views for displaying the task hierarchy and how to switch between explorer views.

Exchanging explorer views

As you now have a node hierarchy, let's have a more thorough look at the various explorer views that you might want to use. The Explorer & Property Sheet API offers several explorer views to display node hierarchies in different ways. Displaying a partly restricted hierarchy would be done best with a tree. BeanTreeView is the explorer view suitable for this scenario. You can switch from a ListView to a BeanTreeView by changing a single line of code.

1. After opening the OverviewTopComponent in the Matisse GUI Builder, select the JScrollPane and modify its property **Custom Creation Code** to the following line:

   ```
   new BeanTreeView();
   ```

2. Restart the application. Notice that the representation of the task hierarchy is changed to a tree.

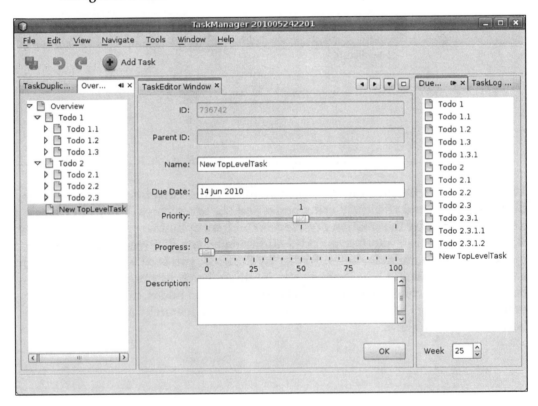

The root node `Overview` has no purpose other than providing `Children` for the view. Let's hide it by modifying the constructor of `OverviewTopComponent`.

```
private OverviewTopComponent() {
// ...
    em.setRootContext(root);
    em.getRootContext().setDisplayName("Overview");
    ((BeanTreeView) this.jScrollPane1).setRootVisible(false);
// ...
```

After a restart of the application the `TopLevelTasks` are shown as root nodes.

To summarize, you have seen how flexible the concept of Nodes and explorer views is. With one line of code, you have changed the representation from a `ListView` to a `BeanTreeView`. In standard Swing, that's an achievement that would have required you to completely change the component model, together with considerable changes to the controller. Several explorer views from the package `org.openide.explorer.view` work in exactly the same way, though some of them work with different superclasses. Views displaying additional information, such as the `OutlineView`, however, require a little bit more work.

Speaking of the `OutlineView`, this is a very powerful Explorer view that displays nodes in a table. The leftmost column of the table contains a tree of nodes. Additional columns contain a set of properties of the current row's node. A complex view of this kind lets you display nodes together with their properties in a single view, which is a very normal thing to expect in a large application of the kind typically found on the NetBeans Platform.

Lazy child creation

More often than not, when dealing with large amounts of data, the calculation and display of child elements is slow. In fact, retrieving data from a filesystem or database can take several seconds, on a good day. Expanding a Node and, thus, the lazy creation of child elements, is done on the EDT, which will freeze the UI. During this time, no UI updates are performed and user gestures are ignored, making the UI unusable for the duration of the process. That is the reason why creating the child elements is done in a different thread. Meanwhile, you should inform the user that child elements are being created and are about to be displayed. During this time, normally a wait cursor and a status message are shown.

Ever since the use of NetBeans Platform 6, the ChildFactory class offers support for creating child elements asynchronously. Like Children.Keys, ChildFactory works by mapping keys to Nodes and can simply be used to replace Children. Keys altogether. To create a Children instance that defers child creation to a ChildFactory, you must call the Children.create() method. This method uses the ChildFactory class, together with a flag that, if true, causes children to be created in a separate thread.

In the following example, you simulate the ChildFactory use case by letting the current thread sleep for some time while children are being created.

1. Modify the TaskChildren class as shown in the following code snippet. You can test the new behavior by restarting the application and then expanding a TaskNode, while trying to use the rest of the application at the same time!

    ```
    @Override
    protected void addNotify() {
        super.addNotify();
        try {Thread.sleep(30000);} catch (InterruptedException ex) {
        }
        this.setKeys(task.getChildren());
    }
    ```

2. In order to prevent the application from freezing while expanding a TaskNode, create a new class named TaskChildFactory, extending ChildFactory. You will use this class to create children asynchronously, while also notifying the user of progress done. The methods of a ChildFactory are very similar to those of Children.Keys:

    ○   createKeys() creates the child elements and adds them to the list passed to the method. You need to fill that list with the subtasks of the Task.

    ○   createNodesForKey() creates the nodes corresponding to the passed key and returns them. Here you return a TaskNode for the Task that is passed.

- ○ Notification of progress is the responsibility of the `ChildFactory`. It has its own wait node, showing that the child elements are being created.

3. Change the `TaskNode` as follows, so that the `TaskChildFactory` is used, instead of the `TaskChildren`, when creating nodes:

```
public TaskNode(Task task) {

    this(task, Lookups.singleton(task));

}

public TaskNode(Task task, Lookup lookup) {

    super(Children.create(new TaskChildFactory(task), true), lookup);

    this.setName(task.getId());

    this.setDisplayName(task.getName());
    this.setIconBaseWithExtension
        ("com/netbeansrcp/overview/Task.png");

    task.addPropertyChangeListener(this);

}
```

4. After you set a dependency on the Progress API, you can use it to display the current progress integrated in the NetBeans Platform progress bar. The `ProgressHandleFactory` creates `ProgressHandle` objects, which display progress and, optionally, enables the user to cancel the progress display. Progress can be displayed with a definite or an indefinite runtime.

5. For the example application, you display progress in percentiles, with a minimum of 0 and a maximum of 100. You create a `ProgressHandle` to show the start of the process, display the progress, and then show the completion of the task.

6. Finally, the children list needs to be updated when the list of subtasks is changed. To this end, you register a `PropertyChangeListener` that updates the children list as required.

The preceding text is expressed in code as follows:

```
public class TaskChildFactory extends ChildFactory<Task> implements
    PropertyChangeListener {

    private Task task;

    public TaskChildFactory(Task task) {
        this.task = task;
        task.addPropertyChangeListener(this);
    }

    protected boolean createKeys(List<Task> arg0) {
        final long delay = 500;
        ProgressHandle handle =
            ProgressHandleFactory.createHandle("Creating
            subtasks...");
        handle.start(100);

        try {Thread.sleep(delay);} catch (InterruptedException ex) {
        }

        handle.progress(25);

        try {Thread.sleep(delay);} catch (InterruptedException ex) {
        }

        handle.progress(50);
        try {Thread.sleep(delay);} catch (InterruptedException ex) {
        }

        handle.progress(75);

        try {Thread.sleep(delay);} catch (InterruptedException ex) {
        }

        handle.finish();

        arg0.addAll(this.task.getChildren());

        return true;
    }

    @Override
    protected Node[] createNodesForKey(Task arg0) {
        return new TaskNode[] { new TaskNode(arg0) };
    }
```

```
public void propertyChange(PropertyChangeEvent arg0) {
    if (Task.PROP_CHILDREN_ADD.equals(arg0.getPropertyName())
    || Task.PROP_CHILDREN_REMOVE.equals(arg0.getPropertyName())) {
        this.refresh(true);
    }
  }
}
```

In the preceding code, take note of the following:

- The Task is passed to the constructor. It is stored there and used for creating the child elements. The `TaskChildrenFactory` itself is registered as `PropertyChangeListener` to the Task.

- The method `createKeys()` is responsible for creating the keys. In the example application, the keys are the subtasks, which need to be added to the list received by the `createKeys()` method.

- To show that child creation is done asynchronously, let's delay the thread for half a second multiple times. As you will see, the application remains responsive during the child creation process. And, while the keys are created, the `ChildFactory` shows a "wait node".

- Next, you implement the integration with the NetBeans Platform progress bar. Using the `ProgressHandleFactory`, you create a `ProgressHandle` with an initial text, set the target progress to **100**, and then display it. During the creation of the children, you update the progress continuously and, finally, stop displaying it.

- The method `createNodesForKey()` is responsible for creating and returning the `TaskNode` that corresponds to the passed subtask.

- When the list of subtasks is changed, the method `propertyChange()` is called which results in a call to `refresh()` to update the list of child nodes. The boolean flag declares that the nodes are updated in the current thread.

Now restart the application and expand a task. Expanding the task takes several seconds. While the task is expanded, a "wait node" showing an hourglass and "Please Wait" is displayed. Additionally, you see a progress bar in the bottom-right corner of the application. During the expansion of the task, the progress bar shows the current progress and disappears when it is finished.

To summarize, in this section you have learned how to create a node's children asynchronously while keeping the application responsive, how the `ChildFactory` notifies the user about lengthy operations, and how this information can be used to display a progress bar.

Context-sensitive actions

Another advantage of the Nodes API is its support for context-sensitive actions. These are actions that only make sense in the context of a particular object. For example, if you click **Save** in the **File** menu, you don't expect a random document to be saved. Rather, you expect a very specific document to be saved, that is, the current document that you have been working on by editing and changing it. This variant of the context-sensitive action can be implemented by combining the `ActionsGlobalContext` with a `LookupListener`.

However, many context-sensitive actions are not made available from global menus and toolbars. Instead, they are found in the context menu of the object for which the actions exist. In this section, you learn about this second variant of the context-sensitive action, in particular, context-sensitive actions that are found in context menus and that relate to specific objects, such as, as in this case, the `Task` object. In this scenario, the Nodes API is useful, in that each `Node` can provide an array of Actions that are displayed in the Node's context menu and that can then be invoked from there. One of these actions can be assigned as the default action, that is, the action that is invoked when the user double-clicks on a `Node`.

The ability of being context-sensitive, here expressed via the connection between a `Node` and an `Action`, is described by the `ContextAwareAction` interface, specifically via its method `createContextAwareInstance(Lookup)`, which returns an `Action`.

Any `Action` or `ActionListener` can be registered as a `ContextAwareAction` in the `layer.xml` file, as shown below. Here an `Action` defined in `action.pkg.YourAction` is enabled if the object `org.netbeans.api.actions.Openable` is available in the `Lookup`. This simplified registration mechanism means that you do not need to deal with the low-level details of subclassing the `ContextAwareAction`, described in the remainder of this section.

```
<file name="action-pkg-ClassName.instance">
  <attr name="instanceCreate"
    methodvalue="org.openide.awt.Actions.context"/>
  <attr name="type" stringvalue="org.netbeans.api.actions.Openable"/>
  <attr name="selectionType" stringvalue="ANY"/>
  <attr name="delegate" newvalue="action.pkg.YourAction"/>
</file>
```

In some scenarios, though, you might still need to use the `ContextAwareAction` directly within your code, by subclassing it, instead of using the registration defined above. For example, above you can see that the `Action` is enabled if one specific object is available in the `Lookup`, that is, the `Openable` object. If your business scenario requires multiple different objects to be available, the above registration is insufficient, requiring you to understand and use the `ContextAwareAction` class in your code. Even more commonly, you might want to check the setting of a property, in addition to checking for the mere presence of an object, before enabling an `Action`. The registration above does not let you support a more fine-grained enablement strategy of this kind. Therefore, let's spend some time looking at how to work with the `ContextAwareAction` in your code, so that you will be able to use it yourself when one of these more complex scenarios arise.

Though contextually-aware Actions work with the `ContextAwareAction` class, it is not the `ContextAwareAction` itself that is invoked when the user clicks a menu item, toolbar button, or keyboard shortcut. Instead, the `ContextAwareAction` is both an interface and a factory for the actual `Action` that needs to be performed. Typically, the `ContextAwareAction` and the `Action` that it manages are defined in separate classes. The `Action` that needs to be invoked context-sensitively has, as a rule, a constructor, which receives the context in the form of a `Lookup`, while implementing the methods `isEnabled()` or `actionPerformed()`, depending on the content of the `Lookup`.

If, for example, you need to connect an `Action` to the context menu of a node which, in turn, represents a model object, you can create an `Action` that provides an implementation of `ContextAwareAction`. By means of `createContextAwa reInstance(Lookup)`, a further `Action` is created, making use of the received `Lookup` to determine its enablement. The `Lookup` is automatically the `Lookup` of the selected `Node`, so that you need to implement `setEnabled` in such a way that the `actionPerformed` can only be invoked if the appropriate model objects are found in the `Lookup`.

In the example application, you begin to create Actions that let the user create new tasks, copy existing tasks, edit tasks, and delete tasks. These Actions need to appear in the context menu of `TaskNodes`, as well as in the global toolbar of the application. When invoked on a `TaskNode`, the Actions operate on the context of the `Node`. In this case, the Explorer view calls `createContextAwareInstance(Lookup)` indirectly and passes the selected `Node` to the `Lookup`, to make the correct context available to the `Action`. In the global toolbar, however, the `Action` looks in the `ActionsGlobalContext` to see if a Task is selected.

Therefore, the `Action` is more than a `ContextAwareAction`, it is also a factory for Actions. The two approaches have a lot in common, in both cases, that is, in the `Node` and in the toolbar, you listen to the `Lookup`, setting the enablement of the `Action` based on the content of the `Lookup`, and calling the same `Action` on the Task retrieved from the `Lookup`. As a result, it makes sense to create the Actions as a single class to be used in the `Node` context menu, as well as in the global toolbar.

Creating the Edit Task Action

You now start by working on the `Action` for editing tasks. First of all, you implement an `EditAction` as a global `Action` shown in a toolbar, while listening to the `ActionsGlobalContext` for the presence of Tasks and adapting the Action's enablement accordingly. When invoked, the `Action` shows a Task in the `TaskEditor`. Once you have gone through this first phase, you make the `Action` available to the context menu of the `TaskNode`.

The steps below describe the code that follows:

1. In the **TaskActions** module, create a class named `EditAction` and let it extend `AbstractAction`, while letting it listen to the `ActionsGlobalContext` via a `LookupListener`.

2. Display the `Action` in the toolbar by implementing the `Presenter.Toolbar` interface.

3. Set the required dependencies, which are the `Lookup` API and Utilities API, on the module.

4. You now need to create two constructors in the `EditAction`. One provides the `ActionsGlobalContext` and registers a `LookupListener` on it. The other enables the class to be instantiated with a `Lookup` received from the components that needs to context-sensitively make use of the `EditAction`.

5. As it implements `Presenter.Toolbar`, the `EditAction` needs to implement `getToolbarPresenter()`. You need to implement it such that the same `JButton` is returned, for visualizing the `Action` in the toolbar.

6. When a change notification is received, the `resultChanged()` is automatically called. Here you check whether at least one Task is found in the `Lookup` and then activate the `Action` itself, as well as the `JButton` that visualizes it in the toolbar.

7. The `Action` is performed in the method `actionPerformed()`, which uses the helper method `openInTaskEditor()` to open the current Task. As the method `openInTaskEditor()` will be used by other classes too, make the helper method static so that it will be accessible elsewhere.

From the above instructions, below is the first version of our `Action`, which you will continue to work on throughout this section, later adding the `ContextAwareAction` implementation:

```
public class EditAction extends AbstractAction implements
   LookupListener, Presenter.Toolbar {

    private Lookup.Result<Task> result;
    private JButton toolbarBtn;

    public EditAction() {
        this(Utilities.actionsGlobalContext());
    }

    public EditAction(Lookup lookup) {

        super("Edit Task...", newImageIcon
          (ImageUtilities.loadImage(
          "com/netbeansrcp/taskactions/Universal.png")));

        this.result = lookup.lookupResult(Task.class);
        this.result.addLookupListener(this);
        this.resultChanged(new LookupEvent(result);
    }

    public void actionPerformed(ActionEvent arg0) {
        if (null != this.result && 0 <
          this.result.allInstances().size()) {
            Task task =
            this.result.allInstances().iterator().next();
            EditAction.openInTaskEditor(task);
          }
    }

    public static void openInTaskEditor(Task task) {
        TaskEditorTopComponent win =
          TaskEditorTopComponent.findInstance(task);
        win.open();
        win.requestActive();
    }

    public void resultChanged(LookupEvent arg0) {
        if (this.result.allInstances().size() > 0) {
            this.setEnabled(true);
            if (null != this.toolbarBtn) {
                this.toolbarBtn.setEnabled(true);
              }
```

```
            }
        else {
            this.setEnabled(false);
            if (null != this.toolbarBtn) {
                this.toolbarBtn.setEnabled(false);
            }
        }
    }

    public Component getToolbarPresenter() {

        if (null == this.toolbarBtn) {
            this.toolbarBtn = new JButton(this);
        }

        return this.toolbarBtn;
    }
}
```

Let's now turn to the activity of making the Action context-sensitive and available for the TaskNode's context menu.

1. To that end, you need to implement the interfaces ContextAwareAction and Presenter.Popup.

2. As a ContextAwareAction, the EditAction needs to implement the method createContextAwareInstance() such that an Action is returned that will operate on the available Lookup. In the case of the example, you have set up the EditAction such that the Lookup is made available via the constructor. Within the received Lookup, locate the Task and then open it in the TaskEditor, which means that the user is then able to work in the current context. Implement the factory method createContextAwareInstance() such that a new EditAction is created, passing the Lookup into the constructor of the EditAction.

    When called from an Explorer view, the Lookup passed into the EditAction is the Lookup of the selected node which, in this case, is the TaskNode. That means the EditAction opens the Task for the currently selected TaskNode, which is exactly what you wanted to have happened.

3. To show the EditAction in the context menu of a Node, you need to implement Presenter.Popup. In the required method getPopupPresenter(), return a JMenuItem that the user can click to invoke the context-sensitive Action.

4. In short, to make the `EditAction` context-sensitive, you need to implement nothing more than the following two methods:

```
public Action createContextAwareInstance(Lookup lkp) {
    return new EditAction(lkp);
}
public JMenuItem getPopupPresenter() {
    return new JMenuItem(this);
}
```

Finally, you need to register the Action in the layer file, so that it can be contributed to the central registry of the application. On one hand, you need to make the `Action` available to the system and add it to the toolbar. On the other hand, you need to bind it to the context menu of the `TaskNode`.

You've already learned how to register Actions and connect them to the toolbar. For your new `EditAction` in the **TaskActions** module, add the following code snippet as shown in the following layer file:

```
<folder name="Actions">
  <folder name="Task">
    <file name="com-netbeansrcp-taskactions-AddAction.instance"/>
    <file name="com-netbeansrcp-taskactions-EditAction.instance"/>
  </folder>
</folder>

<folder name="Toolbars">
  <folder name="Task">
    <file name="com-netbeansrcp-taskactions-AddAction.shadow">
      <attr name="originalFile" stringvalue=
        "Actions/Task/com-netbeansrcp-taskactions
        AddAction.instance"/>
    </file>
    <file name="com-netbeansrcp-taskactions-EditAction.shadow">
      <attr name="originalFile" stringvalue=
        "Actions/Task/com-netbeansrcp-taskactions
        EditAction.instance"/>
    </file>
  </folder>
</folder>
```

Next, again in the layer file of the **TaskActions** module, let's start building a registry of Actions that will appear in the context menu of TaskNodes. Create the registrations below, which you will connect to the contextual menu via the code in the TaskNode:

```
<folder name="Tasks">
  <folder name="Nodes">
    <folder name="Task">
      <folder name="Actions">
       <file name="com-netbeansrcp-taskactions-EditAction.shadow">
          <attr name="originalFile" stringvalue="Actions/Task/com
            netbeansrcp-taskactions-EditAction.instance"/>
       </file>
      </folder>
      <folder name="PreferredAction">
        <file name="com-netbeansrcp-taskactions-EditAction.shadow">
          <attr name="originalFile" stringvalue="Actions/Task/com
            netbeansrcp-taskactions-EditAction.instance"/>
        </file>
      </folder>
    </folder>
  </folder>
</folder>
```

Note that in the preceding code snippet, the folder structure is one you defined yourself. You can define any folder structure at all in the layer file. From your Java code, you can then read the layer file and find the folders and files that are of interest to you.

Next, you need to change the TaskNode in the **Overview** module to bind the EditAction to the Node's context menu. To that end, override the method getActions(boolean). Via this method, the EditAction will be made available as one of the standard Actions in the context menu of the TaskNode. Let's also make sure that the EditAction is invoked when the user double-clicks the TaskNode. You achieve this by overriding the method getPreferredAction(). The result is as follows:

```
static List<? extends Action> registredActions;
  protected static List<? extends Action> getRegistredActions() {
      if (registredActions == null) {
        registredActions =
          Utilities.actionsForPath("Tasks/Nodes/Task/Actions");
        }
      return registredActions;
    }
@Override
public Action getPreferredAction() {
    return Utilities.actionsForPath
      ("Tasks/Nodes/Task/PreferredAction").get(0);
  }
```

```
@Override
public Action[] getActions(boolean context) {
    List<Action> actions = new ArrayList<Action>();
    actions.addAll(getRegistredActions());
    actions.addAll(Arrays.asList(super.getActions(context)));
    return actions.toArray(new Action[actions.size()]);
}
```

Now that you have bound the `EditAction` to the context menu of the node, let's try it out! Restart the application, which should look similar to the following illustration, choose a task, and then click **Edit Task** in the toolbar.

A second `TaskEditor` opens for the selected task. This means that the `EditAction` found the Task in the `ActionsGlobalContext`.

Next, call up the context menu for another Task, this time from the `TaskNode`, and then select **Edit Task** there. Again a new `TaskEditor` opens for the Task, this time using the `Lookup` of the `Node` to obtain the context for the `EditAction`.

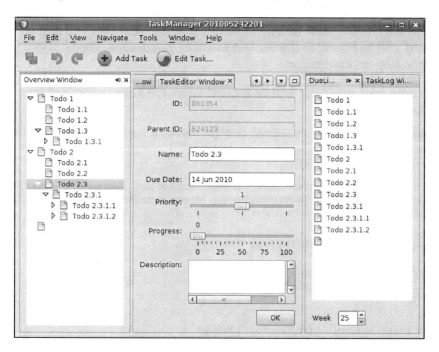

To summarize, you have made an `Action` context-sensitive in two different ways.

1. Firstly, you created an `Action` that you added to the global toolbar, where you generally have no context available. However, here you made use of the `ActionsGlobalContext` to obtain an object on which the `Action` was able to operate.

2. Secondly, you turned the `Action` into a `ContextAwareAction` and bound it to the context menu of a `TaskNode`. Invoked from the context menu of the `TaskNode`, the `Action` operates on an object obtained from the `Lookup` of the `TaskNode`, which is the current `Task` object in the `Lookup` of the `TaskNode`.

To round off this section dealing with context-sensitive Actions, let's create the remaining Actions context-sensitively. You'll create Actions for adding tasks, copying tasks, and deleting tasks.

Creating the Add Task Action

The `Action` for creating new tasks will be called `AddNewAction`, will appear in the toolbar, and will be bound to the context menu of `TaskNodes`. The behavior will differ depending on the context:

- A new `TopLevelTask` will be created when the `Action` is called from the toolbar

- When called from a `TaskNode` context menu, a new subtask will be created

The class outlined above is defined as follows:

```
public class AddNewAction extends AbstractAction implements
    ContextAwareAction, LookupListener, Presenter.Popup,
    Presenter.Toolbar {

    private Lookup.Result<Task> result;

    public AddNewAction() {
        this("Create New Task...");
    }

    private AddNewAction(Lookup lookup) {

        this("Create New Subtask...");
        this.result = lookup.lookupResult(Task.class);
        this.result.addLookupListener(this);
        this.resultChanged(new LookupEvent(result));
    }
    private AddNewAction(String label) {
```

```java
            super(label, new ImageIcon(ImageUtilities.loadImage
              ("com/netbeansrcp/taskactions/Add.png")));
        }


    public void actionPerformed(ActionEvent arg0) {

        TaskManager taskMgr =
          Lookup.getDefault().lookup(TaskManager.class);

        Task task = null;
        if (null != this.result && 0 <
          this.result.allInstances().size()) {

              task = this.result.allInstances().iterator().next();

              task = taskMgr.createTask("", task.getId());

            }
        else {

            task = taskMgr.createTask();
          }

        EditAction.openInTaskEditor(task);
      }

    public Action createContextAwareInstance(Lookup arg0) {
        return new AddNewAction(arg0);
      }

    public void resultChanged(LookupEvent arg0) {
        if (this.result.allInstances().size() > 0) {
            this.setEnabled(true);
          }
        else
          {
            this.setEnabled(false);
          }
      }

    public JMenuItem getPopupPresenter() {
        return new JMenuItem(this);
    }

    public Component getToolbarPresenter() {
        return new JButton(this);
      }
}
```

The preceding code largely parallels the previously discussed EditAction, but with one important difference relating to constructors:

- TopLevelTasks do not need a context, that is, a Lookup is not needed for creating these tasks, unlike earlier when you created the EditAction. Therefore, when the AddNewAction is invoked from the toolbar, the default constructor is used. A corresponding label is set, though no LookupListener is set, as that isn't needed. The actionPerformed() method is used to check the value of the Lookup. If it is set to null a new TopLevelTask is created.

- However, when AddNewAction is invoked from a TaskNode context menu, the constructor receives a Lookup containing the current Task object. The check in actionPerformed() notices this and the first task is retrieved from the Lookup. The Action constructor is again responsible for setting an appropriate label in the context menu.

In both cases, the new task is opened in a TaskEditor, via the static helper method from the EditAction.

Creating the Copy Task Action

Now that the user is able to create new Tasks, let's make it possible for an existing Task to be the basis of a new Task, that is, let's provide the copy functionality. Name the Action AddDuplicateAction and implement it, as with the previous Action, similarly to the EditAction:

```
public class AddDuplicateAction extends AbstractAction implements
    ContextAwareAction, LookupListener, Presenter.Popup,
    Presenter.Toolbar {
    private Lookup.Result<Task> result;

    public AddDuplicateAction() {
        this(Utilities.actionsGlobalContext());
    }

    private AddDuplicateAction(Lookup lookup) {

        this("Copy Task...");

        this.result = lookup.lookupResult(Task.class);
        this.result.addLookupListener(this);
        this.resultChanged(new LookupEvent(result));

        this.resultChanged(null);
    }
    private AddDuplicateAction(String label) {
        super(label, new ImageIcon(ImageUtilities.loadImage
```

```
                                ("com/netbeansrcp/taskactions/Duplicate.png")));
        }
    public void actionPerformed(ActionEvent arg0) {

        if (null != this.result && 0 <
          this.result.allInstances().size()) {
            Task original =
          this.result.allInstances().iterator().next();
            TaskManager taskMgr =
              Lookup.getDefault().lookup(TaskManager.class);
            Task newTask = null;
            String pId = original.getParentId();
            if (null != pId && ! "".equals(pId)) {
                newTask = taskMgr.createTask
                  (original.getName(), original.getParentId());
            }
            else {
                newTask = taskMgr.createTask();
                newTask.setName(original.getName());
            }
            newTask.setDescr(original.getDescr());
            newTask.setDue(original.getDue());
            newTask.setPrio(original.getPrio());
            newTask.setProgr(original.getProgr());
            EditAction.openInTaskEditor(newTask);
        }
    }

    public Action createContextAwareInstance(Lookup arg0) {
        return new AddDuplicateAction(arg0);
    }

    public void resultChanged(LookupEvent arg0) {
        if (this.result.allInstances().size() > 0) {
            this.setEnabled(true);
        }
        else {
            this.setEnabled(false);
        }
    }

    public JMenuItem getPopupPresenter() {
        return new JMenuItem(this);
    }

    public Component getToolbarPresenter() {
        return new JButton(this);
    }
}
```

As with the previous Actions, the AddDuplicateAction observes the
ActionsGlobalContext from the toolbar, while also working with the
TaskNode Lookup from the TaskNode context menu. In both cases, the
method actionPerformed() retrieves the selected task from the Lookup
of the selected Node.

If the template task has a parent task, the new duplicate task is created as a subtask
with the same parent; otherwise a new TopLevelTask is created. In the end, all
values from the template task, except the ID, are copied into the newly duplicated
task, which is then opened in a TaskEditor.

Creating the Delete Task Action

Let's now add an Action for deleting tasks. As this Action complements the
AddNewAction, it can be implemented very similarly. Called from the toolbar, it
queries the ActionsGlobalContext for the selected task and then deletes that task.
Called from the context menu of a TaskNode, it deletes the node.

```java
public class RemoveAction extends AbstractAction implements
    ContextAwareAction, LookupListener, Presenter.Popup,
    Presenter.Toolbar {

    private Lookup.Result<Task> result;
    private JButton toolbarBtn;

    public RemoveAction() {
        this(Utilities.actionsGlobalContext());
    }

    public RemoveAction(Lookup lookup) {

        super("Delete Task...",
          new ImageIcon(ImageUtilities.loadImage(
          "com/netbeansrcp/taskactions/Remove.png")));

        this.result = lookup.lookupResult(Task.class);
        this.result.addLookupListener(this);
        this.resultChanged(new LookupEvent(result));
    }
    public void actionPerformed(ActionEvent arg0) {

        if (null != this.result && 0 <
          this.result.allInstances().size()) {

          Task task = this.result.allInstances().iterator().next();
```

```
                    TaskManager taskMgr =
                            Lookup.getDefault().lookup(TaskManager.class);
                    if (null != taskMgr && null != task) {
                        taskMgr.removeTask(task.getId());
                    }
                }
            }
        }

        public Action createContextAwareInstance(Lookup arg0) {
            return new RemoveAction(arg0);
        }

        public void resultChanged(LookupEvent arg0) {
            if (this.result.allInstances().size() > 0) {
                this.setEnabled(true);
                if (null != this.toolbarBtn) {
                    this.toolbarBtn.setEnabled(true);
                }
            }
            else {
                this.setEnabled(false);
                if (null != this.toolbarBtn) {
                    this.toolbarBtn.setEnabled(false);
                }
            }
        }

        public JMenuItem getPopupPresenter() {
            return new JMenuItem(this);
        }

        public Component getToolbarPresenter() {

            if (null == this.toolbarBtn) {
                this.toolbarBtn = new JButton(this);
            }

            return this.toolbarBtn;
        }
    }
```

Connecting the Actions to the User Interface

As the final activity in this section, you need to add the new Actions to the context menu of the `TaskNode`, and optionally to the toolbar. This requires no changes to the `TaskNode` class, as it is already loading Actions from the layer file.

You need to adjust the `layer.xml` to declare the Actions:

```
<folder name="Actions">
  <folder name="Task">
    <file name="com-netbeansrcp-taskactions-AddAction.instance"/>
      <file name="com-netbeansrcp-taskactions-
        AddNewAction.instance"/>
      <file name="com-netbeansrcp-taskactions-
        AddDuplicateAction.instance"/>
      <file name="com-netbeansrcp-taskactions-
        AddDuplicateAction.instance"/>
      <file name="com-netbeansrcp-taskactions-EditAction.instance"/>
      <file name="com-netbeansrcp-taskactions-
        RemoveAction.instance"/>
  </folder>
</folder>
```

Next, you need to specify which of the Actions should appear in the toolbar:

```
<folder name="Toolbars">
  <folder name="Task">
    <file name="com-netbeansrcp-taskactions-AddAction.shadow">
      <attr name="originalFile" stringvalue="Actions/Task/com-
        netbeansrcp-taskactions-AddAction.instance"/>
    </file>
    <file name="com-netbeansrcp-taskactions-EditAction.shadow">
      <attr name="originalFile" stringvalue="Actions/Task/com-
        netbeansrcp-taskactions-EditAction.instance"/>
    </file>
    <file name="com-netbeansrcp-taskactions-RemoveAction.shadow">
      <attr name="originalFile" stringvalue="Actions/Task/com-
        netbeansrcp-taskactions-RemoveAction.instance"/>
    </file>
  </folder>
</folder>
```

Finally, you need to specify which of the Actions should appear in the `TaskNode` context menu:

```
<folder name="Tasks">
  <folder name="Nodes">
    <folder name="Task">
      <folder name="Actions">
        <file name="com-netbeansrcp-taskactions-AddNewAction.shadow">
          <attr name="originalFile" stringvalue="Actions/Task/com-
            netbeansrcp-taskactions-AddNewAction.instance"/>
```

```
                <attr name="position" intvalue="100"/>
            </file>
            <file name="com-netbeansrcp-taskactions-
              AddDuplicateAction.shadow">
                <attr name="originalFile" stringvalue="Actions/Task/com-
                  netbeansrcp-taskactions-AddDuplicateAction.instance"/>
                <attr name="position" intvalue="200"/>
            </file>
            <file name="Separator0.instance">
              <attr name="instanceClass"
                stringvalue="javax.swing.JSeparator"/>
              <attr name="position" intvalue="300"/>
            </file>
            <file name="com-netbeansrcp-taskactions-EditAction.shadow">
                <attr name="originalFile" stringvalue="Actions/Task/com-
                  netbeansrcp-taskactions-EditAction.instance"/>
                <attr name="position" intvalue="400"/>
            </file>
            <file name="Separator1.instance">
              <attr name="instanceClass"
                stringvalue="javax.swing.JSeparator"/>
              <attr name="position" intvalue="500"/>
            </file>
            <file name="com-netbeansrcp-taskactions-RemoveAction.shadow">
                <attr name="originalFile" stringvalue="Actions/Task/com-
                  netbeansrcp-taskactions-RemoveAction.instance"/>
                <attr name="position" intvalue="600"/>
            </file>
            <file name="Separator2.instance">
              <attr name="instanceClass"
                stringvalue="javax.swing.JSeparator"/>
              <attr name="position" intvalue="700"/>
            </file>
        </folder>
        <folder name="PreferredAction">
          <file name="com-netbeansrcp-taskactions-EditAction.shadow">
              <attr name="originalFile" stringvalue="Actions/Task/com-
                netbeansrcp-taskactions-EditAction.instance"/>
          </file>
        </folder>
      </folder>
    </folder>
</folder>
```

Start the application; invoke the new Actions from the toolbar and also from the context menu of the `TaskNode`:

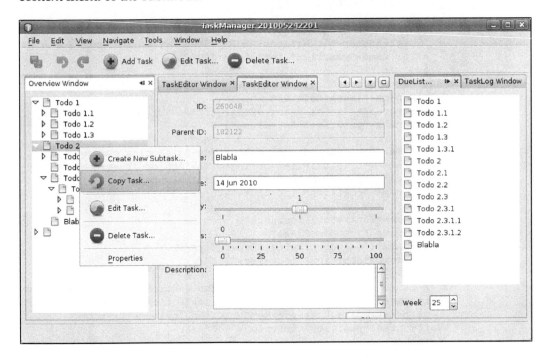

Decorating nodes

There may be situations where you are not really satisfied by an existing node hierarchy. You may want to construct a new node hierarchy, based on the original nodes, but with different behavior. For example, you may want to provide different icons or filter out child nodes, while wanting to keep the rest of the behavior of the original node.

Initially, you might attempt to add more code to the existing node, or the node's children, overriding the relevant methods to obtain the required behavior. In the first place, this approach would be cumbersome and inflexible, given that a flexible alternative exists. Secondly, however, this approach might not be possible in all cases. Think, for example, of nodes that are defined in modules over which you have no control.

The decorator pattern, familiar with other areas of Java, provides a useful approach, letting you create a filter for a node that does not quite meet your requirements. In dealing with Java streams, for example, you have a BufferedInputStream, which is an InputStream that owns another InputStream, the first InputStream delegating the actual reading to the second InputStream. The first InputStream implements additional behavior, namely the buffering of the data, reducing the number of real read activities. Thus, the additional behavior is added to the decorated InputStream at runtime, dynamically. Its behavior is changed, without requiring a subclass. In the same way, you can decorate existing nodes and children to change their behavior.

> **FilterNode** is used as a decorator for nodes, enabling dynamic changes to the appearance and behavior of a node.

To that end, the Nodes API provides the FilterNode class. You pass the node that needs to be decorated to it, generally delegating all of the original node's method calls. If you want to change the behavior of an existing node, you only need to decorate it via a FilterNode subclass, overriding the corresponding methods. If you want to influence the generation of the hierarchy, you can pass the FilterNode an instance of a subclass of FilterNode.Children, which creates the FilterNode for the child elements of the decorated node.

In the example application, let's provide the possibility of filtering the tasks in the OverviewTopComponent according to their priority, that is, let's display only those tasks that conform to a certain priority. To achieve this, you add a JButton to a TopComponent, for filtering the tasks according to a priority, together with another JButton for resetting the filter. When the **Priority** button is clicked, the node hierarchy is decorated with a FilterNode. The FilterNode uses a FilterNode.Children that only creates FilterNodes for nodes that wrap tasks of a particular minimum priority, ignoring all the remaining tasks by filtering them out.

Creating a FilterNode

In this section, you focus on creating a FilterNode for the representation of nodes, with a FilterNode.Children for the actual filtering, together with a TopComponent for displaying the user interface.

1. Create a new module named **PriorityFilter**, with **com.netbeansrcp. priorityfilter** as the code name base.

2. Set dependencies on the **TaskModel** module, the Nodes API, and the Explorer & Property Sheet API.

3. Importantly, set a dependency on the **Overview** module, as you will be referring to the `OverviewTopComponent` which is found in that module. Before you can do so, however, you need to make the main package of the **Overview** module public, so that its classes are made generally available to the other modules in the application.

4. Create a class named `PriorityFilterNode`. The class extends `FilterNode` and provides a constructor where you pass a node, together with a minimum priority.

5. To create its child elements, a `PriorityFilterNode` creates a `FilterNode.Children` instance, which filters tasks corresponding to the given priority.

   The implementation is very simple:

```
public class PriorityFilterNode extends FilterNode {

    public PriorityFilterNode(Node arg0, Task.Priority prio) {
        super(arg0, new PriorityFilterChildren(arg0, prio));
    }

    public Node getOriginal() {
        return super.getOriginal();
    }

}
```

In the code above, take note of the following:

- The method `getOriginal()` is marked protected in `FilterNode`. However, later you will need to be able to access the decorated node. For this reason, you override the method with public access.

- You need a `FilterNode.Children` subclass for the filtering of the child elements. To that end, create a class named `PriorityFilterChildren`, letting it extend `FilterNode.Children`.

Within the `PriorityFilterChildren`, the method `copyNode()` is responsible for returning the decorated node. That is where you create the create `PriorityFilterNode`.

> `createNode()` is responsible for mapping the original node to any number of `FilterNodes`, while `copyNode()` creates the decorated nodes.

The method `createNode()` is responsible for returning any number of decorated nodes. Here the mapping from original node to a `FilterNode` takes place. The standard implementation maps every original node to exactly one `FilterNode` and, for its creation, it calls `copyNode()`. For this reason, `createNode(..)` is the right place to deal with filtering:

```
public class PriorityFilterChildren extends FilterNode.Children {
    private Task.Priority prio;
    public PriorityFilterChildren(Node arg0, Task.Priority prio) {
        super(arg0);
        this.prio = prio;
    }

    @Override
    protected Node copyNode(Node arg0) {
        return new PriorityFilterNode(arg0, this.prio);
    }

    @Override
    protected Node[] createNodes(Node arg0) {

        Task task = arg0.getLookup().lookup(Task.class);

        if (null != task && 0 >=
          this.prio.compareTo(task.getPrio())) {
            return new Node[] { this.copyNode(arg0) };
        }

        return new Node[] {
            };
    }
}
```

- The node providing the children and the required priority is passed to the constructor. Its only job is to save the two values.

- As discussed, the method `copyNode()` creates a decorated `PriorityFilterNode` for the `TaskNode` that is passed and returns it.

- `createNodes()` looks for a task in the `Lookup` of the node that is passed and checks its priority, if applicable. If the priority exceeds the specified minimum, the method returns a `PriorityFilterNode` created by `copyNode()`. If it is less than the required minimum, it does not return a node, so that the node is filtered out.

Now you have set up the filter. Somehow the user needs to control the filter, as described below.

1. Create a `TopComponent` in the **output** mode, with `PriorityFilter` as class name base.

2. In the Matisse GUI builder, add four `JButtons` to the new `TopComponent`. Assign names and icons so that the buttons look as shown below.

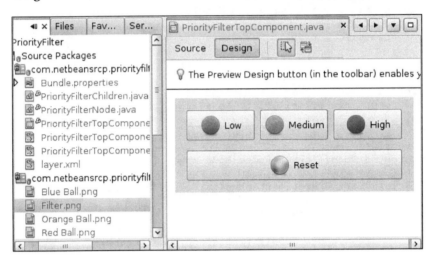

 You can get the icons used above from the sources on this book's website.

3. Register an `ActionListener` on each of the buttons. Then define the handlers as follows:

```java
private void jButton1ActionPerformed(java.awt.event.ActionEvent evt) {
    this.filter(Task.Priority.LOW);
}

private void jButton2ActionPerformed(java.awt.event.ActionEvent evt) {
    this.filter(Task.Priority.MEDIUM);
}

private void jButton3ActionPerformed(java.awt.event.ActionEvent evt) {
    this.filter(Task.Priority.HIGH);
}

private void jButton4ActionPerformed(java.awt.event.ActionEvent evt) {
    this.filter(null);
}
```

Above, the method `filter()` is called with different priorities, impacting the decoration of the node hierarchy. The `filter()` method is described later, followed by the code.

To start with, the filter needs to find the `OverviewTopComponent`, which it can do via the `WindowManager`, which knows all the `TopComponents` registered in the application. As the `OverviewTopComponent` is itself an `ExplorerManager.Provider`, you can get its `ExplorerManager` via its `getExplorerManager()`. Then you can obtain the root node.

The root node could be a `PriorityFilterNode`, which you have already set. In this case you need to ask it for its original node and use that node as the root node. If a priority has been passed to the method, it should be used as the minimum priority and a corresponding `PriorityFilterNode` is created for the original root node. If no priority has been passed, an existing filter should be removed, so that the original root node is used without decoration.

The new root node that has been detected in this way now needs to be set as the new root node of the `ExplorerManager`.

The implementation is straightforward and looks as follows:

```
private void filter(Task.Priority prio) {

    OverviewTopComponent tc =
        (OverviewTopComponent)
          WindowManager.getDefault().
          findTopComponent("OverviewTopComponent");

    Node root = tc.getExplorerManager().getRootContext();

    if (root instanceof PriorityFilterNode) {
        root = ((PriorityFilterNode) root).getOriginal();
    }
    Node newRoot =
        (null != prio) ? new PriorityFilterNode(root, prio) : root;

    tc.getExplorerManager().setRootContext(newRoot); }
```

Restart the application. It should look as shown in the following screenshot. Create some tasks with different priorities. If you click the filter buttons, the number of displayed nodes in the overview should increase/decrease accordingly.

When you click on the **Clear** button, you remove the filter, displaying all the tasks again.

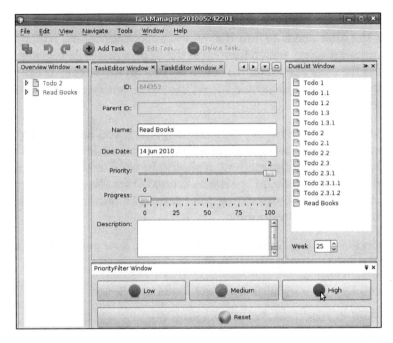

To summarize, you have seen how existing node hierarchies can be decorated. In other words, you learned how the view, as well as the number of displayed nodes, can be modified via node decoration, which can be used regardless of whether you created the decorated node yourself. The only requirement for node decoration is that you have access to the `ExplorerManager` that controls the node you want to decorate.

Displaying properties

When you create property sheets, you give the user a quick overview of the properties of an object, together with the values of those properties. Used in moderation, property sheets are an important instrument for the visualization of details, as you have seen while using the "Matisse" GUI Builder. In general, a property sheet presents a table containing two columns; properties in the first column, values in the second.

Typically, though not necessarily in all cases, values in the right column can be edited. Either the value can be edited directly within the table itself or within an external property editor that is opened by clicking the **...** ellipsis button.

As a table providing a very long list of properties could quickly become very confusing, you can split properties into subsets, each with their own table in the sheet.

In the example application, if you want to see the value of a Task property, you currently need to open a task into the `TaskEditor`. Let's now change the application so that the properties of tasks are displayed in the **Properties** window.

To that end, properties in the example application need to be divided into three groups.

1. The first group contains the ID of the task as well the ID of the parent task. Both values are fixed, so that they should be displayed as read-only.

2. The second group contains all other properties, except the description, and those values should be writable.

3. The third group contains the detailed description, as it does not relate directly to any of the other properties, and can be useful to display on its own.

Creating a Property sheet

The `Node` class provides the method `createSheet()`, whose job it is to return a `Sheet` object. A `Sheet` object contains `Sheets.Sets`, for displaying properties. In this section, you override the `createSheet()` method, create a Sheet, add a `Sheet.Set` for all the subsets of properties, and, finally, you return the Sheet. At the same time, you need to set meaningful display names for the `Sheet.Sets`, as well as add the properties that need to be displayed.

The `PropertySupport` class helps in the creation of properties, as its inner classes provide a scope for read-only, read-write, and reflection-based properties. In the case of reflection-based properties, you often only need to instantiate the `PropertySupport.Reflection`, while in other cases you need to create subclasses, overriding `getValue()` or `setValue(Object)` where relevant.

With the above general description in mind, add the code below to the `TaskNode` class:

```java
@Override
protected Sheet createSheet() {

    final Task task = getLookup().lookup(Task.class);

    Sheet sheet = Sheet.createDefault();
```

```
Sheet.Set setProps = sheet.createPropertiesSet();
setProps.setDisplayName("identification");
sheet.put(setProps);

Property<String> idProp = new PropertySupport.ReadOnly<String>(
        "id", String.class, "ID", "identification number") {

        public String getValue()
                    throws IllegalAccessException,
InvocationTargetException {
                return (null != task) ? task.getId() : "";
        }
};

Property<String> parentIdProp = new PropertySupport.ReadOnly<String>(
        "parent-id", String.class, "parent-ID",
        "identification number of parent task") {

        public String getValue()
                    throws IllegalAccessException,
                                        InvocationTargetException {
                return (null != task) ? task.getParentId() : "";
        }
};

setProps.put(idProp);
setProps.put(parentIdProp);


Sheet.Set setExp = sheet.createExpertSet();
setExp.setDisplayName("properties");
sheet.put(setExp);
try {

        Property nameProp = new PropertySupport.Reflection<String>(
                task, String.class, "name");
        nameProp.setName("name");
        nameProp.setDisplayName("name");
        nameProp.setShortDescription("name");

        Property dueProp = new PropertySupport.Reflection<Date>(
                task, Date.class, "due");
        dueProp.setName("due");
        dueProp.setDisplayName("due date");
        dueProp.setShortDescription("due date");

        Property<Task.Priority> prioProp =
                new PropertySupport.Reflection<Task.Priority>(
                        task, Task.Priority.class, "prio");
        prioProp.setName("prio");
```

```
        prioProp.setDisplayName("priority");
        prioProp.setShortDescription("priority");

        Property progrProp = new PropertySupport.ReadWrite(
                "progr", Integer.class, "Progress", "Progress") {

                public Object getValue()
                        throws IllegalAccessException,
                                            InvocationTargetException {
                            return (null != task) ? task.getProgr() : 0;
                }
                public void setValue(Object arg0)
                        throws IllegalAccessException,
                                            IllegalArgumentException,
                                            InvocationTargetException {
                            if (null != task && (arg0 instanceof Integer)) {
                                task.setProgr(((Integer) arg0).intValue());
                            }
                }
        };

        setExp.put(nameProp);
        setExp.put(dueProp);
        setExp.put(prioProp);
        setExp.put(progrProp);

    } catch (NoSuchMethodException ex) {
        ex.printStackTrace();
    }


    Sheet.Set setDescr = new Sheet.Set();
    setDescr.setName("description");
    setDescr.setValue("tabName", " description ");
    sheet.put(setDescr);

    try {

        Property descrProp = new PropertySupport.Reflection<String>(
                task, String.class, "descr");
        descrProp.setName("descr");
        descrProp.setDisplayName("description ");
        descrProp.setShortDescription("description ");
        setDescr.put(descrProp);
    } catch (NoSuchMethodException ex) {
        ex.printStackTrace();
    }

    return sheet;
}
```

Now start the application again, open the **Properties** window (**Window | Properties**), and select a TaskNode in the overview. The **Properties** window now displays the properties you defined via the preceding code.

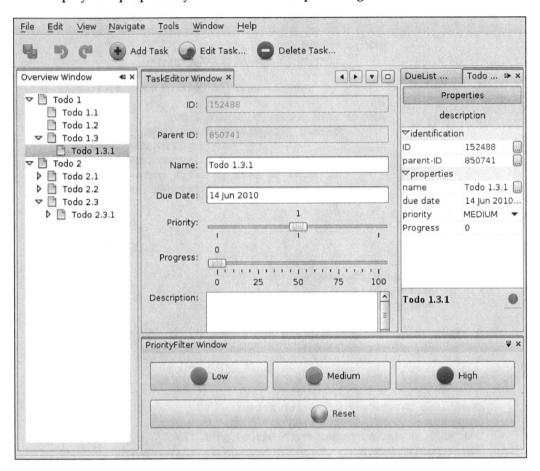

To summarize, you have successfully enhanced the application by integrating support for the **Properties** window. In doing so, you learned how to include read-only, read-write, and reflection-based properties. As you built the sheet yourself, you were able to decide which properties should be displayed, how to group them, and in which tabs to place the groups.

Inplace property editors

Property editors let you influence *how* properties are edited; they are familiar from the world of JavaBeans. In the **Properties** window, a Property editor is opened when the user clicks the small ... elipsis button next to the related property value. However, the NetBeans Platform provides an optional enhancement to Property editors, known as **inplace editors**. An inplace editor, unlike the Property editor, is not opened by explicitly clicking a button. Rather, it is an editor used directly in the value cell, becoming available as soon as the user places the cursor within the cell.

An inplace editor is a custom editor, specifically tailored towards the needs of the values for which it is created. In the example application, you will create an inplace editor for the priority value. When the value cell of the priority is clicked, a `JSlider` will appear, so that the user can set the task priority more intuitively than made possible by the Property editor.

The inplace editor is named `PriorityEditor`. It extends `PriorityEditorSupport` and implements `ExPropertyEditor`. The required method `attachEnv()` is called to create the link between the `PriorityEditor` and the property, as well as to provide supporting information about it. You need to register the `InplaceEditor.Factory` for the property, as it is, as the name implies, responsible for creating an `InplaceEditor` for a particular property.

To simplify this activity, let's combine the `PropertyEditorSupport`, the `InplaceEditor`, and the `InplaceEditor.Factory` in the same class. You create an instance of the class in the `getInplaceEditor()` method. The implementation of `InplaceEditor` contains quite a number of base methods, which are mostly implemented directly, not needing much more explanation, as the names of the methods are mostly self-explanatory. Especially the methods `getValue()` and `setValue()`, for reviewing and setting the value, are interesting, as the property to edit is of the type `Task.Priority` and a `JSlider` works with `int`. Therefore, in these methods, a mapping from the Priority to the `int` and from the `int` to the Priority needs to take place.

The preceding text is expressed in code as follows:

```
public class PriorityEditor extends PropertyEditorSupport
   implements ExPropertyEditor, InplaceEditor.Factory {
      public void attachEnv(PropertyEnv arg0) {
         arg0.registerInplaceEditorFactory(this);
      }

      public InplaceEditor getInplaceEditor() {
      return new PriorityInplaceEditor();
      }
```

```
static class PriorityInplaceEditor
  implements org.openide.explorer.propertysheet.InplaceEditor {
    private PropertyEditor editor;
    private PropertyModel model;
    private JSlider slider;

    public PriorityInplaceEditor() {
        this.slider = new JSlider(0, 2);
        this.slider.setSnapToTicks(true);
    }

    public void connect(PropertyEditor arg0, PropertyEnv
      arg1) {
        this.editor = arg0;
        this.reset();
    }

    public JComponent getComponent() {
        return this.slider;
    }

    public void clear() {
        this.editor = null;
        this.model = null;
    }

    public Object getValue() {
        switch (this.slider.getValue()) {
            case 0:
              return Task.Priority.LOW;
            case 1:
              return Task.Priority.MEDIUM;
            case 2:
              return Task.Priority.HIGH;
        }
          return Task.Priority.MEDIUM;
    }

    public void setValue(Object arg0) {
        Task.Priority prio = (Priority) arg0;
        switch (prio) {
            case LOW:
              this.slider.setValue(0);
            break;
            case MEDIUM:
              this.slider.setValue(1);
            break;
```

```
                  case HIGH:
                    this.slider.setValue(2);
                  break;
              }
          }
        public boolean supportsTextEntry() {
            return true;
          }

        public void reset() {
            Priority val = (Priority) this.editor.getValue();
            this.setValue(val);
          }

        public void addActionListener(ActionListener arg0) {
          }

        public void removeActionListener(ActionListener arg0) {
          }

        public KeyStroke[] getKeyStrokes() {
            return new KeyStroke[0];
          }

        public PropertyEditor getPropertyEditor() {
            return this.editor;
          }

        public PropertyModel getPropertyModel() {
            return this.model;
          }

      public void setPropertyModel(PropertyModel arg0) {
          this.model = arg0;
        }

    public boolean isKnownComponent(Component arg0) {
        return arg0 == this.slider ||
          this.slider.isAncestorOf(arg0);
      }
    }
  }
```

Next, you need to assign the `PriorityEditor` to the property. Therefore, change the `TaskNode` as follows:

```
// ...

PropertySupport.Reflection<Task.Priority> prioProp =
  new PropertySupport.Reflection<Task.Priority>(
    task, Task.Priority.class, "prio");
      prioProp.setName("prio");
      prioProp.setDisplayName("priority");
      prioProp.setShortDescription("priority");

      prioProp.setPropertyEditorClass(PriorityEditor.class);
// ...
```

Start the application again, select a `TaskNode` in the overview, and click in the value cell for the priority. In the place of the text in the Property editor, you now see a `JSlider` instead.

To summarize, you have improved the visualization of Task properties by creating a custom inplace editor for the priority property. Instead of the default text area for setting the priority of the property, you now have a `JSlider`, matching the UI component in the TaskEditor used for adjusting the priority of the current task.

Adding widgets

Over the years, the NetBeans Visual Library API has become one of the most popular features of the NetBeans Platform. Providing a set of widgets for general purpose visualization of data structures, the Visual Library API can enrich an application with drag-and-drop widgets containing a wide range of predefined features.

Programming with the Visual Library API is comparable to programming in Swing. You build a component hierarchy consisting of a tree of modifiable elements, of which the following are the most commonly used classes:

Swing	Visual Library
JComponent	Widget
no equivalent	Scene
JGlassPane	LayerWidget
Label	LabelWidget
Image	ImageWidget

There are many other widget classes available, each with their own predefined properties, actions, layouts, and borders. Typical actions include MoveAction and ResizeAction, for example. See the NetBeans Platform javadoc for full descriptions of the many classes provided by the Visual Library API.

Creating a first scene

In this section you create the simplest Visual Library Scene, just to see what can be done with a very small amount of code.

1. Create a new module named **TaskOrganizer**, with code name base **org. netbeansrcp.taskorganizer**.

2. Use the **New Window** wizard to create a new window in the editor mode, opening when the application starts, with **TaskOrganizer** as the class name prefix.

3. By default, the Visual Library API is not available to the **TaskManager** application. The New NetBeans Platform Application template that you used in the beginning of this book includes many NetBeans modules by default, but the Visual Library API is not one of these. Right-click the application node, that is, the **TaskManager** node, choose **Properties**, and then put a checkmark next to the Visual Library item in the **platform** cluster within the **Libraries** panel.

4. Now you can set a dependency on the Visual Library API, in your **TaskOrganizer** modules.

5. Drag a JScrollPane onto the TopComponent. Switch to the **Source** view and then add the following code to the end of the constructor:

```
Scene scene = new Scene();

LayerWidget lw = new LayerWidget(scene);
scene.addChild(lw);

LabelWidget labelWidget = new LabelWidget(scene, "hello world");
labelWidget.setFont(new Font("Helvetica", Font.BOLD +
                              Font.ITALIC, 16));
labelWidget.getActions().addAction(ActionFactory.
        createMoveAction());
lw.addChild(labelWidget);

jScrollPane1.setViewportView(scene.createView());
```

As you can see, you have instantiated a new scene and added a `LayerWidget`. On top of the `LayerWidget`, all the other widgets can be added. Here you have a `LabelWidget`, with a predefined `MoveAction` assigned to it. Once the scene's component is added to the `JScrollPane`, you can run the application again, which should result in a window being shown containing a label that can be dragged, as shown below:

Integrating a scene into the Task Manager

Now that you have a basic idea of the fundamentals of the Visual Library API, let's apply it to the example application. You start by make the **TaskNode** in the `OverviewTopComponent` draggable. Then you create a new `Scene` using **VMDGraphScene**, which is one of the `Scene` subclasses. **VMD** stands for **Visual Mobile Designer**, which is a set of tools in NetBeans IDE from which the Visual Library was extracted.

At the end of this section, you will be able to drag a node form the **Overview** window and drop it into your **TaskOrganizer** window, with this result:

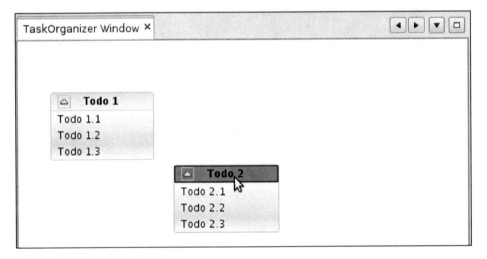

To achieve the above, do the following:

1. At the end of the `OverviewTopComponent` constructor, add this statement, which is all that you need to enable a node to be dragged from the `BeanTreeView`:

   ```
   ((BeanTreeView) this.jScrollPane1).setDragSource(true);
   ```

2. In the **TaskOrganizer** module, set a dependency on the **TaskModel** module and the Nodes API module.

3. Create a new `Scene` class that extends `VMDGraphScene`. Get the `Task` object from the `Lookup` of the `Node` and use its name and `children` to set the content of the node and pin of the `VMDWidget`, as follows:

   ```
   public class TaskScene extends VMDGraphScene {

       private LayerWidget mainLayer;

       public TaskScene() {

           mainLayer = new LayerWidget(this);

           addChild(mainLayer);

           getActions().addAction(ActionFactory.createAcceptAction(
                                       new AcceptProvider() {

               @Override
               public ConnectorState isAcceptable(Widget widget,
                           Point point, Transferable transferable) {
                   Node node = NodeTransfer.node(transferable,
                               NodeTransfer.DND_COPY);
                   if (node != null && node.getLookup().lookup(
                               Task.class) != null) {
                       return ConnectorState.ACCEPT;
                   } else {
                       return ConnectorState.REJECT_AND_STOP;
                   }
               }

               @Override
               public void accept(Widget widget, Point point,
                           Transferable transferable) {
                   Node node = NodeTransfer.node(transferable,
                               NodeTransfer.DND_COPY);
                   Task task = node.getLookup().lookup(Task.class);
                   createNode(task.getName());
                   List<Task> children = task.getChildren();
   ```

```
                            for (Task subTask : children) {
                                createPin(task.getName(), subTask.getName());
                            }
                    }
            }));


    }

    private void createNode(String nodeID) {
        ((VMDNodeWidget) addNode(nodeID)).setNodeName(nodeID);
    }

    private void createPin(String nodeID, String pinID) {
        ((VMDPinWidget) addPin(nodeID, pinID)).setPinName(pinID);
    }


}
```

Note the following:

- You have extended VMDGraphScene, which enables you to create nested widgets. Each widget consists of a Node, which provides the header of the widget. The children of the widget are called Pins, which in the preceding code are defined by the children of the Task retrieved from the Lookup.

- The Scene class has an acceptAction, which is one of the predefined actions provided by the Visual Library. Here this action is used to retrieve the Task from the Lookup and populate the Node and Pins of each VMDNodeWidget.

- Finally, in the TaskOrganizerTopComponent, change the code that creates the Scene, to the following:

  ```
  Scene scene = new TaskScene();
  jScrollPanel.setViewportView(scene.createView());
  ```

Though this introduction to the Visual Library is brief, you should now understand where it fits into the NetBeans Platform and how easily you can use it to visualize the underlying data structures of your applications.

Summary

In this chapter, you learned about Nodes and Explorer views. Nodes represent model objects, which are displayed in explorer views. Explorer views can be easily interchanged because of the indirection provided by the shared ExplorerManager. Node support for contextual menus, node decoration, property sheets, inplace editors, and widgets have also been covered in this chapter.

7
File System

The File System API provides unified access to virtual filesystems, which can be implemented in a variety of ways. Data in the local filesystem of the operating system can be stored in virtual filesystems, in the form of XML files or JAR archives or in memory. That's an indication of how broad your understanding of files and filesystems needs to be in the context of NetBeans Platform. Files are simply units for storing hierarchically arranged data in a virtual filesystem which can be identified by a name. Therefore, a filesystem is simply a namespace for fileobjects. It represents hierarchical storage for file-like data, with a single root folder that offers support for a variety of notifications.

A NetBeans `FileObject` class is a storage unit in a filesystem. It contains either data or further `FileObjects`. The `FileObject` does not know anything about its content and structure; it contains nothing more than a stream of bytes. `FileObjects` are comparable to `java.io.File` but offer additional support for file change notifications, file locking, and the storage of module-specific attributes.

As part of the example application that you continue to develop in the next sections, you use the local filesystem of the operating system to store tasks permanently. A `TopLevelTask` is treated as a unit containing all its subtasks, which are then stored in a file.

The topics covered in this chapter will teach you the following:

- What kinds of filesystem exist
- How to access the local filesystem
- How to work with `FileObjects` and their attributes
- How to listen to changes on `FileObjects`

Central registry

Accessing the local filesystem of the operating system is certainly the most obvious usage of a filesystem, but it is, in fact, not the most commonly used in the context of the NetBeans Platform. You have already met this particular filesystem: the central registry, which is also called the System FileSystem.

Whenever you want to influence the configuration of the application, you modify a `layer.xml` file in one of the modules. As the content of XML files is hierarchically structured, it is able to include XML elements with the names of the relevant filesystem, folder, or file.

At the startup of the application, the NetBeans Platform merges the `layer.xml` files of all the modules into a single virtual filesystem, with the folders and files corresponding to features in the application. In short, the names, attributes, and content of these files represent various aspects of the NetBeans Platform's configuration.

Accessing the local FileSystem

Let us now use the local filesystem to store tasks. When the application starts, a predefined folder is searched for task files, which are then loaded into the application.

Storing and loading of tasks in `FileObjects` is done by the **TaskManager** via the predefined folder on the local filesystem. Therefore, you use the NetBeans Platform `LocalFileSystem` class to access the local filesystem and point to the root of the predefined folder.

During this task, you make use of the FileSystem API so that the required tasks can be found programmatically.

```
public class TaskManagerImpl implements TaskManager {

    // ...
    private FileObject root;
    public TaskManagerImpl() {
        // ...

        try {
            File file = new File("/Users/jpe/tasks/");
            LocalFileSystem fs = new LocalFileSystem();
            fs.setRootDirectory(file);
            this.root = fs.getRoot();
```

```
        }
      catch (Exception ex) {
          Exceptions.printStackTrace(ex);
        }

    // ...
```

Now you need to implement two methods, one for storing a `TopLevelTask` in a file and the other for loading it.

As you do not want long-term backup in this simple example, you simply use default serialization to store and load a task, as well as its subtasks.

Usage of the virtual filesystem means that you do not need to think about how the `FileObjects` are actually saved to the filesystem, as every `FileObject` provides a built-in `InputStream` and `OutputStream`.

As you can see in the following code snippet, the filename of the file to be saved is built from its ID, together with the custom file extension `.tsk`:

```
// ...
FileObject save(Task task);
void save(Task task, FileObject fo);
Task load(FileObject fo);
// ...


TaskManagerImpl.java

public FileObject save(Task task) {

    FileObject fo = null;
    try {

        fo = this.root.createData(task.getId()+".tsk");
        this.save(task, fo);
      }
    catch (IOException ex) {
        Exceptions.printStackTrace(ex);
      }

    return fo;
  }


public void save(Task task, FileObject fo) {
    ObjectOutputStream oOut = null;
    try {

        oOut =  new ObjectOutputStream(new
          BufferedOutputStream(fo.getOutputStream()));
```

```
            oOut.writeObject(task);
        }
    catch (Exception ex) {

        Exceptions.printStackTrace(ex);
        }
    finally {
        try {
            oOut.close();
            }
        catch (IOException ex) {
            Exceptions.printStackTrace(ex);
            }
        }
    }
}


    public Task load(FileObject fo) {
        Task task = null;
        ObjectInputStream oIn = null;

        try {

            oIn =   new ObjectInputStream(new
              BufferedInputStream(fo.getInputStream()));
            task = (Task) oIn.readObject();

            if (!this.topLevelTasks.contains(task)) {
                this.topLevelTasks.add(task);
                this.pss.firePropertyChange(PROP_TASKLIST_ADD, null, task);
            }
        }
    catch(Exception ex) {

        Exceptions.printStackTrace(ex);
        }
    finally {
        try {
            oIn.close();
            }
        catch (IOException ex) {
            Exceptions.printStackTrace(ex);
            }
        }

    return task;
    }
```

The preceding code implements the functionality for saving and loading tasks.

Now, you add dummy data to try out the new code. For these purposes, you delete all the tasks from the root folder, create and save tasks together with their subtasks, delete them from working memory, and load the tasks from storage again. After the final loading process, the created tasks are restored.

```java
public TaskManagerImpl() {

    this.topLevelTasks =
            new ArrayList<Task>();
    this.pss = new PropertyChangeSupport(this);


    try {
        File file = new File("/Users/jpe/tasks/");

        LocalFileSystem fs = new LocalFileSystem();
        fs.setRootDirectory(file);
        this.root = fs.getRoot();

    }
    catch (Exception ex) {
        Exceptions.printStackTrace(ex);
    }

    this.deleteTasks();


    Task t1 = this.createTask();
    t1.setName("Todo 1");
    Task t2 = this.createTask("Todo 1.1", t1.getId());
    t2 = this.createTask("Todo 1.2", t1.getId());
    t2 = this.createTask("Todo 1.3", t1.getId());
    this.createTask("Todo 1.3.1", t2.getId());


    Task t3 = this.createTask();
    t3.setName("Todo 2");
    t2 = this.createTask("Todo 2.1", t3.getId());
    t2 = this.createTask("Todo 2.2", t3.getId());
    t2 = this.createTask("Todo 2.3", t3.getId());
    Task t4 = this.createTask("Todo 2.3.1", t3.getId());
    t2 = this.createTask("Todo 2.3.1.1", t3.getId());
    t2 = this.createTask("Todo 2.3.1.2", t3.getId());


    this.save(t1);
    this.save(t3);

    System.out.println("Count of known TopLevelTasks before deleting:
            " + this.topLevelTasks.size());

    this.removeTask(t1.getId());
```

```
            this.removeTask(t3.getId());

            System.out.println("Count of known TopLevelTasks after deleting: " +
                    this.topLevelTasks.size());

            this.loadTasks();
            System.out.println("Count of known TopLevelTasks after loading: " +
                    this.topLevelTasks.size());
        }


    private void loadTasks() {

        for (FileObject fo : this.root.getChildren()) {

            if ("tsk".equalsIgnoreCase(fo.getExt())) {

                this.load(fo);
            }
        }
    }


    private void deleteTasks() {
        for (FileObject fo : this.root.getChildren()) {

            if ("tsk".equalsIgnoreCase(fo.getExt())) {

                try {

                    fo.delete();
                }
                catch (IOException ex) {
                    Exceptions.printStackTrace(ex);
                }
            }
        }
    }
```

After restarting the application, you see two tasks and the following output:

```
Count of known TopLevelTasks before deleting: 2
Count of known TopLevelTasks after deleting: 0
Count of known TopLevelTasks after loading: 2
```

You have learned how to access the local filesystem through the FileSystem API. As an example, you used directories in the local filesystem to create and delete files. Also remember that the FileSystem API enables you to write code that is not tied to a specific filesystem.

Providing additional attributes

Another useful capability of the FileSystem API is that it allows you to save
`FileObjects` with application-specific attributes. These attributes are key-value
pairs and are saved in XML files with the file extension `.nbattrs`.

To take a quick look at this aspect of the API, you expand the `.tsk` files with an
attribute that registers when the file was last saved. When the task is stored, the
attribute is set on the `FileObject`; when the task is loaded, the registered time is
displayed. To that end, extend the methods for the saving and loading of tasks
as follows:

```
private void save(Task task, FileObject fo) {

    // ...
    oOut.writeObject(task);

    fo.setAttribute("saved",
      SimpleDateFormat.getInstance().format(new Date()));

    // ...

}


private Task load(FileObject fo) {

    // ...
    task = (Task) oIn.readObject();

        System.out.println
          ("Loaded: " + task + "[" + fo.getAttribute("saved") + "]");

    // ...
}
```

Run the application again. The `saved` attributes are stored within the files. As the
existing tasks are not always removed and recreated, you will comment in the
constructor of `TaskManagerImpl` everything regarding deleting tasks but not the
storing of the task. If necessary, start the application again. In the output you should
now be able to see which tasks have been loaded and when they were last saved.

You have seen how easily attributes can be assigned to `FileObjects`. The attributes
are stored permanently. Even after you quit the application, the attributes can
be restored upon restart. The FileSystem determines the implementation of how
the attributes are stored; in case of the `LocalFileSystem`, the XML files with the
`.nbattrs` extension are used.

Listening to file changes

On top of everything else offered by the FileSystem API, FileObjects are observable. You can define FileChangeListeners for notifications about changes to a folder or file that is of interest to you, using the addFileChangeListener() method. As the usage of this feature is fairly trivial and the **TaskManager** doesn't really deal with folders and files that need to be monitored, an example will not be shown here.

Summary

In this chapter, you've been introduced to the FileSystem API. The API can be used to access the central registry or any other filesystem created on top of the NetBeans Platform. In the example application, you accessed the local filesystem, worked with attributes, and also learned about listening to file changes.

In the next chapter, you learn about the NetBeans data system, which is a level above the filesystem, giving you access to the content of FileObjects.

8

Data System

The NetBeans Platform's Datasystems API lets your application recognize new types of files, while providing a standardized approach for programmatically accessing file content. While the File System API, introduced in the previous chapter, is used for managing files, file content is handled separately, via the Datasystems API.

The topics covered in this chapter will teach you the following:

- How to provide support for new file types.
- How to provide an interface to the contents of a file.
- How objects representing file content can change their capabilities dynamically, depending on their state. For example, when a Task has changed, the capability of being saved is added dynamically to the object.
- How to implement "icon badging", that is, how to change an icon context-sensitively.

Building on the example application, you define a new file type for Tasks. In other words, you extend the application to support newly created Task files. You examine how, when the application encounters a Task file, the related support is activated and support is made available for the file dynamically.

Support for new file types

Let's start by extending the **TaskManager** with basic support for Task files. Before doing so, however, let's get acquainted with the basic elements involved in this feature, as well as the responsibilities of each of the elements in the feature used to represent files within applications based on the NetBeans Platform.

As you learned in the previous chapter, FileObjects are responsible for managing and representing folders and files. Though they manage folders and files, FileObjects know nothing about the content of files.

On the other hand, `DataObjects` are responsible for managing and representing the content of a file. `DataObjects` are elements of a resource management system representing stored entities within files. A single `DataObject` may represent the content of one or more files and provide various features for dealing with them.

The `DataLoader` is the bridge between a `FileObject` and a `DataObject`. It is able to determine whether it is responsible for a particular file's content and then creates a corresponding `DataObject`.

Nodes are responsible for the visualization of model elements, that is, `DataObjects`. A `Node` displays an object, in this case, a `DataObject` in an explorer view. `Nodes` visualize `DataObjects` by providing them with formatted names and icons, as well as with the `Actions` a user can perform on them. The bridge between the `DataObject` and the `Node` is the `DataObject` itself, as it creates its own corresponding `Node`.

If a file is to be displayed in a view, a `FileObject` needs to be created to represent the file. A `DataObject` must be identified for this `FileObject`, which provides access to the file content, through the `Lookup` offering capabilities, such as the capability of opening and the capability of saving.

In order to create a `FileObject` for the `DataObject`, a pool of registered `DataLoaders` is provided. Each individual `DataLoader` is asked whether it is responsible for the `FileObject`. Once the appropriate `DataLoader` has been identified, it creates a matching `DataObject`, which then creates a `Node`. The `Node` determines the visualization of the `DataObject`, such as its name and icon, as well as its `Actions` and capabilities. An explorer view is a NetBeans Platform Swing component for displaying a `Node`.

In short, the preceding infrastructure gives you a clean separation between file management (`FileObject`), file type detection (`DataLoader`), access to file content (`DataObject`), and user interaction (node and explorer views).

Creating support for Task files

Now that you know the basic responsibilities of the various elements involved, let's examine the construction of each of these elements.

1. First, to support the new files in the example application, create a new module named **TaskFileSupport**, using the **Code Name Base com.netbeansrcp.taskfilesupport**.

2. Declare the module's dependency on the Datasystems API and the **TaskModel** module.

3. You can create all the files to provide basic support for new file types via a wizard in the IDE. Right-click the module project and then choose **New | File Type**.

4. On the first page of the wizard, define the MIME type of the file (`application/x-task`) and describe how it should be identified (via the extension `tsk` or `task`). Available options for recognizing files are the file extension and, for XML files, the namespace of the root element.

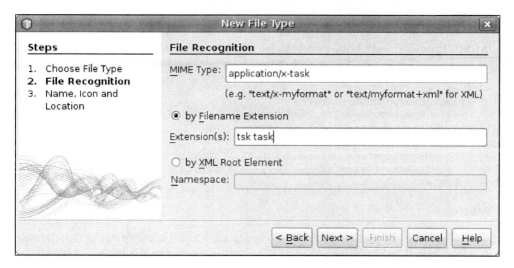

5. On the second page of the wizard, specify `TopLevelTask` as the prefix for the files that are to be created, as well as the **Task.png** icon.

6. Click **Finish** to allow the IDE to generate the files used to recognize the new file type. In the Projects window, you should now see a new `DataObject` class, a MIME type resolver, a new `PNG` file, a template file, and new entries in the layer file, `project.xml` file, and `Bundle.properties` file.

Examining the generated files

When the NetBeans Platform first encounters a file, for example, when the user tries to open a file into the application, the `DataLoader` registered in the layer for the file's file type is identified. That `DataLoader` is a factory, creating the `DataObject` for the file type. Determining which `DataLoader` is responsible for creating a file type's `DataObject` is done via MIME type registration, which is again done in the layer file.

In the case of the example application, the **New File Type** wizard created and registered a file type which maps both the extensions .tsk and .task to the MIME type application/x-task:

```
<MIME-resolver>
  <file>
    <ext name="tsk"/>
    <ext name="task"/>
    <resolver mime="application/x-task"/>
  </file>
</MIME-resolver>
```

The MIME type defined above needs to be registered in the layer. This is done in the folder Services/MIMEResolver, as follows, by the **New File Type** wizard you used:

```
<folder name="Services">
  <folder name="MIMEResolver">
    <file name="TopLevelTaskResolver.xml"
      url="TopLevelTaskResolver.xml">
    <attr name="displayName"
      bundlevalue="com.netbeans.rcp.taskfilesupport.
      Bundle#Services/MIMEResolver/TopLevelTaskResolver.xml"/>
    </file>
  </folder>
</folder>
```

You do not need to implement the DataLoader directly. Through using the default DataLoader provided by the NetBeans Platform, mapped in the layer file, the DataLoader adds the MIME types to a list of file extensions. In other words, the MIME type is resolved to a list of file extensions through the registered mapping.

Customizing the DataObject

Now that you have generic functional support for the TaskFileType, let's customize it to your very specific needs.

- You need to customize the TopLevelTaskDataObject, as it represents the contents of a Task file. Let's make it externally available to the Task hierarchy. Though you could retrieve it via a getter, you would then force developers using the DataObject to cast to the TopLevelTaskDataObject. Therefore, instead it makes sense to publish the Task via the Lookup. A developer making use of the DataObject can then use a simple DataObject, looking in its Lookup for a Task object.

- Once you have the Task object, the DataObject is able to evaluate and use it, because you have already implemented various features in the **TaskManager**. For example, as a first step, you need to extend the constructor of TopLevelTaskDataObject so that, through the **TaskManager**, a Task is loaded for the FileObject, represented by the current DataObject.

- The `DataObject` is responsible for creating a `Node` to display to the user. The wizard has generated code in the `DataObject` for creating a corresponding `Node`. However, let's continue to use the existing `TaskNode` from the **Overview** module. Therefore, you need to set a dependency, mentioned as follows, on the **Overview** module, which provides the `TaskNode` you want to reuse.

Take the following steps to implement the above changes:

1. Set a dependency in the **TaskFileSupport** module on the **Overview** module.

2. Make the following changes in the `TopLevelTaskDataObject`:

```
public class TopLevelTaskDataObject extends MultiDataObject {

    private InstanceContent ic;
    private Lookup lookup;
    private TaskManager taskMgr;

    public TopLevelTaskDataObject(FileObject pf,
      TopLevelTaskDataLoader loader)
        throws DataObjectExistsException, IOException {

        super(pf, loader);

        this.ic = new InstanceContent();
        this.lookup = new AbstractLookup(this.ic);

        this.taskMgr = Lookup.getDefault().
        lookup(TaskManager.class);
        if (null != this.taskMgr) {

            Task task = this.taskMgr.load(pf);
            this.ic.add(task);
        }
    }

    protected Node createNodeDelegate() {
        return new TaskNode(this.lookup.lookup(Task.class),
            this.lookup);
    }

    @Override
    public Lookup getLookup() {
        return this.lookup;
    }
}
```

In the **Overview** module, change the `TaskNode` as follows:

```
public TaskNode(Task task) {
    this(task, Lookups.singleton(task));
}
public TaskNode(Task task, Lookup lookup) {

    super(Children.create(new TaskChildFactory(task), true), lookup);

    this.setName(task.getId());
    this.setDisplayName(task.getName());
    this.setIconBaseWithExtension
      ("com/netbeansrcp/overview/Task.png");

    task.addPropertyChangeListener(this);

}
```

As `ToplevelTasks` are now represented by the `TopLevelTaskDataObject`, you need to refactor various parts of your application.

Refactoring the TaskModel

Let's start by changing the `TaskManager` class in the **TaskModel** module.

Currently, you have three methods for creating, deleting, and editing `TopLevelTasks`. These now no longer work with a Task, but with a `DataObject`:

```
public interface TaskManager {

    DataObject createTask();
    List<DataObject> getTopLevelTasks();

    // ...
```

When creating `TopLevelTasks`, you now also need to save the Task in a file. And, when deleting a Task, you need to remember to delete the file as well. In both cases, you need to return `DataObjects` instead of Tasks.

Therefore, change the implementation of the `TaskManagerImpl` class accordingly:

```
public class TaskManagerImpl implements TaskManager {

    // ...

    private Map<Task, DataObject> doByTask;

    // ..

    public synchronized DataObject createTask() {

        DataObject dao = null;

        try {
```

```
        Task task = new TaskImpl();
        FileObject fo = this.save(task);
        dao = DataObject.find(fo);
        if (null != dao) {
            this.doByTask.put(task, dao);
        }

        this.topLevelTasks.add(task);
        this.pss.firePropertyChange(PROP_TASKLIST_ADD, null,
          task);
      }
    catch (DataObjectNotFoundException ex) {
        Exceptions.printStackTrace(ex);
      }

    return dao;
  }


public synchronized void removeTask(String id) {

    Task task = this.getTask(id);
    if (null != task) {

        Task parent = this.getTask(task.getParentId());
        if (null != parent) {

            parent.remove(task);
          } else {

            DataObject dao = this.doByTask.get(task);
            if (null != dao) {
                try {

                    dao.getPrimaryFile().delete();
                    this.doByTask.remove(task);
                  }
                catch (IOException ex) {
                    Exceptions.printStackTrace(ex);
                  }
              }
          }

        this.topLevelTasks.remove(task);
        this.pss.firePropertyChange(PROP_TASKLIST_REMOVE, parent,
          task);
      }
  }


public List<DataObject> getTopLevelTasks() {
    return Collections.unmodifiableList
      (new ArrayList<DataObject>(this.doByTask.values()));
  }
```

When you create the new Task, you now save it in a newly created file, using the existing method save(). You return the corresponding FileObject. However, you do not want to return a FileObject, but a DataObject. Therefore, you need to convert the FileObject into a DataObject. To do this, you invoke DataObject. find() and pass in the FileObject, which performs the above described process of file identification.

You have also implemented the deletion of a Task. If you delete a Task which doesn't have a parent Task, it must be a TopLevelTask. You get the appropriate DataObject from the above described map; ask it for its FileObject and delete it. Then, to clean up the map, you remove the remaining entries.

The class TopLevelTasks has changed very little. Instead of a list of Tasks, you now return a list of DataObjects, which you get from the map.

You have now done everything necessary to implement file support for Tasks. However, if you now try to compile the whole project, you see a lot of compilation errors because you have not yet adapted the other classes that use **TaskManager** to the new signatures. In each module you need to declare a dependency on the Datasystems API and the Nodes API. Then refactor the other modules described as follows:

Refactoring the DueList module

In the previous section, you changed the **TaskManager** to return DataObjects instead of Tasks. Therefore, you need to change the TaskChildren class in the **DueList** module as follows, after setting a dependency on the Datasystems API:

```
protected Collection<Node> initCollection() {

    // ...
      List<Task> dueTasks = new ArrayList<Task>();

        if (null != this.taskMgr) {

            List<DataObject> topLevelTaskDaos =
              this.taskMgr.getTopLevelTasks();
            for (DataObject dao : topLevelTaskDaos) {
                Task topLevelTask =
                  dao.getLookup().lookup(Task.class);
                this.findDueTasks(topLevelTask, dueTasks);
            }
        }
    // ...
```

Refactoring the TaskEditor module

Similarly, you need to refactor the **TaskEditor** module. Again, start by adding a dependency on the Datasystems API. Next, change the `actionPerformed()` method as follows:

```
public void actionPerformed(ActionEvent e) {

    TaskManager taskMgr =
      Lookup.getDefault().lookup(TaskManager.class);
        if (null != taskMgr) {
            Task task =
              taskMgr.createTask().getLookup().lookup(Task.class);
            // ...
```

Next, in the same vein, still in the **TaskEditor** module, change this line:

```
this.task = this.taskMgr.createTask();
```

To this line:

```
this.task = this.taskMgr.createTask().getLookup().lookup(Task.class);
```

In the `TaskEditorTopComponent`, you need to make a similar change, from this constructor:

```
private TaskEditorTopComponent(TaskManager taskMgr) {
    this((taskMgr != null) ? taskMgr.createTask() : null);
}
```

To this constructor:

```
private TaskEditorTopComponent(TaskManager taskMgr) {
    this((taskMgr != null) ?
    taskMgr.createTask().getLookup().lookup(Task.class) : null);
}
```

Refactoring the TaskActions module

Both the `AddDuplicateAction` and the `AddNewAction` classes need to change, in accordance with the change you made in the **TaskModel** module:

```
public void actionPerformed(ActionEvent arg0) {
    if (null != this.result && 0 < this.result.allInstances().size()) {
        // ...
      }
    else {
       newTask =
         taskMgr.createTask().getLookup().lookup(Task.class);
       newTask.setName(original.getName());
      }
          // ...
```

Refactoring the Overview module

Only the class `TopLevelTaskChildren` in the **Overview** module has experienced
significant changes. Up until now, it created `TaskNodes`. Now, however, this is done
by the `DataObject`. Therefore, the `TopLevelTaskChildren` must use `DataObjects`
as keys and delegate the creation of the Nodes to the key:

```
public class TopLevelTaskChildren extends Children.Keys<DataObject>
   implements PropertyChangeListener {
// ...

      protected Node[] createNodes(DataObject arg0) \ {
         return new Node[]{arg0.getNodeDelegate()};
         }
   // ...
   }
```

Now you have updated all the classes that use **TaskManager**. Your file support is
complete. It only lacks a small test to verify that the new feature in the application
works correctly.

Trying out the New Task File Support

There are still some Task files in the folder where you saved the results of the
exercises for the last chapters. Let's use these Task files to check whether the new file
support actually works. In `TaskManagerImpl`, within the **TaskModel** module, you
need to modify the existing method `loadTasks()` for testing purposes.

The `loadTasks` method should no longer use file extensions to identify Task files in a
given directory. Instead, the `loadTasks` method will now let the `DataObject` do the
work instead.

If a file is a Task file, the registered `DataLoader` creates and assigns the corresponding
`TopLevelTaskDataObject`. This `DataObject` is then registered in the map that links
Tasks and `DataObject`.

The `TopLevelTaskChildren` of the **Overview** module identifies the `TopLevelTasks`
to be displayed in the **TaskManager**, so that the registered Tasks stored in the
directory can be displayed.

To trigger the **TaskManager** and the instantiation of `TopLevelTaskDataObjects`,
you will load the Tasks as late as possible. You will check via a flag whether
initialization should occur.

Therefore, if it is still there, remove the call to `loadTasks()` from the constructor of the `TaskManagerImpl` class. Then modify the `loadTasks()` method as follows:

```
// ...
  private boolean tasksLoaded;
// ...

  private void loadTasks() {

      if (this.tasksLoaded) {
          return;
      }
      this.tasksLoaded = true;

      FileObject[] entries = this.root.getChildren();
      for (FileObject fo : entries) {
          try {
              DataObject dao = DataObject.find(fo);
              if (null != dao) {
                  this.doByTask.put(dao.getLookup().lookup
                      (Task.class), dao);
              }
          }
          catch (DataObjectNotFoundException ex) {
              Exceptions.printStackTrace(ex);
          }
      }
  }
// ...
```

Run the **TaskManager** again. Although you have not created demo data, some Tasks should be visible. You created these in the previous chapter, while one is newly created by the **TaskEditor**.

To summarize, you have now created support for a new file type, that is, a feature enabling the NetBeans Platform to recognize Task files. You used the **New File Type** wizard to define and register the new file type. As a result, the default `DataLoader` is registered in the layer file. The `DataLoader` is registered such that it is responsible for processing files that match the registered file type. The `DataLoader` is a factory for the `DataObject` that represents the content of the matched files. The `DataObject` knows how to evaluate these specific files. In evaluating these specific files, the `DataObject` makes the `TopLevelTask` available in its `Lookup`. The `DataObject` also supports the creation of the `TaskNode`, which represents the `TopLevelTask` in the explorer views.

Your support for Task files is currently based on file content. The `TopLevelTasks` are made available to the end user via `DataObjects` and Nodes. However, other typical features for dealing with file content, specifically those that relate to dynamic changes to the content of the files, are still missing. The next section explores these aspects in detail.

Context-sensitive capabilities

In this section, you learn how DataObjects can provide capabilities to deal with the content of files. In the end, capabilities should be provided transparently, that is, the developer of the capabilities should not need to know what kind of DataObject will use them nor how DataObjects will dynamically make the capabilities available.

To illustrate this point, let's extend the example application to let the DataObject make the capability of being saved available. The DataObject should make the save capability available only when the underlying Task has actually changed.

The NetBeans Platform Cookie class lets you provide the capabilities that DataObjects can make available for dealing with file content. To understand the concept "Cookie", mentally replace it with the word "capability", and then everything becomes much clearer. For example, a SaveCookie is, in fact, a SaveCapability. The term "Cookie" is mostly deprecated in new NetBeans Platform code and is interesting in so far as you are likely to come across it a lot, as older NetBeans Platform code tends to make use of it. The more current approach is to use the Lookup instead of the Cookie class, that is, to put objects representing capabilities into the Lookup of a DataObject when you want to add new capabilities to a DataObject. When you want to remove a capability, remove the capability object from the Lookup of the DataObject.

As you will come across the term Cookie, despite not needing to create them directly in your code anymore, it is worth knowing that a Cookie is both a design pattern and an implementation of the Node.Cookie interface or one of its subinterfaces. For example, when integrating with the NetBeans Platform functionality for saving objects, you need to work with the SaveCookie interface, which is an object that provides the save capability. As a result, a capability to save a DataObject needs to implement the SaveCookie interface, as follows:

```
public class TopLevelTaskDataObject extends MultiDataObject {

    // ...

    private class TopLevelTaskSaveCapability implements SaveCookie {

        public void save() throws IOException {

            FileObject fo = TopLevelTaskDataObject.this.getPrimaryFile();

            Task task = TopLevelTaskDataObject.this.getLookup().
                lookup(Task.class);

            TopLevelTaskDataObject.this.taskMgr.save(task, fo);
        }
    }

}
```

In the code above, the inner class `TopLevelTaskSaveCapability` implements, via `SaveCookie`, a subinterface of `Node.Cookie`. It is therefore itself a `Cookie` which is, in this case, a capability of being saved. The `save()` method, required to be implemented when you implement the `SaveCookie` class, takes both the `FileObject` as well as the Task of the surrounding `TopLevelTaskDataObject` and tells the **TaskManager** to save this task to the `FileObject`.

Now, the `TopLevelTaskSaveCapability` functionality needs to be made available to the developer making use of the `TopLevelTaskDataObject`. As you have already seen, the standard way to make something available externally in a flexible way is to put it into the `Lookup`. Therefore, you put the `TopLevelTaskSaveCapability` into the `DataObject`'s `Lookup`. What this means is that you are hiding the save functionality behind a standard interface for saving `DataObjects`, that is, the NetBeans Platform's `SaveCookie` interface.

A developer wanting to create a save capability for a `DataObject` should have no idea that the `TopLevelTaskDataObject` is being dealt with, nor how to save such a `TopLevelTaskDataObject`. The developer should only know that `DataObjects` can in principle be stored through a `SaveCookie` and that the `DataObject` must be asked whether it makes such a capability available. If a `DataObject` makes this capability available, the developer has only to call its `save()` method, without needing to know how it is saved nor even what is being saved. According to this principle, for the developer of the capability, it is only important to know that an object is capable of being saved.

Another advantage of this approach is how dynamic it is. That is, a `DataObject` can dynamically change its capabilities. If it is in a state that can be saved, it makes a `SaveCookie` available in its `Lookup`. If it is not capable of being saved, the capability is removed from the `Lookup` of the `DataObject`, meaning that the `SaveCookie` is no longer available. That means that the `DataObject` is able to adapt its capabilities to its current state.

Let's now return to the example application. You want to extend the `TopLevelTaskDataObject` to make the save capability available, so that the `TopLevelTaskDataObject` can be saved, but only if the underlying Task has changed. Then, when the changes are actually saved, the `DataObject` loses the capability to save again, until the next time that changes are made to it.

Creating a save capability

To implement a save capability, you need to register a `PropertyChangeListener` for the Task, create a `TopLevelTaskSaveCapability` for when changes occur, and place the `TopLevelTaskSaveCapability` in the `Lookup` of the `TopLevelTaskDataObject`. When the capability is executed, it must detach itself from the `Lookup`.

Turning the above explanations into code, to dynamically adapt the capabilities of your `DataObject` to its state, the following few changes are needed in the `TopLevelTaskDataObject`:

```java
public class TopLevelTaskDataObject extends MultiDataObject
  implements PropertyChangeListener {

    // ...

public TopLevelTaskDataObject(FileObject pf,
  TopLevelTaskDataLoader loader) throws DataObjectExistsException,
    IOException {
    // ...

    if (null != this.taskMgr) {
        Task task = this.taskMgr.load(pf);
        task.addPropertyChangeListener(this);
        this.ic.add(task);
    }
}

public void propertyChange(PropertyChangeEvent arg0) {

    SaveCookie saveCookie =
      this.getLookup().
        lookup(SaveCookie.class);

    if (null == saveCookie) {
        this.ic.add(new TopLevelTaskSaveCookie());
    }
}

private class TopLevelTaskSaveCookie implements SaveCookie {

    public void save() throws IOException {
        FileObject fo = TopLevelTaskDataObject.this.getPrimaryFile();
        Task task = TopLevelTaskDataObject.this.getLookup().
          lookup(Task.class);
            TopLevelTaskDataObject.this.taskMgr.save(task, fo);
            TopLevelTaskDataObject.this.ic.remove(this);
    }
  }
}
```

The preceding code assumes that you have worked through the previous sections, during which time you informed the Task about changes, through its `PropertyChangeListener`.

However, this is not yet the case for the subtasks. You currently only fire `PropertyChangeEvents` for changes on a Task's attributes, but not on changes on the attributes of the subtasks.

Therefore, `TaskImpl` needs to implement `PropertyChangeListener`, and you need to propagate the events of the subtasks.

```
public interface Task extends Serializable {
    // ...
    String PROP_CHILDREN_MODIFICATION = "children_modified";
}
```

In `TaskImpl`:

```
public class TaskImpl implements Task, PropertyChangeListener {
    // ...
    public void addChild(Task subTask) {
        this.children.add(subTask);
        this.pss.firePropertyChange(PROP_CHILDREN_ADD, null,
          this.children);
    }
    public boolean remove(Task subTask) {
        boolean res = this.children.remove(subTask);
        subTask.removePropertyChangeListener(this);
        this.pss.firePropertyChange(PROP_CHILDREN_REMOVE, null,
          this.children);
        return res;
    }

    public void propertyChange(PropertyChangeEvent evt) {
        this.pss.firePropertyChange
          (PROP_CHILDREN_MODIFICATION, evt.getOldValue(),
            evt.getNewValue());
    }
}
```

Invoking the Save capability

The `DataObject` is now able to make a context-sensitive capability available, but still lacks the Action enabling the user to see and to invoke the capability.

In general, there is a standard Action for each standard Cookie, which is for each capability offered by the NetBeans Platform. The Action searches for the corresponding Cookie in the `Lookup` of the received `Node` and then calls its methods. For example, the `SaveCookie`, which is a standard capability in the NetBeans Platform has an accompanying `SaveAction`, which is also provided by the NetBeans Platform. Therefore, to make the save capability available to the `Node`, you need to return a `SaveAction` to the `TaskNode`. This action is context-sensitive in two ways:

1. It is enabled only on the `Node` for which it was called
2. It is enabled only when the `DataObject` beneath the `Node` has changed

However, let's assume that you want to place the **Action** not only in the context menu of the `TaskNode`, but also in the global task toolbar. Let's assume, in addition, that you also want to change the **Action's** appearance, depending on its state, via an icon and display name.

Therefore, as you have all these custom requirements, let's focus on writing a custom `SaveAction`. For the context-sensitive icon changes, you will make use of a concept called "icon badging". Icon badging involves merging several icons into one, in order to visualize the current state of an object represented by a `Node`. Icon badging is very useful when visualizing whether a Task is capable of being saved or not.

Unlike the other context-sensitive `Actions` you created, the `SaveAction` will not subclass `ContextAwareAction` directly. Instead, the new approach to working with context-sensitive `Actions` will be used instead. As mentioned in the Nodes chapter, new functionality has been added to the NetBeans Platform allowing plain `ActionListeners` and `AbstractActions` to be enabled based on registrations in the layer file. As shown below, you can use the **New Action** wizard to map an **Action** to an object which, when present in the `Lookup`, will cause the Action to be enabled.

1. In the **TaskActions** module, right-click the main package and choose **New | Action**.

2. In the **New Action** wizard, specify that a new context-sensitive **Action** should be created that is sensitive to the `SaveCookie` class, as shown in the illustration as follows:

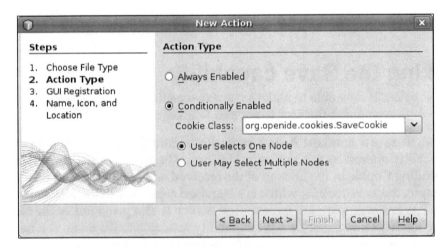

3. Click **Next**, choose **Task** in the **Category** drop-down list. Deselect all other checkboxes and then click **Next**. Set `SaveAction` as the **Class Name**, with **Save** as the **Display Name**. Use the `Orange Ball.png` file as the icon you would like to display. Then click **Finish**.

4. Unlike the other `Actions` you created, the code you need for this particular context-sensitive class is very simple:

```
public final class SaveAction implements ActionListener {

    private final SaveCookie context;
    public SaveAction(SaveCookie context) {
        this.context = context;
      }

    public void actionPerformed(ActionEvent ev) {
        try {
            context.save();
          }
        catch (IOException ex) {
            Exceptions.printStackTrace(ex);
          }
      }

  }
```

The preceding context is provided via the layer file, as follows:

```
<file name="com-netbeansrcp-taskactions-SaveAction.instance">
    <attr name="delegate"
      methodvalue="org.openide.awt.Actions.inject"/>
    <attr name="displayName"
      bundlevalue="com.netbeansrcp.taskactions.Bundle#CTL_SaveAction"/>
    <attr name="iconBase"
      stringvalue="com/netbeansrcp/taskactions/resources/Orange
        Ball.png"/>
    <attr name="injectable"
      stringvalue="com.netbeansrcp.taskactions.SaveAction"/>
    <attr name="instanceCreate"
      methodvalue="org.openide.awt.Actions.context"/>
    <attr name="noIconInMenu" boolvalue="false"/>
    <attr name="selectionType" stringvalue="EXACTLY_ONE"/>
    <attr name="type" stringvalue="org.openide.cookies.SaveCookie"/>
</file>
```

The `SaveAction` listens to the `Lookup` for `SaveCookies` (see the "type" attribute in the XML snippet above). When exactly one `SaveCookie` is found (see the "selectionType" attribute in the XML snippet above), the `SaveAction` is enabled (see the "injectable" attribute in the XML snippet above).

Next, register the new `SaveAction` in the layer, within the `Tasks/Nodes/Task/ Actions` folder, at position `450`:

```
...
<file name="com-netbeansrcp-taskactions-SaveAction.shadow">
    <attr name="originalFile" stringvalue="Actions/Task/com-
       netbeansrcp-taskactions-SaveAction.instance"/>
    <attr name="position" intvalue="450"/>
</file>
...
```

The `SaveAction` is now made available in the context menu of the `TaskNode`. It is enabled when the `SaveCookie` is made available. When the user invokes the `SaveAction`, the `SaveCookie` in the `Lookup` is located, the `save()` method is called, and the related `DataObject` is saved.

Providing Icon Badging

Now let's customize the icon of the `TaskNode` to reflect the state of the `DataObject`. If the `DataObject` makes a `SaveCookie` available, the icon for the `SaveAction` should be added to the `TaskIcon` in a minimized form. This merge is achieved by the method `ImageUtilities.mergeImages()`.

The `TaskNode` and the `ToplevelTaskDataObject` share the same `Lookup`, so that you only need to return the icon to be displayed in the `TaskNode`, without worrying about whether the `SaveCookie` is located in the `TaskNode`'s own `Lookup` or not.

As a result, your icon badging functionality is implemented as follows:

```
// ...
private Lookup.Result result;
private boolean saveable = false;
public TaskNode(Task task, Lookup lookup) {
    // ...
    this.result = this.getLookup().lookup(SaveCookie.class);
    this.result.addLookupListener(this);
}

@Override
public Action[] getActions(boolean arg0) {
    // ...
    actions.add(new SaveAction());
    actions.add(null);
    // ...
}
public void resultChanged(LookupEvent arg0) {
    SaveCookie save = this.getLookup().lookup(SaveCookie.class);
    if (false == this.saveable && null != save) {
        this.saveable = true;
```

```
            this.fireIconChange();
        }
        if (this.saveable && null == save) {
            this.saveable = false;
            this.fireIconChange();
        }
    }

    @Override
    public Image getIcon(int arg0) {
        Image std = super.getIcon(arg0);
        if (this.saveable) {
            Image badge = ImageUtilities.loadImage
                ("com/netbeansrcp/overview/Orange Ball small.png");
            return ImageUtilities.mergeImages(std, badge, 5, 5);
        }
        return std;
    }
```

When you run the application again and make a change to a task, the icon badging in the **Overview** window shows that the task is saveable:

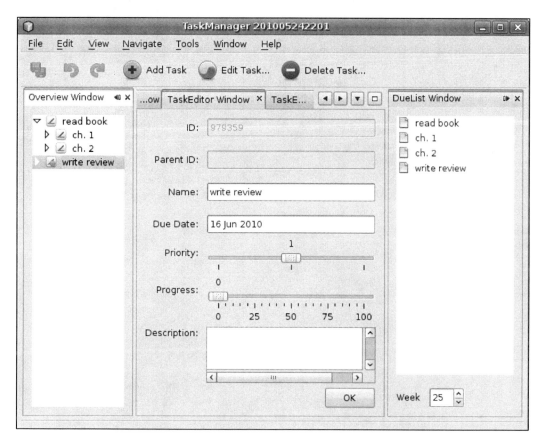

Summary

In this chapter, you added support for Task files. You started by using the **New File Type** wizard in the IDE, which creates a MIME type resolver, together with supporting files, such as a `DataObject`. The `DataObject` is created for file types of the MIME type `application/x-task`. The `DataLoader` mapped in the layer is the factory for creating `DataObjects` as needed. You also saw how context-sensitive file-based features, such as a save capability and icon badging, can be implemented.

9
Dialogs

In this chapter, you learn how to use the NetBeans Dialogs API to interact with the user. You start by looking at simple notifications and then at the set of standard dialogs that the Dialogs API provides. Next, you focus on how to integrate your existing complex dialogs into your application, in particular, focusing on multi-step dialogs, which are often called "wizards".

The topics covered in this chapter will teach you the following:

- How to create notifications
- How to use standard dialogs
- How to integrate complex dialogs
- How to create wizards

Notifications

Let's start by looking at simple notifications. Simple notifications include information dialogs, warning messages, and failure notifications.

The `NotifyDescriptor` class is responsible for describing the notification, that is, the message itself and the options available to the user when responding to the message. The `NotifyDescriptor.Message` class is responsible for pure notifications without the possibility of receiving a response from the user, much like a `JOptionPane`. It provides the simplest form of communication with the user. It describes a dialog, which is shown via the `DialogDisplayer` class. The `DialogDisplayer` class is implemented as a singleton. It can create dialogs to be displayed immediately or delayed in the EDT.

Let's now demonstrate these classes in action. In the example application, you'll inform the user of the tasks shown by the filter. The following steps introduce the code that follows:

1. You need an instance of `NotifyDescriptor.Message` if you need to provide a simple notification without the possibility of reaction from the user.

2. You can pass the constructor a message and, optionally, a message type, which can be either an information message or a warning message. Depending on the type used, a corresponding icon is shown. In this case, you want to inform the user that specific tasks are no longer shown. Therefore you use the message type `NotifyDescriptor.INFORMATION.MESSAGE`.

3. Pass the `NotifyDescriptor` to the `notify()` method of the singleton instance of the `DialogDisplayer`.

4. The filtering of tasks is handled in the **PriorityFilter** module. Specifically, the filtering code is provided by the `filter()` method in the `PriorityFilterTopComponent` class. Find that method and enhance it with the code shown as follows, after declaring a dependency on the Dialogs API.

The preceding steps are expressed in code as follows:

```
private void filter(Task.Priority prio) {
    OverviewTopComponent tc = (OverviewTopComponent)
      WindowManager.getDefault().findTopComponent
        ("OverviewTopComponent");
    Node root = tc.getExplorerManager().getRootContext();

    if (root instanceof PriorityFilterNode) {
        root = ((PriorityFilterNode) root).getOriginal();
    }

    Node newRoot = (null != prio) ? new PriorityFilterNode
      (root, prio) : root;
    tc.getExplorerManager().setRootContext(newRoot);

    String msg = "";
    if (null != prio) {

        String prioTxt = "";
        switch (prio) {
            case LOW:
                prioTxt = "low";
                break;
```

```
                case MEDIUM:
                    prioTxt = "medium";
                    break;
                case HIGH:
                    prioTxt = "high";
            }
            msg = "Only Tasks with priority\n" + prioTxt + " or higher
              are shown.";

        }
    else {
            msg = "All tasks are shown independent of priority";
        }

        NotifyDescriptor d = new NotifyDescriptor.Message
            (msg, NotifyDescriptor.WARNING_MESSAGE);
        DialogDisplayer.getDefault().notify(d);
    }
```

Start the application and filter the tasks in the overview. When you do so, you are notified of tasks that are shown:

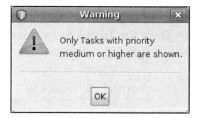

To summarize, you have extended the application with a simple notification in a dialog. To that end, you used the `NotifyDescriptor` class, displaying the dialog via the `DialogDisplayer` class.

Standard dialogs

Let's now take a look at some slightly more complex dialogs that enable user interaction. These are implemented just as simply as the notification shown in the previous section. Once again, you use the `NotifyDescriptor` class and display the described dialog via the `DialogDisplayer` class.

In this case, the `NotifyDescriptor` is a `NotifyDescriptor.Confirmation` or a `NotifyDescriptor.InputLine`. These give the user the possibility of confirming or aborting the dialog and, in the latter case, of typing a single-line text.

In the example application, let's enable the user to confirm the deletion process, prior to the deletion actually taking place. Deleting a task is currently done in the RemoveAction class, within the **TaskActions** module. Now you need to add code to this class.

The following steps explain the code that follows:

1. Create an instance of NotifyDescriptor.Confirmation to display a confirmation dialog.

2. Pass the constructor the message, a dialog title, an option type, and a message type. The option type defines the combination of the **Yes**, **No**, **OK**, and **Cancel** buttons you want to use. The message type is the same as the message type used in the previous section. In this case, you need a **Yes** and a **No** button for displaying a warning. For that you use NotifyDescriptor. YES_NO_OPTION and NotifyDescriptor.WARNING_MESSAGE. You can give a default answer by setting up the buttons setValue(...) method of DialogDisplayer. In this case, the NO_OPTION would make sense.

3. The value of the clicked button is returned by the **DialogDisplayer** via the notify() method.

   In the RemoveAction within the **TaskActions** module, the steps above can be implemented as follows, requiring a dependency in the **TaskActions** module on the Dialogs API:

```
public void actionPerformed(ActionEvent arg0) {

    if (null != this.result && 0 < this.result.allInstances().size()) {
        Task task = this.result.allInstances().iterator().next();
        String msg = "Do you really want to delete the task " +
          task.getId() + " ?";
        NotifyDescriptor d = new NotifyDescriptor.Confirmation
          (msg,"Delete Task"NotifyDescriptor.YES_NO_OPTION,
            NotifyDescriptor.WARNING_MESSAGE);
        d.setValue(NotifyDescriptor.NO_OPTION);

        Object res = DialogDisplayer.getDefault().notify(d);
          if (null != res && DialogDescriptor.YES_OPTION == res) {

            TaskManager taskMgr =
              Lookup.getDefault().lookup(TaskManager.class);
            if (null != taskMgr && null != task) {
               taskMgr.removeTask(task.getId());
             }
          }
       }
     }
   }
```

Start the application and try to delete a task. A dialog box pops up asking if you really want to delete the task. The task is only deleted if the message is confirmed.

To summarize, you have seen how easy it is to use standard dialogs. As an example, you used a simple confirmation dialog. Next, you used a NotifyDescriptor. Confirmation, displaying it via a DialogDisplayer. Using the method setValue(), you selected an answer button. The answer chosen by the user is the return value of the notify() method. In addition, a question with a single-line text as answer can be created via NotifyDescriptor.InputLine, with the return value available via the method getInputText().

Custom dialogs

Often the NetBeans Platform standard dialogs are not as flexible as you would like them to be. More typically, you need to create your own dialogs, containing your own domain-specific Swing components. In this section, you focus on single-pane dialogs, while the next section examines the support for wizards, that is, multi-pane dialogs.

Let's say that, in the example application, you want to provide another Action in the toolbar. This Action allows filtering of tasks by priority, similar to the PriorityFilterTopComponent. However, while PriorityFilterTopComponent provides several buttons for the different priorities, let's say that the new Action should use a dialog to enable the user to set how the filtering should be done.

As the logic to filter tasks remain the same, whether used from the `TopComponent` or from the new dialog that you will create, let's reuse the filtering logic in the `Action`.

1. In the **PriorityFilter** module, create a new helper class named `Filter`.

2. Move the filtering logic from the `PriorityFilterTopComponent` to the new `Filter` class:

```
public class Filter {

    public static void filter(Task.Priority prio) {
        // paste filter code from the PriorityFilterTopComponent here
    }
}
```

3. Back in the `PriorityFilterTopComponent`, reuse the filter method as follows:

```
private void filter(Task.Priority prio) {
    Filter.filter(prio);
}
```

Now let's create an Action that manages the filtering via a dialog. You need to create your own dialog, enabling the user to set a priority via a radio button.

The main difference from the previously displayed standard dialogs is the usage of the `Descriptor` class. While you previously used the `NotifyDescriptor` class, you will now use the `DialogDescriptor` class instead. The `DialogDescriptor` class extends `NotifyDescriptor`, providing additional capabilities for displaying custom content, while also giving you control over dialog features such as modality, button look and feel, and context-sensitive help. Just like the `NotifyDescriptor`, the `DialogDescriptor` is displayed via a `DialogDisplayer`.

1. Start by creating a `JPanel` for the custom content of the dialog. To that end, in the **PriorityFilter** module, create a `JPanel` called **FilterPanel**.

2. On the **FilterPanel**, using the Matisse GUI Builder, add a `JLabel` and a `JButtonGroup` with four `JRadioButtons`. The result should be as shown in the following screenshot. Adding the `JRadioButtons` to the `JButtonGroup` is done via the property **buttonGroup** in the **Properties** window, for each of the `JRadioButtons`.

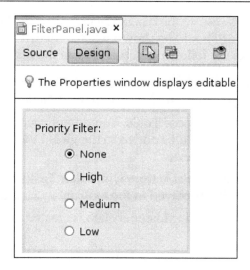

The purpose of the `FilterPanel` is to allow the selection of a priority. Therefore, you should introduce a method that returns the selected priority, as follows:

```
public class FilterPanel extends javax.swing.JPanel {
    /** Creates new form FilterPanel */
    public FilterPanel() {
        initComponents();
    }
    public Priority getPriority() {
        if (this.jRadioButton2.isSelected())     return Priority.HIGH;
        if (this.jRadioButton3.isSelected())     return
          Priority.MEDIUM;
        if (this.jRadioButton4.isSelected())     return Priority.LOW;
        return null;
    }

    // ...
```

You can pass the `FilterPanel` to the `DialogDescriptor`, as the `JPanel` is the custom content. The dialog should be shown when a related `Action` from the task toolbar is activated. Take the following steps to create the `Action`:

1. In the **PriorityFilter** module, use the **New Action** wizard, as described in the Actions chapter, to create an "Always Enabled" action. Click **Next**.

2. In the **Category** field, choose **Tools**. You do not need an entry in a menu. However, an entry should be added to the global toolbar **Task**, after the **RemoveAction**. Click **Next**.

3. Name the class **FilterTasksAction**, with **Filter Tasks** as the display name. Choose an icon to be displayed in the toolbar.

4. Click **Finish** and the **ActionListener** class is created and registered in the `layer.xml` file.

5. In the toolbar, you want to see not only the icon, but also the textual name of the Action. Therefore, override, just as you did for the other Actions, the `getToolbarPresenter()` method, returning a corresponding JButton.

6. The `FilterAction` should display a dialog which, in turn, should contain the `FilterPanel` you created earlier. You need to create a `DialogDescriptor` with a constructor that should receive an instance of the JPanel, together with a title, a modality flag, an option type, an option preselection, and an `ActionListener` for the buttons.

7. Instead of the option types, you could pass a list of custom options and their alignment, together with a help context, neither of which you need to do in the context of the example application. Instead, you display the created `DialogDescriptor`, as usual, via the `DialogDisplayer`. The result is returned by the `display()` method and you can read the selected priority directly in the `FilterPanel`.

The preceding steps describe the following code:

```
public final class FilterTasksAction extends AbstractAction implements
    Presenter.Toolbar {
    private JButton toolbarBtn;
    @Override
    public void actionPerformed(ActionEvent e) {
        FilterPanel filterPanel = new FilterPanel();
        DialogDescriptor dd = new DialogDescriptor
                            (filterPanel,"Priority
                            Filter",true,DialogDescriptor.
                            OK_CANCEL_OPTION,
                            DialogDescriptor.OK_OPTION,
                            null);
        Object result = DialogDisplayer.getDefault().notify(dd);
        if (null != result && DialogDescriptor.OK_OPTION == result) {
```

```
                    Filter.filter(filterPanel.getPriority());
                }
            }
        }

        @Override
        public Component getToolbarPresenter() {
            if (null == this.toolbarBtn) {
                this.toolbarBtn = new JButton(this);
            }
            return this.toolbarBtn;
        }
    }
```

In the example, you do not need dynamic behavior during the display of the dialog box; therefore you need to pass "null" instead of an ActionListener, when creating the DialogDescriptor.

Now start the application again. When you click **Filter Tasks**, the dialog box shown in the following screenshot appears. It requires the user to specify a priority. If the dialog is cancelled, no filtering takes place; if you confirm the dialog, it is filtered, using the selected priority.

To summarize, you have seen how you can create dialogs with custom content. The dialog is displayed, as usual, via the DialogDisplayer class. However, instead of a NotifyDescriptor class, the DialogDescriptor class is used to define the content to be displayed. For example, you can pass a JPanel to a DialogDescriptor, with custom content, which gives you control over the content and appearance of the dialog you create.

Wizards

Though custom dialogs are an improvement over standard dialogs, they're often not sufficient either. Especially when a lot of information needs to be gathered during a single process, a single-pane dialog is limiting. In this section, you learn how to create multi-pane dialogs, which are normally called "wizards".

Creating a wizard

In the example application, let's create a wizard to manage the creation of new tasks. You will create it in the **TaskActions** module, taking the following steps to do so.

1. NetBeans IDE provides a wizard for creating new wizards. To use this wizard, choose **New | Wizard** from the context menu of the **TaskActions** module.

2. On the first page of the wizard, as shown in the illustration below, first select the type of registration. A custom wizard is not registered in the **New File** wizard, needing to be called programmatically from somewhere in your code instead. Choosing **New File** wizard will result in layer entries being added that will register the wizard in the **New File** dialog box of the application.

3. For custom wizards, you can choose if the wizard should pass through a sequence of separate panels, in linear fashion or dynamically, based on the choices made by the user. The first option creates code that lets the user pass through the sequence of panels forward and backward, without branching off or skipping panels. The second creates code that, by default, gives you full control over the order of the panels and allows a dynamic order of the panels to be created.

4. You also need to specify how many panels should be created for the new wizard. For the example, let's create a custom wizard, that is, with its own registration, that is, not registered in the layer but invoked from your own code, with a static panel sequence, and three panels.

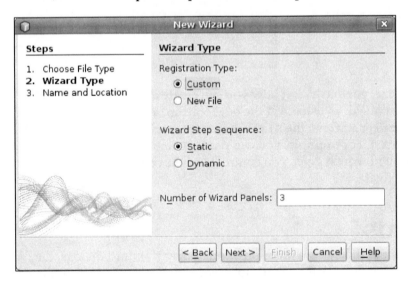

5. On the second page of the wizard, shown as follows, specify a **Class Name Prefix** for the classes to be generated, as well as the destination package. For the example, set **NewTask** as the prefix and **com.netbeansrcp.taskactions. wizards** as the package.

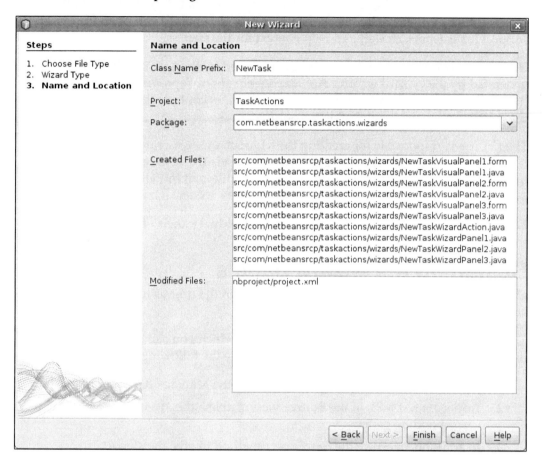

6. When you click **Finish** in the wizard, the following classes are created:

   ° An action to invoke the wizard named **NewTaskWizardAction**

   ° Three **WizardDescriptor.Panels** with the prefix **NewTaskWizardPanel**

   ° Three JPanels with the prefix **NewTaskWizardVisualPanel**

Each of the JPanels is responsible for visually representing a step in the wizard.

The **WizardDescriptor.Panels** are responsible for controlling the step. These manage the JPanels at the beginning of the step, by reading the settings, initializing the JPanels with these settings, and saving the entered data before the user continues with the next step. They also check the validity of the entered values and provide support for listeners, as well as a help context for the step.

In custom wizards, a WizardDescriptor is created by the Action class that is generated by the Wizard wizard. A WizardDescriptor represents the description of the dialog, manages the WizardDescriptor.Panels, controls the iteration through the panels, and manages global dialog settings.

The Action is responsible for creating the WizardDescriptor, to initialize it with WizardDescriptor.Panels, and to create via the DialogDisplayer the corresponding dialog, and to display it. In addition, it initializes both the WizardDescriptor and the JPanels with property values.

Let's now start with the visual design of the individual panels of the wizard.

Designing the wizard panels

On the first page of the wizard, you need to inform the user as to whether they are creating a TopLevelTask or a subtask.

The JPanel for this step requires only a JLabel, which you can access from the outside to set the text dynamically. Therefore, take the following steps:

1. Open the NewTaskVisualPanel1 class in the Matisse GUI Builder.

2. Add a JLabel and, in the **Source** view, publish the JLabel via a corresponding getter.

3. In addition, override the getName() method to give the step a reasonable name.

4. To let all steps have a panel with the same size, for this panel as well as all following JPanels, set the preferredSize property to 460,300.

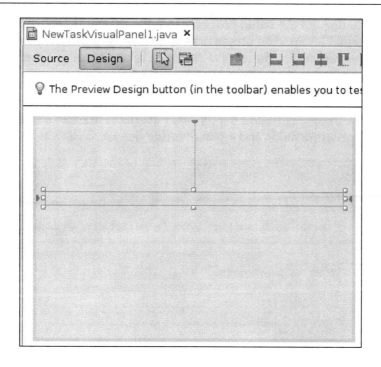

```
public final class NewTaskVisualPanel1 extends JPanel {

    public NewTaskVisualPanel1() {
        initComponents();
    }

    public JLabel getInfoLabel() {
        return this.jLabel1;
    }
    public @Override String getName() {
        return "Introduction";
    }
    // ...
```

5. On the second page of the wizard, let the user set the name of the task, its
    due date, priority, and current progress.

To this end, open the `NewTaskVisualPanel2` class and add four `JLabels`, two
`JTextFields`, and two `JSliders`, as seen in the illustration in the next page.
Set the labeled `JLabels` to the same size, align them to the right, and set the
`horizontalAlignment` property to `TRAILING`.

For the first JSlider, set the **value** property to **1**, the **maximum** property to **2**, and the **majorTickSpacing** property to **1**. Enable the **paintTicks** and **snapToTicks** properties. For the second JSlider, set the **value** property to **0**, the **majorTickSpacing** property to **25** and the **minorTickSpacing** property to **5**. Enable the properties **paintLabels**, **paintTicks**, and **snapToTicks**.

Finally, make the JTextField and the JSlider available to other modules in the application via getter methods and again override the getName() method.

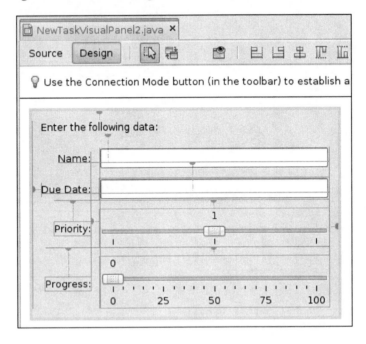

```java
public final class NewTaskVisualPanel2 extends JPanel {

    public NewTaskVisualPanel2() {
        initComponents();
    }

    public JSlider getPriority() {
        return jSlider1;
    }

    public JSlider getProgress() {
        return jSlider2;
    }
    public JTextField getNameField() {
        return jTextField1;
    }

    public JTextField getDue() {
```

```
        return jTextField2;
    }

    @Override
    public String getName() {
        return "Details";
    }

    // ...
```

6. Last but not least, let's turn to the third panel. Here you want to ask the user to provide a detailed description of the task. Open the NewTaskVisualPanel3 class and then add a JLabel and a JTextArea. Make these components available to the other classes in the module via getter methods and override getName().

```
public final class NewTaskVisualPanel3 extends JPanel {

    /** Creates new form NewTaskVisualPanel3 */
    public NewTaskVisualPanel3() {
        initComponents();
    }
    public JTextArea getDescription() {
        return this.jTextArea1;
    }
    public @Override String getName() {
        return "Description";
    }

    // ...
```

The graphic design of the individual steps is completed. Now let's turn to examining how the wizard steps are controlled.

Controlling the wizard panels

The `WizardDescriptor.Panel` class controls the wizard panels, fulfilling the following responsibilities:

- Creation of the visual representation of the step. This task is handled by the `getComponent()` method which is already completely implemented and must be extended only by any possible initializations.

- Reading the settings for the step, initializing the visual panel, and storing the settings. For these tasks the methods `readSettings(...)` and `storeSettings(...)` are provided. The wizard does not currently operate with generics, so that an object is passed to these methods. This object is actually the `WizardDescriptor` and is used to store the settings that are stored with `putProperty(...)` and read out with `getProperty(...)`.

- Checking the validity of entered values and supporting listeners. This responsibility is mapped to the methods `isValid()` and add and `removeChangeListener(...)`.

- Supporting context-sensitive help by returning a help context via the `getHelp()` method.

Before you proceed with the coding of each wizard panel, prepare the storage of the settings in the properties of the `WizardDescriptor`. To do this, you need to create an interface with constants for the property names to the separate settings.

1. In the package **coms.netbeansrcp.taskactions.wizards**, create a Java interface named **NewTaskConstants**.

2. Define the content of your new class as follows.

   ```
   public interface NewTaskConstants {
       String PARENT_ID = "PARENT_ID";
       String NAME = "NAME";
           String DUE = "DUE";
           String PRIORITY = "PRIORITY";
           String PROGRESS = "PROGRESS";
           String DESCRIPTION = "DESCRIPTION";

   }
   ```

3. Turn to the first wizard panel, which should display whether a `TopLevelTask` or a subtask is created with, where relevant, the ID of the parent. To achieve this, pass the ID of the parent task to the panel. If it is set, create a subtask, else create a `TopLevelTask`.

4. Passing the value takes place via the properties of `WizardDescriptor`, which are passed to the `readSettings()` method. In this method, you read the intended property `PARENT_ID` and remember the value.

5. The visual representation of the panel is provided by the `getComponent()` method, where you create and initialize a `NewTaskVisualPanel1`. In this case, you provide the information label with accompanying text.

Based on the preceding steps, the implementation of the first wizard panel therefore looks as follows:

```
public class NewTaskWizardPanel1 implements WizardDescriptor.Panel {
    private NewTaskVisualPanel1 component;
    public Component getComponent() {

        if (component == null) {
            component = new NewTaskVisualPanel1();
        }

        return component;
    }

    public HelpCtx getHelp() {
        return HelpCtx.DEFAULT_HELP;
    }
    public boolean isValid() {
        return true;
    }
    public final void addChangeListener(ChangeListener l) {
    }
    public final void removeChangeListener(ChangeListener l) {
    }
    public void readSettings(Object settings) {
        WizardDescriptor wd = (WizardDescriptor) settings;
        String parentId = (String)
          wd.getProperty(NewTaskConstants.PARENT_ID);
        String txt = "";
        if (null == parentId) {
            txt =    "You want a Task without parent" +" Create
              Task...";
        }
        else {
            txt =    "You want to create a Subtask for the task
              with the ID..." + parentId;
        }
            ((NewTaskVisualPanel1) this.getComponent()).
              getInfoLabel().setText(txt);
    }
    public void storeSettings(Object settings) {
    }
}
```

Validating entered values

Use the second panel of the wizard to ask for the details of the task to be created. The values entered by the user need to be stored. To this end, you use the method storeSettings(). This method stores the values as properties in the WizardDescriptor. The entered values need to be validated. To query the validity of the panel, the method isValid() is used. The state of the panel is monitored via a ChangeListener.

In the example application, only the input of the date should be validated, as the conversion of text to date is error-prone. Therefore, register a DocumentListener on the Document of the JTextField for the date input. When the text changes, the listener checks the validity and sets it accordingly.

Following the instructions in the preceding paragraphs, implement the NewTaskWizardPanel2 class as follows:

```java
public class NewTaskWizardPanel2 implements WizardDescriptor.Panel,
    DocumentListener {

    private NewTaskVisualPanel2 component;
    private WizardDescriptor wd;
    private boolean valid = true;
    private ChangeSupport cs = new ChangeSupport(this);

    public Component getComponent() {
        if (component == null) {
            component = new NewTaskVisualPanel2();
            this.component.getDue().
              setText(DateFormat.getDateInstance().
                format(new Date()));
            this.component.getDue().getDocument().
              addDocumentListener(this);
        }
        return component;
    }

    public HelpCtx getHelp() {
        return HelpCtx.DEFAULT_HELP;
    }

    public void readSettings(Object settings) {

        this.wd = (WizardDescriptor) settings;
    }

    public void storeSettings(Object settings) {

        this.wd.putProperty(NewTaskConstants.NAME,
          this.component.getNameField().getText());
```

```
        try {
            this.wd.putProperty(NewTaskConstants.DUE,
              DateFormat.getDateInstance().
                parse(this.component.getDue().getText()));
        }
        catch (Exception e)  {
        }

        Priority prio = null;
        switch (this.component.getPriority().getValue()) {
            case 0:
                prio = Priority.LOW;
                break;
            case 1:
                prio = Priority.MEDIUM;
                break;
            case 2:
                prio = Priority.HIGH;
                break;
        }
        this.wd.putProperty(NewTaskConstants.PRIORITY, prio);
        this.wd.putProperty(NewTaskConstants.PROGRESS,
          this.component.getProgress().getValue());
    }
    public boolean isValid() {
        return this.valid;
    }

    public void addChangeListener(ChangeListener arg0) {
        this.cs.addChangeListener(arg0);
    }

    public void removeChangeListener(ChangeListener arg0) {
        this.cs.removeChangeListener(arg0);
    }

    public void insertUpdate(DocumentEvent arg0) {
        this.changeDue();
    }

    public void removeUpdate(DocumentEvent arg0) {
        this.changeDue();
    }
    public void changedUpdate(DocumentEvent arg0) {
        this.changeDue();
    }

    private void changeDue() {
        boolean old = this.valid;
        try {
            DateFormat.getDateInstance().
              parse(this.component.getDue().getText());
            this.wd.putProperty("WizardPanel_errorMessage", null);
```

```
                   this.valid = true;
              }
          catch (Exception ex) {
              this.wd.putProperty("WizardPanel_errorMessage",
                "Due date not formatted correctly!");
              this.valid = false;
          }
          if (old != this.valid) {
              this.cs.fireChange();
          }
      }
  }
```

The exchange of data takes place in the readSettings() method and the storeSettings() method. As you do not pass in any data, the readSettings() only stores the WizardDescriptor. On the other hand, in the storeSettings() method, the fields of the NewTaskVisualPanel2 are read and, if necessary, converted to data types corresponding to task properties. Then they are written into a property of the WizardDescriptor via the putProperty() method.

For validation, first of all, the initialization of the NewTaskVisualPanel2 in getComponent() is important. Here you can immediately register the NewTaskWizardPanel2 itself as a listener on the Document of the JTextField for the date input. Once the text of the due date is changed, the corresponding listener method is called, delegating its call to changeDue().

In changeDue(), check whether the text can be converted to a date and set the validity flag to valid. If the date input is invalid, set the property WizardPanel_errorMessage in the WizardDescriptor. The value of the property appears as an error message at the bottom of the dialog, as shown in the screenshot on the next page. If the date input is valid, set the property to null so that the displayed error message is deleted.

You have to provide support for a listener for the validity so that a dynamic change of validity and the related dynamic display of the error messages work. For this file methods addChangeListener and removeChangeListener are responsible. You extend NewTaskWizardPanel2 with an attribute of the type ChangeSupport which is analogous to the already discussed PropertyChangeSupport. As a result, you do not need to manage these listeners yourself.

In the methods used to register and unregister the ChangeListener you delegate the call to this ChangeSupport. To notify the registered listeners about changes to the validity of current inputs you only have to call the method fireChange() on the ChangeSupport in changeDue(). The displayed error message changes dynamically as you type in the due date.

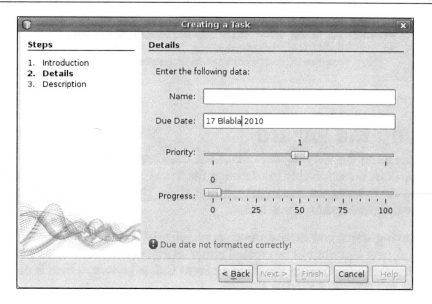

The third panel of the wizard asks the user for the detailed description of the task. Again, here you need to save the entered value via the `storeSettings()` method. If you followed the implementation of the previous panel, the implementation does nothing special:

```
public class NewTaskWizardPanel3 implements WizardDescriptor.Panel {
    private NewTaskVisualPanel3 component;
    public Component getComponent() {
        if (component == null) {
            component = new NewTaskVisualPanel3();
        }
        return component;
    }

    public HelpCtx getHelp() {
        return HelpCtx.DEFAULT_HELP;
    }

    public boolean isValid() {
        return true;
    }

    public final void addChangeListener(ChangeListener l) {
    }

    public final void removeChangeListener(ChangeListener l) {
    }

    public void readSettings(Object settings) {
    }
```

```
    public void storeSettings(Object settings) {
        WizardDescriptor wd = (WizardDescriptor) settings;
        wd.putProperty(NewTaskConstants.DESCRIPTION,
          this.component.getDescription().getText());
    }
}
```

Invoking the wizard

Let's now focus on the `NewTaskWizardAction` class created by the Wizard wizard. The `Action` class is responsible for defining the `WizardDescriptor`, initializing it, and displaying it, using the `DialogDisplayer` class. The Wizard wizard generated most of the code needed for these tasks.

In the following steps, you extend the responsibility of the `Action` by letting it create new tasks. A new task should be created either as a `TopLevelTask` or as a subtask. The deciding factor is whether the ID of a parent task is known, which is determined by whether an ID is passed to the `Action`.

You begin by subclassing `ActionListener`, rather than `CallableSystemAction`. As discussed in the chapter on Actions, subclassing `ActionListener` is simpler and more idiomatic than subclassing `CallableSystemAction`. The Wizard wizard should probably have created an `ActionListener` class for you, instead of a `CallableSystemAction` class and, if you want to start contributing to the NetBeans Platform community by submitting issues in the NetBeans Issuezilla, this would be a good time to start doing so!

Once you have changed the code so that `ActionListener` is subclassed, you rewrite the signature of the existing `actionPerformed()` method to receive the parent ID. If the ID is set, a subtask is created for the specified task. If the IDE is not set, a `TopLevelTask` is created. To remain compliant with the `Action` interface, you introduce a new `actionPerformed()` method that delegates to your new `actionPerformed(String)` method and passes null as the parent ID.

Following the preceding description, the class `NewTaskWizardAction` now looks as follows:

```
public final class NewTaskWizardAction implements ActionListener {

    private WizardDescriptor.Panel[] panels;

    public void actionPerformed(ActionEvent e) {
        this.actionPerformed ("");
    }

    public void actionPerformed(String parentId) {
```

```
WizardDescriptor wizardDescriptor =
  new WizardDescriptor(getPanels());
wizardDescriptor.setTitleFormat(new MessageFormat("{0}"));
wizardDescriptor.setTitle("Creating a Task");

wizardDescriptor.putProperty("WizardPanel_image",
  Utilities.loadImage("com/netbeansrcp/taskactions" +
      "/TaskBackground.png"));
wizardDescriptor.putProperty(NewTaskConstants.PARENT_ID,
  parentId);

Dialog dialog =
  DialogDisplayer.getDefault().createDialog
    (wizardDescriptor);
dialog.setVisible(true);
dialog.toFront();
boolean cancelled = wizardDescriptor.getValue() !=
  WizardDescriptor.FINISH_OPTION;
if (!cancelled) {
    TaskManager taskMgr = Lookup.getDefault().
      lookup(TaskManager.class);

    if(null != taskMgr) {
        Task task = null;
        if (null != parentId) {

            task =   taskMgr.createTask
              ((String) wizardDescriptor.getProperty
              (NewTaskConstants.NAME), parentId);
        }
        else {
            task =
            taskMgr.createTask().getLookup
            ().lookup(Task.class);

            task.setName
              ((String)wizardDescriptor.getProperty
              (NewTaskConstants.NAME));
        }

        task.setDue((Date) wizardDescriptor.getProperty
          (NewTaskConstants.DUE));
        task.setPrio((Task.Priority)
          wizardDescriptor.getProperty
          (NewTaskConstants.PRIORITY));
        task.setProgr((Integer)
          wizardDescriptor.getProperty
          (NewTaskConstants.PROGRESS));
        task.setDescr((String)
          wizardDescriptor.getProperty
          (NewTaskConstants.DESCRIPTION));
          }
}
```

```
    }

        private WizardDescriptor.Panel[] getPanels() {
            if (panels == null) {
                panels =new WizardDescriptor.Panel[]{new
                    NewTaskWizardPanel1(),
                    new NewTaskWizardPanel2(),
                    new NewTaskWizardPanel3()};
                String[] steps = new String[panels.length];
                for (int i = 0; i < panels.length;i++) {
                    Component c = panels[i].getComponent();
                    steps[i] = c.getName();
                    if(c instanceof JComponent) {
                        JComponent jc = (JComponent) c;
                        jc.putClientProperty
                            ("WizardPanel_contentSelectedIndex",new
                            Integer(i));
                        jc.putClientProperty("WizardPanel_contentData",
                            steps);
                        jc.putClientProperty
                            ("WizardPanel_autoWizardStyle",
                              Boolean.TRUE);
                        jc.putClientProperty
                            ("WizardPanel_contentDisplayed",
                              Boolean.TRUE);
                        jc.putClientProperty
                            ("WizardPanel_contentNumbered",
                              Boolean.TRUE);
                    }
                }
            }
            return panels;
        }


    }


}
```

When required, the method `getPanels()` creates a `WizardDescriptor.Panel[]` and initializes it with instances of the three `NewTaskWizardPanels`. It iterates over this array, obtains each `JPanel` from the `WizardDescriptor.Panel`, transfers the name to a `String[]`, and sets some of the following listed client properties on the `JPanel`.

WizardPanel_autoWizardStyle	Boolean	Activates the automatic laying out of the wizard and leads to the verifying of the following properties.
WizardPanel_contentDisplayed	Boolean	Provides a list of the steps on the right side with the background image.
WizardPanel_helpDisplayed	Boolean	Turns on the help display and, if steps are displayed, the help and content panes are put into tabbed pane.
WizardPanel_contentNumbered	Boolean	Provides the numbering of steps.
WizardPanel_ contentSelectedIndex	Integer	Provides the index of the step, starting at 0.
WizardPanel_contentData	String[]	Provides the step names displayed in the content pane.
WizardPanel_image	Image	Provides the image displayed as background of the content pane.
WizardPanel_errorMessage	String	Provides the error message for the invalid state of the panel.
WizardPanel_helpURL	URL	Provides the URL of the help topics for this panel.

These properties can usually be placed in either the JPanel or the WizardDescriptor, although the helpURL can only be set on the JPanel, while the error message can only be set on the WizardDesriptor.

As previously discussed, the method actionPerformed() calls actionPerformed(String) with a null argument. This method, in turn, is responsible for the real action and creates a WizardDescriptor, to which it passes the WizardDescriptor.Panels obtained from the getPanels() method.

Next, the format for the title, and the title itself, are set, where the placeholder {0} is replaced by the name of the JPanel and the placeholder {1} is replaced by the name returned from the WizardDescriptor.Iterator. By default, the name returned is an indication of which step is being displayed.

Next, you set properties on the WizardDescriptor, for specifying a background image and the ID of the parent task. The dialog described by the WizardDescriptor is created and displayed via the DialogDisplayer.

As usual, the return of the `display()` method is the result of the wizard. If the wizard has not been cancelled, you obtain the `TaskManager` from the Lookup and use it to create a new Task. The task properties are set by the values specified in the `WizardDescriptor`. At this point, you have completely implemented the `Action` and now need to integrate it into the existing `AddNewAction`.

The `actionPerformed()` method of the `AddNewAction` must no longer create and open a new Task. It should leave this to the `AddNewWizardAction`. Remove the related calls on the `TaskManager` and, instead, get the `AddNewWizardAction` and call it. Depending on whether a `TopLevelTask` or a subtask should be created, pass the ID of the parent task, so that the method now looks as follows:

```
public void actionPerformed(ActionEvent arg0) {

    Task task = null;
    if (null != this.result && 0 < this.result.allInstances().size()) {

        task = this.result.allInstances().iterator().next();

        SystemAction.get(NewTaskWizardAction.class).
          performAction(task.getId());

    }
    else {

        SystemAction.get(NewTaskWizardAction.class).performAction();
    }

}
```

Start the application and initiate the creation of a new task. This no longer opens a `TaskEditor` with a new **Task** but, instead, the recently created wizard. The following three images show what you should see as you step through your newly created wizard.

In the first step, you see the introduction to the wizard as shown in the following screenshot:

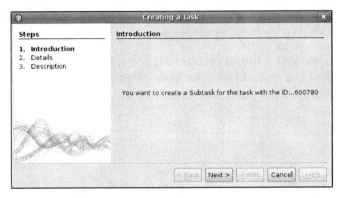

The details needed for defining a new task are shown in the second step, as shown in the following screenshot:

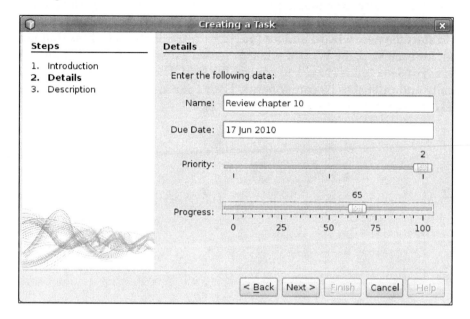

In the third step, the description of the task is defined, as shown in the following screenshot:

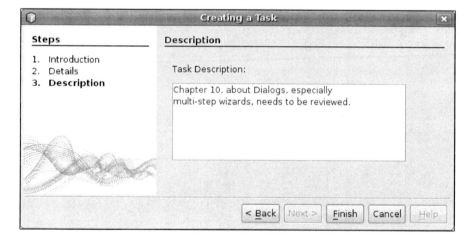

Summary

You have learned how to create notifications, dialogs, and wizards. Most of the focus of this chapter has been on creating a wizard. The Wizard wizard created an Action to start the new wizard and a `WizardDescriptor` to control the dialog. In addition, for each step, the Wizard wizard created a `JPanel` for graphic display and a `WizardDescriptor.Panel` to control the step. The `JPanel` visualizes a step graphically and publishes its components. The `WizardDescriptor.Panel` creates, manages, and controls the `JPanel`.

10
Settings

When you want to let the user configure the application, the NetBeans Platform provides two sets of APIs to help you:

- Options Dialog and SPI: It lets you create panels that integrate with the NetBeans Platform Options window, so that you have a centralized location where you can integrate with an extensible user interface for the user to define the application's settings.

- Utilities API: It provides a NetBeans-specific Java Preferences API implementation. Though you can continue to program against the standard JDK Preferences class when you use the NetBeans-specific implementation, the configuration data is stored in the NetBeans Platform user directory, rather than in the location where the standard preferences class would normally put it.

In this chapter you extend the Options window so that the user is able to configure a user-specific storage location for the tasks handled by the **Task Manager**.

Options window

Two different extension points are provided for integrating panels into the Options window as follows:

- The Options window offers several Primary Panels, identified by their large icons along the top of the Options window. These Primary Panels can be used to configure the most important groupings of settings in an application.

- Secondary Panels are provided so that you can provide panels with less important settings needed for configuring the application. For example, one of the default Primary Panels is named "Miscellaneous", containing Secondary Panels within it.

Integrating with the Options window

For the sample application that you are creating, you need to create a Primary Panel to configure the path pointing to the location where the tasks are stored. Extensions to the Options window can be provided in a new module or within the same module that provides the feature which the Options window extension complements. In this instance, that is, for the sample application, you provide the extensions to the Options window in a new module.

1. Create a new module named **Preferences** with **org.netbeansrcp.preferences** as the **Code Name Base**. Set a dependency on the Utilities API, which provides the NbPreferences class. Also set a dependency on the FileSystem API, so that you can access the local filesystem via the LocalFileSystem class.

2. Within the **org.netbeansrcp.preferences** main package, create a new package named **api**. Within the **api** package, create a Java interface named **Preferences** to provide access to the settings provided by the module:

```
public interface Preferences {
    String PATH_CHANGED = "path_changed";
    void setPersistencePath(String path);
    File getPersistencePath();
    void addPropertyChangeListener(PropertyChangeListener
        listener);
    void removePropertyChangeListener(PropertyChangeListener
        listener);
}
```

The implementation of this interface needs to create the module's settings, aided by the **NetBeans Preferences** API.

Preferences

Via the NbPreferences API class, you can create a Preferences object for the root of a configuration or for a specific class within the configuration. If you create a Preferences object for a class, the path to the location of the configuration is defined by the name of the code name base of the module, together with the name of the file, within the NetBeans Platform user directory. The settings themselves are saved as properties, with the filename using the .properties extension.

Setting and using a Preference

For the sample application, you need to store the settings for the **Preferences** module, so that the path and the filename should be as shown in the following screenshot:

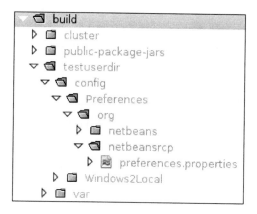

Create a new class named `PreferencesImpl`, for implementing your `Preferences` interface. The implementation uses a preference named `DIRECTORY` to load and store the absolute path to the location for storing tasks. You also need to be able to inform other modules of changes to the setting, to which end you include support for a `PropertyChangeListener`. Taking these considerations into account, our implementation needs to be defined as follows:

```
public class PreferencesImpl implements Preferences {

    private PropertyChangeSupport pss = new
      PropertyChangeSupport(this);

    public void setPersistencePath(String path) {
        this.pss.firePropertyChange(PATH_CHANGED,
          this.getPersistencePath(), path);
        NbPreferences.forModule(PreferencesPanel.class).
            put("DIRECTORY", path);
}

    public File getPersistencePath() {
```

```
        String taskDir = NbPreferences.forModule(PreferencesPanel.class).
            get("DIRECTORY",new LocalFileSystem().
            getRootDirectory().getAbsolutePath());

        File file = new File(taskDir);
        return file;
    }

    public synchronized void addPropertyChangeListener
        (PropertyChangeListener listener) {
            this.pss.addPropertyChangeListener(listener);
        }

    public synchronized void removePropertyChangeListener
        (PropertyChangeListener listener) {
            this.pss.removePropertyChangeListener(listener);
        }
}
```

 The PreferencesPanel, referred to in the preceding code, does not exist yet. You create it later in this section; until then, a red error underline will be shown in the editor.

1. To register the preceding class in the META-INF/services folder, let the module depend on the Lookup API. Then annotate the PreferencesImpl class as follows:

   @ServiceProvider(service=Preferences.class)

2. Right-click the main package and choose **New | Other | Module Development |** Options **Panel** and click **Next**. The Options **Panel** wizard opens, enabling you to create a new Options window extension.

3. On the first page, as shown in the screenshot on the next page, you need to decide whether to provide a Primary Panel or a Secondary Panel. Create a **Primary Panel** named **Task Manager**, with **task manager** as the **Keywords**. The keywords enable the user to quickly open the Options window from the **Quick Search** field in the application, if you choose to support this feature.

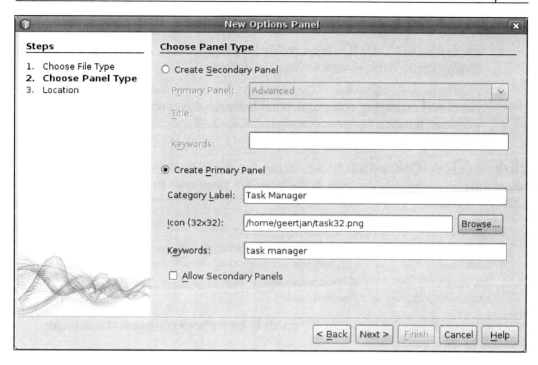

4. As always, the second page, as shown in the following screenshot, offers the possibility to specify a name prefix to be used for the created classes.

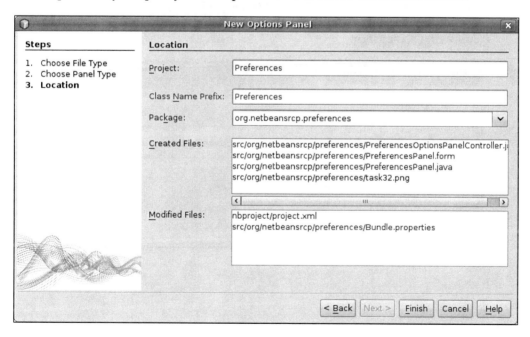

When you click **Finish**, the wizard generates two classes:

1. `PreferencesPanel`: It is responsible for visualization, loading, and storing of configuration data, as well as data validation.

2. `PreferencesOptionsPanelController`: It is responsible for creating the panel and managing communication between the panel and the Options window. It uses a `PropertyChangeListener` to monitor the state of the panel.

The `PreferencesOptionsPanelController` has the following class annotation that, at compile time, generates entries in the layer file to register the Options panel in the Options window:

```
@OptionsPanelController.TopLevelRegistration
 (categoryName      = "#OptionsCategory_Name_Preferences",
  iconBase          = "org/netbeansrcp/preferences/task32.png",
  keywords          = "#OptionsCategory_Keywords_Preferences",
  keywordsCategory  = "Preferences")
```

Now you can design the layout of the panel to let the user configure the storage location of their tasks:

1. Open the **PreferencesPanel** and change the layout to **BorderLayout**.

2. Add a JLabel, a JTextField, and a JButton. The `editable` property of the JTextField needs to be deselected because you will provide a JFileChooser for setting the path. After these steps the dialog should look as shown in the following screenshot:

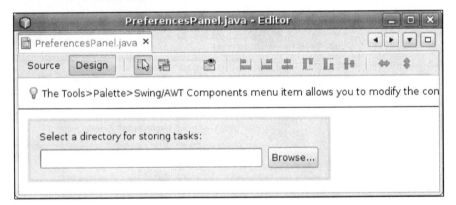

3. Register an `ActionListener` on the JButton, so that you can open a JFileChooser when the JButton is clicked and update the JTextField with the path to the selected directory. The content of the `ActionListener` should be as follows:

```
JFileChooser chooser = new JFileChooser();

chooser.setFileSelectionMode(JFileChooser.DIRECTORIES_ONLY);

int rc = chooser.showOpenDialog(this);

if (JFileChooser.APPROVE_OPTION == rc) {
    this.jTextField1.setText(chooser.getSelectedFile().
      getAbsolutePath());


}
```

4. Next, you need to implement loading, storing, and validation of the preferences. For each of these tasks, a separate method is provided in the `PreferencesPanel` class: `load()` to load the preferences, `store()` to save them, and `isValid()` for validation purposes. Implement them as follows:

```
void load() {
    this.jTextField1.setText(Lookup.getDefault().lookup
      (Preferences.class).getPersistencePath().getAbsolutePath());
  }

void store() {
    Lookup.getDefault().lookup(Preferences.class).
    setPersistencePath(this.jTextField1.getText());
  }

boolean valid() {
    return new File(this.jTextField1.getText()).isDirectory();
  }
```

5. Start the application again and open the Options window. You should be able to see your **Task Manager** Primary Panel, including the icon that you specified, as shown in the following screenshot. Select a folder, close the Options window, and exit the application. When you restart the application, notice that the selected value continues to be shown in the Options window.

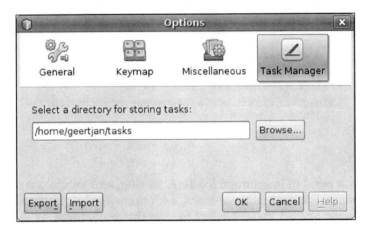

Summary

You have learned how to use the NbPreferences class to store application-specific settings in the NetBeans Platform user directory via the default Java Preferences API. In addition, you have learned how to attach a new Primary Panel to the Options window, which is the centralized location for integrating user interfaces for configuring the features provided by the modules making up the application. Most of the required classes were generated automatically by a wizard, with only a few manual tweaks required to complete this application requirement. You only needed to design a JPanel and to read and write configuration data using the Java Preferences API.

Though you didn't learn how to add a Secondary Panel to the Miscellaneous panel, there's no magic there, either. The same approach is taken for the Primary Panel, except that you specify in the Options Panel wizard that you would like to create a Secondary Panel rather than a Primary Panel. The wizard then creates all the required classes, with you only needing to design the JPanel to display the configuration settings, as well as the logic to read and write the required settings.

11
Help

When you are writing the documentation for your application, the NetBeans Platform lets you integrate HTML files from different modules into a single application-wide helpset. For this, the open sourced JavaHelp API, which is the standard help system for Java applications, is used under the hood.

In this chapter, you learn how to create help sets for the features in your application. You integrate help sets from different modules into a single helpset available from the application's **Help** menu, while you also learn how to create context-sensitive help sets by linking help topics to GUI components.

Creating a helpset

In this section, you are shown how to create a helpset for dealing with tasks in the sample application. If JavaHelp is invoked for a `TaskNode` (when the user clicks *F1* while a `TaskNode` is selected), a help topic appears to define to the user what a task is.

To get started, you need to create a helpset in the **Overview** module, as this is the module that contains the `TaskNode` class, which is the class that you need to document.

- Right-click the **Overview** module and choose **New | Other | Module Development | JavaHelp Help Set**. Click **Next**.

- The **JavaHelp Help Set** wizard is shown, which you use to create a new helpset as shown in the following screenshot:

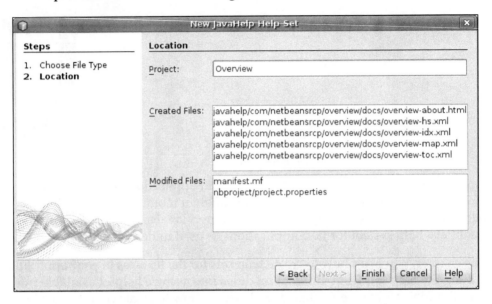

When you click **Finish** in the preceding wizard, the following files are created in a directory named after the code name base, appended by "docs":

- The file `moduleName-about.html` is a template for your first help page and is automatically registered in the map file, the table of contents file, and the index file.
- The file `moduleName-map.xml` is the map file, mapping the ID of a help topic to a URL pointing to the physical HTML file defining the help page.
- The file `moduleName-toc.xml` defines the table of contents of the helpset, associating a title to an ID from the map file, thereby linking it to a help page.
- The file `moduleName-idx.xml` defines the index of the helpset, associating a title to an ID from the map file and, thereby, to a help page.
- The file `moduleName-hs.xml` defines the helpset, combining a map file, table of contents, and index. Additionally, it defines how the helpset can be searched. Compared to the other files, this file rarely if at all needs any modification.
- The file `moduleName-helpset.xml` is not put into the `docs` directory but directly into the module. It defines where the helpset is located and is registered in the layer file.
- The `manifest.mf` is extended to declare the required dependency on the **JavaHelp Support** module.

After you have used the **JavaHelp** wizard to create the basic structure, you need to create the individual help pages.

Each help page is an HTML file. Using the HTML wizard from the directory **docs | New | HTML file**, create an HTML file named `Task.html`, as follows:

```html
<!DOCTYPE HTML PUBLIC "-//W3C//DTD HTML 4.01 Transitional//EN">
<html>
  <head>
    <title></title>
    <meta http-equiv="Content-Type" content="text/html;
      charset=UTF-8">
  </head>
  <body>
    <p>A <code>Task</code> describes a job and has the following
      properties:</p>
    <ul>
      <li>The <b>ID</b> is used for unique identification of a
        Task. It is set automatically and is not editable.</li>
      <li>The <b>parent-ID</b> is used to associate SubTasks to
        their parent Task.</li>
      <li>The <b>name</b> briefly describes the task.</li>
      <li>The <b>dueDate</b> is the date the task is due to be
        completed.</li>
      <li>The <b>priority</b> describes how important the Task is.
        Available priorities are 'low', 'medium' and 'high'.</li>
      <li>The <b>Progress</b> shows how much of the task is done
        already.</li>
      <li>The <b>description</b> is used for a detailed description
        of the task.</li>
    </ul>
  </body>
</html>
```

Next, you need to assign this help page to the map file, shown as follows in the `overview-map.xml` file. As the key under which this help page will be accessed needs to be set in a specific source file, make the key unique by using the fully qualified name of the source file as the name of the key. In this specific context, it will be the fully qualified name of the `TaskNode`:

```xml
<?xml version="1.0" encoding="UTF-8"?>
<!DOCTYPE map PUBLIC "-//Sun Microsystems Inc.//DTD JavaHelp Map
  Version 2.0//EN" "http://java.sun.com/products/javahelp/map_2_0.dtd">
<map version="2.0">
<mapID target="com.netbeansrcp.overview.about" url="overview-
    about.html"/>
<mapID target="com.netbeansrcp.overview.TaskNode"
    url="Task.html"/>
</map>
```

Additionally, you need to add the help page to the table of contents file, shown as follows in a file named `overview-toc.xml`:

```xml
<?xml version="1.0" encoding="UTF-8"?>
<!DOCTYPE toc PUBLIC "-//Sun Microsystems Inc.//DTD JavaHelp TOC
  Version 2.0//EN" "http://java.sun.com/products/javahelp/toc_2_0.dtd">
<toc version="2.0">
    <tocitem text="Overview">
    <tocitem text="About Overview"
             target="com.netbeansrcp.overview.about"/>
    <tocitem text="Task"
             target="com.netbeansrcp.overview.TaskNode"/>
    </tocitem>
</toc>
```

Next, register the help page in the index of the helpset, which is defined as follows in `overview-idx.xml`:

```xml
<?xml version="1.0" encoding="UTF-8"?>
<!DOCTYPE index PUBLIC "-//Sun Microsystems Inc.//DTD JavaHelp Index
  Version 2.0//EN" "http://java.sun.com/products/javahelp/index_2_0.dtd">
<index version="2.0">
    <indexitem text="About Overview"
               target="com.netbeansrcp.overview.about"/>
    <indexitem text="Task"
               target="com.netbeansrcp.overview.TaskNode"/>
</index>
```

Creating context-sensitive help

NetBeans API classes include methods to enable help contexts to be bound to UI components:

Class	Help Method
TopComponent	TopComponent.getHelpCtx()
SystemAction	SystemAction.getHelpCtx()
Explorer Nodes	Node.getHelpCtx()
Property Sheets	Sheet.setValue("helpID", "id")
Property Set	Node.PropertySet.setValue("helpID", "id")
Custom Property Editor	HelpCtx.setHelpIDString(jpanel, "id")
Dialog	for the entire Dialog: DialogDescriptor.setHelpCtx("id") for a panel: HelpCtx.setHelpIDString(visualPanel, "id")
Wizards	WizardDescriptor.Panel.getHelp()
DataObject	DataObject.getHelpCtx()

In the example application, you bind the `TaskNode` to a help context. Therefore, you need to override the `getHelpCtx()` method, as follows, in the `TaskNode.java` file:

```
@Override
public HelpCtx getHelpCtx() {
    return new HelpCtx(TaskNode.class);
}
```

The class instance is replaced by its fully qualified class name, which matches the previously set key in the map file.

When users start the application and select a task, they can show the applicable help topic by pressing the *F1* key. Additionally, the help topic can be shown programmatically. One way to do this is to open the properties of the task. The **Help** button will be enabled and by pressing it the help is displayed.

The code for showing the help topic programmatically is as follows:

```
String id = "here is the help id from the mapping file";
Help help = Lookup.getDefault().lookup(Help.class);
if (help != null && help.isValidID(id, true).booleanValue()) {
    help.showHelp(new HelpCtx(id));
}
```

In this section, you have created a helpset and you have associated a help page with a node. You did this by using a wizard that created several XML and HTML files and which registered them in the layer file.

You extended those files with an additional help page. The ID of the help page was set as the help context of the node. When JavaHelp is invoked on that node, its help context is requested, which causes the associated help page to be shown.

Combining help sets from different modules

The application consists of not one but several modules. In this section, you create another helpset for one of the other modules. You learn how to combine the application's help sets from different modules and how you can even create links between them.

In the context of the sample application, the wizard steps to create a new task in the **TaskActions** module will be documented. The help topics in the **TaskActions** module will link to the helpset in the **Overview** module, which is where the help topics that define the Tasks are found.

To accomplish that, you will create a new helpset, containing three help pages, in the **TaskActions** module. The help pages will describe the specific wizard steps and contain the content described as follows:

The first page is a simple help page, defined in `NewTaskWizardPanel1.html`:

```
<!DOCTYPE HTML PUBLIC "-//W3C//DTD HTML 4.01 Transitional//EN">
<html>
    <head>
        <title></title>
        <meta http-equiv="Content-Type" content="text/html;
            charset=UTF-8">
    </head>
    <body>
        <p>The first page of the Wizard will show if you are creating
            a Task without a parent task or a Subtask.</p>
    </body>
</html>
```

The second page will contain links to internal and external documentation. Internal help pages are linked using the "`nbdocs`" protocol, within a URL of the following structure:

```
nbdocs://moduleCodeNameBase/pathToHelpFile
```

External websites are not always displayed correctly in the internal Swing browser. It is often easier to display the URL in the system's default external browser. You can start an external browser and open pages into it by embedding an object tag in the help page, as follows:

```
<object
    classid="java:org.netbeans.modules.javahelp.BrowserDisplayer">
    <param name="content" value="urlToRessource">
    <param name="text" value="displayNameofResourceAsHtml">
    <param name="textFontSize" value="fontSize">
    <param name="textColor" value="fontColor">
</object>
```

In the sample application, you will add links to the **Overview** module's helpset and to a Wikipedia article. This results in the following page, defined in `NewTaskWizardPanel2.html`:

```
<!DOCTYPE HTML PUBLIC "-//W3C//DTD HTML 4.01 Transitional//EN">
<html>
    <head>
        <title></title>
        <meta http-equiv="Content-Type" content="text/html;
            charset=UTF-8">
    </head>
    <body>
```

```
    <p>The second page will let you enter the name, the dueDate, the
       priority as well as the current progress.</p>
    <p>For a detailed description of the fields have a look at the
       following documentation: <a href="nbdocs://com.netbeansrcp.overview/
          com/netbeansrcp/overview/docs/Task.html">Task</a>.</p>
       <p>A detailes documentation concerning Tasks can be found here:
          <object classid=
             "java:org.netbeans.modules.javahelp.BrowserDisplayer">
             <param name="content"
                value="http://en.wikipedia.ork/wiki/Task">
             <param name="text" value="Task">
             <param name="textFontSize" value="medium">
             <param name="textColor" value="blue">
          </object>
       </p>
    </body>
 </html>
```

The third page is a simple help page, defined in `NewTaskWizardPanel3.html`:

```
<!DOCTYPE HTML PUBLIC "-//W3C//DTD HTML 4.01 Transitional//EN">
  <html>
    <head>
       <title></title>
       <meta http-equiv="Content-Type" content="text/html;
          charset=UTF-8">
    </head>
    <body>
       <p>The third page lets you display an extended description of
          the Task.</p>
    </body>
  </html>
```

As shown in the following code snippet, these three help pages need to be added to the helpset's map file, which is `taskactions-map.xml`:

```
<?xml version="1.0" encoding="UTF-8"?>
<!DOCTYPE map PUBLIC "-//Sun Microsystems Inc.//DTD JavaHelp Map Version
2.0//EN"
"http://java.sun.com/products/javahelp/map_2_0.dtd">
<map version="2.0">
    <mapID target="com.netbeansrcp.taskactions.about"
             url="taskactions-about.html"/>
    <mapID target="com.netbeansrcp.taskactions.wizards.
                   NewTaskWizardPanel1" url="NewTaskWizardPanel1.html"/>
    <mapID target="com.netbeansrcp.taskactions.wizards.
                   NewTaskWizardPanel2" url="NewTaskWizardPanel2.html"/>
    <mapID target="com.netbeansrcp.taskactions.wizards.
                   NewTaskWizardPanel3" url="NewTaskWizardPanel3.html"/>
</map>
```

Optionally, these pages can be added to the table of contents file and the index file. In `taskactions-toc.xml`, change the content as follows:

```xml
<?xml version="1.0" encoding="UTF-8"?>
<!DOCTYPE toc PUBLIC "-//Sun Microsystems Inc.//DTD JavaHelp TOC
  Version 2.0//EN" "http://java.sun.com/products/javahelp/toc_2_0.dtd">
<toc version="2.0">
    <tocitem text="TaskActions">
    <tocitem text="About TaskActions"
            target="com.netbeansrcp.taskactions.about"/>
    <tocitem text="NewTaskWizard - Step 1"
            target="com.netbeansrcp.taskactions.wizards.
                NewTaskWizardPanel1"/>
    <tocitem text="NewTaskWizard - Step 2"
            target="com.netbeansrcp.taskactions.wizards.
                NewTaskWizardPanel2"/>
    <tocitem text="NewTaskWizard - Step 3"
            target="com.netbeansrcp.taskactions.wizards.
NewTaskWizardPanel3"/>
    </tocitem>
</toc>
```

In `taskactions-idx.xml`, register the topics, shown as follows:

```xml
<?xml version="1.0" encoding="UTF-8"?>
<!DOCTYPE index PUBLIC "-//Sun Microsystems Inc.//DTD JavaHelp Index
Version 2.0//EN"
"http://java.sun.com/products/javahelp/index_2_0.dtd">
<index version="2.0">
    <indexitem text="About TaskActions"
            target="com.netbeansrcp.taskactions.about"/>
    <indexitem text="NewTaskWizard - Step 1"
            target="com.netbeansrcp.taskactions.wizards.
                NewTaskWizardPanel1"/>
    <indexitem text="NewTaskWizard - Step 2"
            target="com.netbeansrcp.taskactions.wizards.
                NewTaskWizardPanel2"/>
    <indexitem text="NewTaskWizard - Step 3"
            target="com.netbeansrcp.taskactions.wizards.
                NewTaskWizardPanel3"/>
</index>
```

Finally, the connection between the GUI components and the helpset needs to be established. The help pages will correspond to the `WizardDescriptor.Panel` that contains the method `getHelp()`. For each of the panels, the method will return a specific help context. This means that the panels need the following modifications:

In `NewTaskWizardPanel1.java`:

```
// ...

public HelpCtx getHelp() {
    return new HelpCtx(NewTaskWizardPanel1.class);
}

// ...
```

In `NewTaskWizardPanel2.java`:

```
// ...

public HelpCtx getHelp() {
    return new HelpCtx(NewTaskWizardPanel2.class);
}

// ...
```

In `NewTaskWizardPanel3.java`:

```
// ...

public HelpCtx getHelp() {
    return new HelpCtx(NewTaskWizardPanel3.class);
}

// ...
```

The recent changes have the consequence that if the user requests help, either by pressing *F1* or by clicking on the **Help** button, the help page associated with the step in the wizard is shown. Getting help in the first step of the wizard will show the help page of the first step. The **Help** page for the second step contains two links. By selecting the first link the help page for the task will be shown. Selecting the second link will open the system's default browser and open the Wikipedia article concerning Tasks. This shows that linking external pages and displaying them in an external browser works as well. A look at the table of contents will show that the Help Sets of the modules **Overview** and **TaskActions** were merged with any manual input from the developer.

With that, everything that is required to create a JavaHelp set and integrate it in the NetBeans Platform has been shown. However, it may be undesirable to have other than your desired ones in the overall help. How to remove predefined helpsets is covered in the next section.

Removing help sets provided by other modules

In this section, you learn how to remove the NetBeans Platform's default help sets from your own application's helpset.

To remove a helpset provided by another module, a "_hidden" entry in the layer file is sufficient to hide the unwanted helpset. The entry must be added within the Services/JavaHelp folder, for the filename of the helpset file of the helpset that you want to hide.

The name of the unwanted helpset file can easily be determined in NetBeans IDE by expanding the module node Important Files | <this layer in context> | Services | JavaHelp. Not only does this node show you the registered help sets, but you can also delete them there, via the node's **Delete** menu item. When you delete a helpset file, a corresponding _hidden file is created in the module's layer file.

Potentially, rather than removing a helpset, you might not want to distribute the complete module that provides the helpset that you do not need. In some scenarios, it might simply be easier to avoid distribution of a module than to unregister a helpset. For example, in standalone applications a VCS System is typically not required. Rather than unregistering the VCS helpset, you'd more likely exclude the module that provides the helpset. How to achieve that is shown in the chapter concerning the branding of an application.

After deleting one or more help sets, your layer file should look as follows:

```
<folder name="Services">
    <folder name="JavaHelp">
      <file name="overview-helpset.xml" url="overview-helpset.xml">
        <attr name="position" stringvalue="3967"/>
      </file>

      <file name="org-netbeans-modules-usersguide-helpset.xml_hidden"/>
          <file name="org-netbeans-modules-java-helpset.xml_hidden"/>
          <file name="org-netbeans-modules-apisupport-project-
            helpset.xml_hidden"/>
          <file name="org-netbeans-modules-profiler-
            helpset.xml_hidden"/>
          <file name="org-netbeans-modules-dbschema-
            helpset.xml_hidden"/>
          <file name="org-netbeans-modules-subversion-resources-
            helpset.xml_hidden"/>
          <file name="org-netbeans-modules-db-helpset.xml_hidden"/>
          <file name="org-netbeans-modules-versioning-system-cvss-
            resources-helpset.xml_hidden" />
    </folder>
  </folder>
```

Restart the application and open the helpset. By looking at the table of contents, you should see that the removed help sets are not included anymore. Ideally, the helpset only contains the help topics that relate to the example application.

In this section, you have cleaned up the helpset such that only the sample application's help topics are shown when running the application. In other words, you removed the default help sets provided by NetBeans IDE. With this step, you now know everything you need to know to make a well-organized helpset available to users of your application.

Summary

In this chapter, you learned how to create new JavaHelp sets. You started by using a wizard in the IDE, which creates all the files that you need for setting up a skeleton helpset. The wizard also registered the files correctly in various parts of your module. Next, you learned how to create context-sensitive help and how to tweak the helpset so that only those helpsets that you actually need are included.

Now that you have created and configured a helpset, let's turn to the topic of branding, that is, you will spend some time learning about how to customize the NetBeans Platform's icons and strings, among many other topics related to wrapping up your application prior to delivering it to your users.

12
Branding

When you are "branding" an application, you are interested in customizing or personalizing those aspects of the application that come from modules provided by the NetBeans Platform itself. Rather than forcing you to change a NetBeans Platform module's sources, you can brand them externally in a number of different ways, as explained in this chapter.

Among other things, in this chapter you learn how to:

- Brand the name of the application launcher
- Brand the strings in the NetBeans Platform's modules
- Brand the splash screen

Application launcher

The name of the application launcher is set in the **Project Properties** dialog of the **TaskManager** application. Right-click the **TaskManager** project node, choose **Properties**, click **Application**, and then type the characters that should form the launcher name:

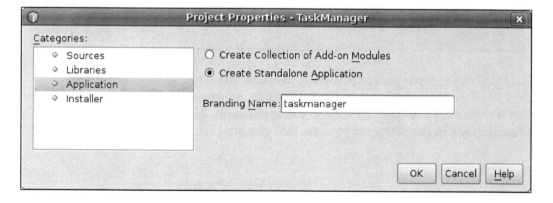

When you create a ZIP distribution of the application, as explained in the next chapter, the launcher name that you have defined previously will be used to create a launcher for the application, for each of the operating systems to which you will distribute the application.

Limiting the set of modules

Next, you probably want to limit the set of NetBeans Platform modules that the application will make available. In the **Libraries** tab of the TaskManager's **Project Properties** dialog (right-click the application and choose **Properties** to open the **Project Properties** dialog), you see a list of modules and a list of groupings of related modules, which are called "clusters", that are required by the application:

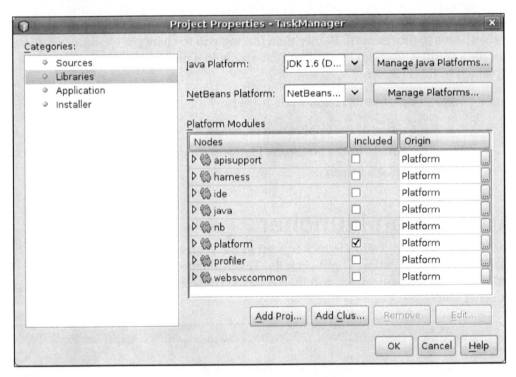

Here you can remove groups of related modules (clusters), as well as individual modules that are superfluous to the application. Whenever you remove a module that is required by another module in the application, a helpful warning message is printed in red in the dialog, to indicate that you are removing a required module.

For the example application, deselect all clusters except for **platform**, although even here you do not need all modules. Within the **platform** cluster, make sure you actually need all the modules in the list before distributing the application to the end user.

Branding editor

A **Branding Editor**, which is a new feature in NetBeans IDE 6.9, lets you customize a number of visual features in the application. Right-click the **TaskManager** project node, choose **Branding**, and then the **Branding Editor** shown in the following sections appears.

Application title and icons

Use the **Basic** tab to define a title that will be shown in the application title bar. Then look at the icons, as shown in the following screenshot. These are the default icons shown in various places in the application, such as the small icon in the top-left of dialogs, as used in the **Branding Editor** itself:

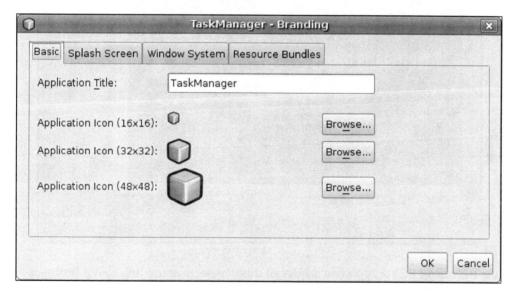

Browse to the icons on disk relevant to your application, using the **Browse...** buttons as shown in the preceding screenshot. These are then copied into the application, overriding the defaults provided by the NetBeans Platform.

Splash screen

A splash screen is a visual placeholder shown to the end user while the modules in the application are loaded and the application, as a whole, starts. The splash screen also shows information about the specific step in the process that is currently being completed. Via a progress bar, the user is informed of the number of steps that are left to be completed.

In the **Branding Editor**, you can adjust all these aspects according to the business needs of your application, as shown in the screenshot above. You can set your own background image as a visual placeholder for the application during startup, as well as the positioning and adjustment of the progress text shown during the startup sequence.

Window system features

Though the NetBeans Platform window system provides many out of the box features, not all end users will find those features useful. For example, some end users are not very technical and will be confused after undocking and moving windows around the screen, as they will not immediately know how to put all the windows back in their original positions. For some end users, you will want to disable the feature that allows windows to be closed. When you do so, the small **x** in the top-right corner of the windows will be removed, so that the end user will not be able to close the windows in the application.

Window system features can be removed per window, via client properties set in the constructor of your **TopComponent** classes. However, it is better if all the windows in an application have the same behavior. You can modify window behavior for the whole application in the **Branding Editor**. Right-click the **TaskManager** project node in the **Projects** window, choose **Branding**, and then choose the **Window System** tab, as shown in the following screenshot:

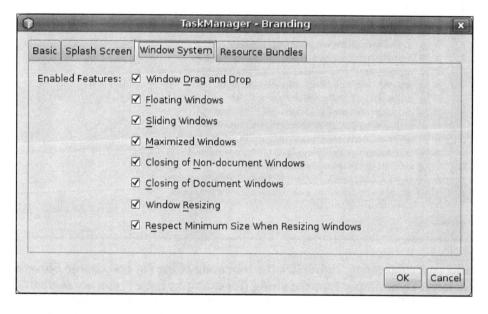

By default, all the window system features are enabled. To disable a feature, uncheck the related checkbox in the pane as shown in the preceding screenshot. Properties are then added to the application `branding` folder (visible in the **Files** window), which override the default properties defined in the NetBeans Platform.

Display texts

All the bundle files in the NetBeans Platform modules in your application can be branded. That means that you're able to override any display texts used in your application, such as menu items and titlebars in dialogs.

In the **Branding Editor**, which you can shown by right-clicking the **TaskManager** project node and choosing **Branding**, choose the **Resource Bundles** tab and then you see a long list of all the bundle files from the NetBeans Platform modules in the application, as shown in the following screenshot:

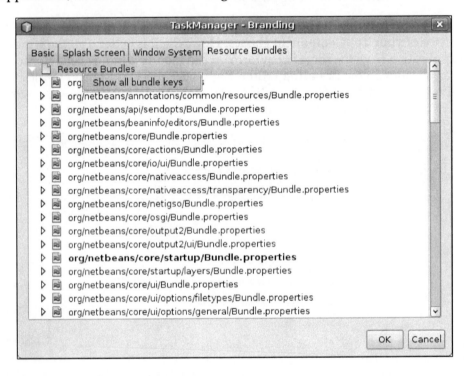

To find a particular string, right-click the root node of the list and choose **Show all bundle keys**. Then simply type the string (for example, **Save** if you are searching for the string defining the Save menu item) when the pane in the **Branding Editor** is active. Then the search string appears in a text field at the bottom of the **Branding Editor** and the first instance matching the search string is found, as shown in the next screenshot. Find the next instance of the matched string by pressing *F3*; continue pressing *F3* and you will continue seeing the next instance, until you find the specific instance you are looking for.

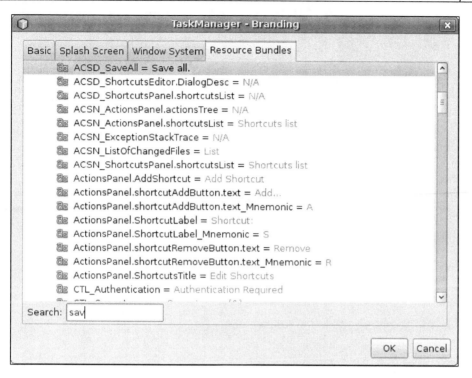

When you find the string you are looking for, right-click it and choose **Add to Branding**. You are then prompted to provide a string that overrides the original string in the NetBeans Platform. When you click **OK**, the string is added to a properties file that you can see in the `branding` folder (in the **Files** window) of the application. When the application is compiled, a JAR is created containing the overridden bundle file, which will override the matching bundle file in the NetBeans Platform.

Summary

In this chapter, you have completed the branding of the application. It now has its own application name, libraries, splash screen, icons, and display texts. In the next chapter, you examine different strategies for distributing the application, as well as features and patches, to its end users.

13
Distribution and Updates

Now that the development cycle of the TaskManager is coming to an end, it is time to think about how best to distribute it. Not only do you need to think about distributing the application itself, but also about how to provide additional features and patches between releases of the application. The modular structure of the application implies that the delivery of plugins should be possible, which is one of the areas explored in this chapter.

Creating a ZIP distribution

The NetBeans Platform lets you distribute your application in one or more different ways, from ZIP archive, to webstart-enabled, to installer-based. In this section, you learn about these standard distribution mechanisms for NetBeans Platform applications.

The distribution of a ZIP archive lets you provide the complete application to your end users, that is, all the modules and their configuration files, together with the launcher that starts them. Launchers for Windows and Unix-based systems, as well as Mac OSX distributions, can be created.

Once users receive the ZIP file, they simply need to unpack it and double-click the launcher to start the application.

1. To create such a ZIP distribution for the **TaskManager**, right-click the **project** node in the **Projects** window, and choose **Build ZIP Distribution**. A build script builds the whole application and creates the ZIP archive in the newly created dist folder of the application, which you can see in the **Files** window:

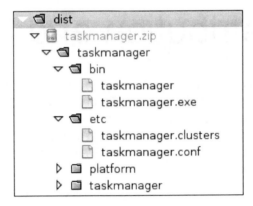

2. Now you can try out the generated launcher. Unzip the ZIP archive created. Then start the launcher relevant for your operating system. The **TaskManager** should now welcome you, starting with its splash screen.

You have learned how to create a ZIP archive for the application, with a minimum of effort. Now that you have created it, you need to distribute it to your users, who simply need to unpack it, and then run the launcher relevant to their operating system.

Even though we have only covered the ZIP distribution, the NetBeans Platform provides support for Mac OSX and web start, in a very similar way. Right-click the **project** node in the **Projects** window, and choose the menu item for creating a Mac OSX distribution, a web start distribution, or both, depending on your business needs. Then read the **Output** window and inspect the **Files** window for the generated results.

Creating an installer

To create an installer for the **TaskManager**, right-click the **project** node and choose
Properties. Use the **Installer** pane, as shown in the following screenshot, to specify
the target operating systems for the installers you would like to create:

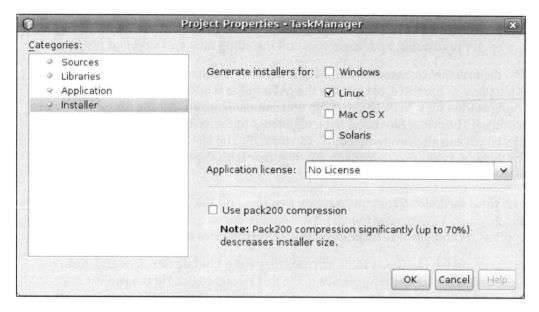

Click **OK**, as shown in the preceding screenshot, and then right-click the **project**
node in the **Projects** window, choosing **Build Installers**. The selected installers are
then built. Open the **Files** window to see the generated installers, which are now
ready to be distributed to the end users.

Enabling online updates

By enabling the application to be updated online, you provide support for dynamic
substitution, loading, and reloading of the modules in your application. A typical use
case for this feature is that it enables you to distribute bug fixes to your end users,
in-between release cycles. Earlier, where the end users would need to wait for the
next release to benefit from bug fixes, you can now simply distribute an individual
patched module to them instead. You can do this regardless of the current state of
the next release of the application.

The support for online updates of NetBeans Platform applications comprises of two components:

1. **Server component** NetBeans Platform AutoUpdate Service polls an update center, defined in XML format, for new and updated modules.

2. **Client component** NetBeans Platform Plugin Manager provides a user interface in a NetBeans Platform application, invoked via **Tools | Plugins**, for registering update centers and installing new and updated plugins.

The deployment format of modules is the **NBM (NetBeans Module)** format. It is simply a ZIP archive, containing the JARs in the module, together with their configuration files. In NetBeans IDE, you can generate an NBM file for each of your modules. These NBM files need to be registered in the Update Center descriptor file, which can also be created in NetBeans IDE. The Update Center then consists of the Update Center descriptor file, together with the modules that are registered within it.

Carry out the following steps to create NBM files and the Update Center descriptor. You register the Update Center descriptor in the sample application and use it to install updates to the modules in the application.

1. Add the NetBeans Platform modules **Auto Update Services** and **Auto Update UI** to the application. Do this by right-clicking the **project** node in the **Projects** window, choosing **Properties**, and then **Libraries**. Select the two modules, as shown in the following screenshot, and then click **OK**:

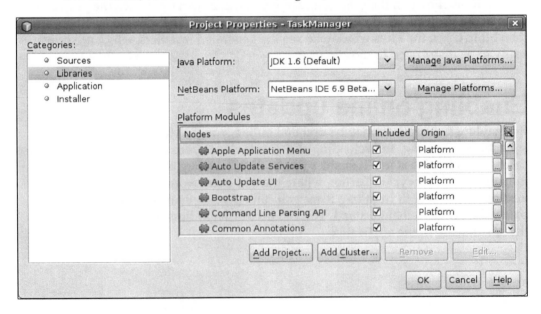

2. Check that the **Plugin Manager** is now available. Do this by right-clicking the application, choosing **Clean All** (to remove the user directory), and then **Run**. The user directory is recreated, while the application restarts. When the application has started, go to the **Tools** menu and notice that you now have a **Plugins** menu item. Choose the **Plugins** menu item and your new **Plugin Manager** opens as shown in the following screenshot:

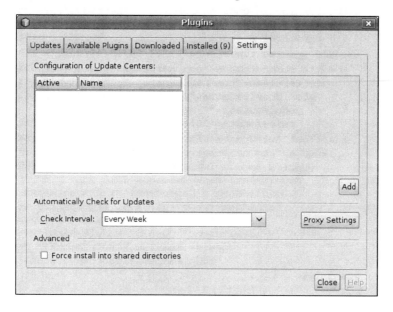

3. Next, let's create NBM files for all the modules in the application. Right-click the **Task Manager** project node and choose **Create NBMs**. Now an NBM file is created for each module. The new NBM files are created in the `build/updates/` directory, as shown in the following screenshot:

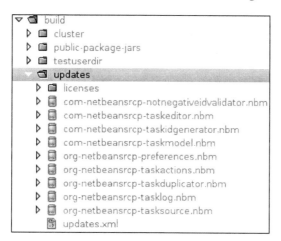

○ One of the preceding files is named `updates.xml`. This is the `Update Center descriptor`. It is an XML file that defines an element for each module, with attributes for information such as the download location and the module's related dependencies.

```
<?xml version="1.0" encoding="UTF-8" ?>
<!DOCTYPE module_updates PUBLIC "-//NetBeans//DTD Autoupdate
    Catalog 2.6//EN" "http://www.netbeans.org/dtds/autoupdate-
        catalog-2_6.dtd">
<module_updates timestamp="09/45/06/02/05/2010">
    <module codenamebase="com.netbeansrcp.notnegativeidvalidator"
        distribution="com-netbeansrcp-notnegativeidvalidator.
          nbm" downloadsize="2907" homepage="" license="AD9FBBC9"
            moduleauthor="" needsrestart="false"
              releasedate="2010/05/02" targetcluster="taskmanager">
    <manifest AutoUpdate-Show-In-Client="true" OpenIDE-
        Module="com.netbeansrcp.notnegativeidvalidator"
          OpenIDE-Module-Implementation-Version="100502" OpenIDE-
            Module-Java-Dependencies="Java &gt; 1.6" OpenIDE-
              Module-Module-Dependencies="com.netbeansrcp.
                taskidgenerator &gt; 1.0, org.openide.util.lookup
                  &gt; 8.2" OpenIDE-Module-Name="NotNegativeI
                    dValidator" OpenIDE-Module-Requires="org.
                      openide.modules.ModuleFormat1" OpenIDE-
                        Module-Specification-Version="1.0"/>
    </module>
    ......
    ...
```

○ Here any URL can be used to describe where the module can be downloaded. The URL is, by default, simply set to the name of the module, which results in a local reference to the |`updates.xml`. For our sample application, you can assume that all the modules are located directly beside the `updates.xml`, meaning that you do not need to change anything in the generated `Update Center descriptor`.

4. Now you need to publish the Update Center descriptor, as well as the modules you want to make available to end users. Do this by uploading the Update Center descriptor file to a web server. For testing purposes, you could put it somewhere locally, together with the various modules.

   ○ In the application, choose **Tools | Plugins**, go to the **Settings** tab, click **Add** and then enter the **URL** to the **Update Center descriptor**.

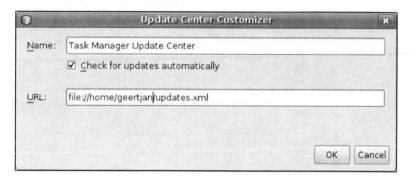

Summary

You have learned that you can create a ZIP distribution, an installer, or a JNLP (webstart) distribution for your application. You have set up and used an Update Center. You did this by creating an **Update Center descriptor**, together with a set of NBM files. You have also learned how to include the **Plugin Manager** in your application. When you deliver the application, the end user can use the **Plugin Manager** to update the application with new features and patches.

Index

F

FileObject class 175
FileObjects changes
listening 182
filesystem
central registry 176
filter() method 161
FilterNode
about 114, 157
creating 157-162
form, Form Builder
components, aligning 29, 30
creating 27-29
laying out 29
size, modifying 31
Form Builder
about 25-27
Connection wizard 27
Design view 26
Event handling 32
form, creating 27-29
form, laying out 29
form components, aligning 29, 30
form size, modifying 31
Form Tester 27
global overview 26
Inspector window 27
Properties window 27
Source view 26

G

generated code
DocumentListener, creating 35
modifying 34, 35
generateID() method 72
getExplorerManager() method 121
getHelpCtx() method 243
getLookup() method 89
getName() method 214
getOriginal() method 158
getPanels() method 227
getPersistenceType() method 45
getPopupPresenter() method 144
getPreferredAction() method 146
getTask method 95
getToolbarPresenter() method 210

global Actions
creating 103-106
pre-application changes 100-102
global Lookup
node 112
GroupLayout 25

H

HelloService class 13
HelpCtx.setHelpIDString() method 242
help method
HelpCtx.setHelpIDString() 242
Node.getHelpCtx() 242
Node.PropertySet.setValue() 242
Sheet.setValue() 242
SystemAction.getHelpCtx() 242
TopComponent.getHelpCtx() 242
WizardDescriptor.Panel.getHelp() 242
help set
combining, from different modules 243-247
creating 239-242
other module help sets, removing 248
horizontalAlignment property 215

I

icon badging 183
providing 200, 201
ImageUtilities.mergeImages() method 200
initCollection() method 119
initComponents() method 44
inplace editors
about 167
PriorityEditor 167-169, 174
installer
creating 261
installing
module 18, 19

J

java.awt.event.KeyEvent 109

K

key-based node hierarchy
about 126
creating 127-131

Thank you for buying
NetBeans Platform 6.9 Developer's Guide

About Packt Publishing

Packt, pronounced 'packed', published its first book "*Mastering phpMyAdmin for Effective MySQL Management*" in April 2004 and subsequently continued to specialize in publishing highly focused books on specific technologies and solutions.

Our books and publications share the experiences of your fellow IT professionals in adapting and customizing today's systems, applications, and frameworks. Our solution based books give you the knowledge and power to customize the software and technologies you're using to get the job done. Packt books are more specific and less general than the IT books you have seen in the past. Our unique business model allows us to bring you more focused information, giving you more of what you need to know, and less of what you don't.

Packt is a modern, yet unique publishing company, which focuses on producing quality, cutting-edge books for communities of developers, administrators, and newbies alike. For more information, please visit our website: www.packtpub.com.

About Packt Open Source

In 2010, Packt launched two new brands, Packt Open Source and Packt Enterprise, in order to continue its focus on specialization. This book is part of the Packt Open Source brand, home to books published on software built around Open Source licences, and offering information to anybody from advanced developers to budding web designers. The Open Source brand also runs Packt's Open Source Royalty Scheme, by which Packt gives a royalty to each Open Source project about whose software a book is sold.

Writing for Packt

We welcome all inquiries from people who are interested in authoring. Book proposals should be sent to author@packtpub.com. If your book idea is still at an early stage and you would like to discuss it first before writing a formal book proposal, contact us; one of our commissioning editors will get in touch with you.

We're not just looking for published authors; if you have strong technical skills but no writing experience, our experienced editors can help you develop a writing career, or simply get some additional reward for your expertise.

Java EE 5 Development with NetBeans 6

ISBN: 978-1-847195-46-3   Paperback: 400 pages

Develop professional enterprise Java EE applications quickly and easily with this popular IDE

1. Use features of the popular NetBeans IDE to improve Java EE development

2. Careful instructions and screenshots lead you through the options available

3. Covers the major Java EE APIs such as JSF, EJB 3 and JPA, and how to work with them in NetBeans

Building SOA-Based Composite Applications Using NetBeans IDE 6

ISBN: 978-1-847192-62-2   Paperback: 300 pages

Design, build, test, and debug service-oriented applications with ease using XML, BPEL, and Java web services

1. SOA concepts and BPEL process fundamentals

2. Build complex SOA applications

3. Design schemas and architect solutions

4. JBI components including service engines and binding components

5. Master the BPEL Designer, WSDL Editor, and XML Schema Designer

Please check **www.PacktPub.com** for information on our titles

Lightning Source UK Ltd.
Milton Keynes UK

173607UK00002BA/4/P